ALMOST GROWN

LAUNCHING YOUR CHILD FROM HIGH SCHOOL TO COLLEGE

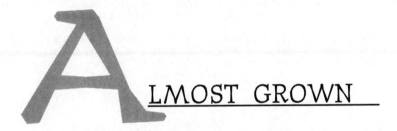

ALMOST GROWN

LAUNCHING YOUR CHILD FROM HIGH SCHOOL TO COLLEGE

PATRICIA PASICK, M.ED., PH.D.

W. W. Norton & Company
New York ◆ London

Copyright © 1998 by Patricia Pasick

For information about permission to reproduce selections from this book, write to Permissions, W. W. Norton & Company, Inc., 500 Fifth Avenue, New York, NY 10110

The text of this book is composed in Simoncini Garamond with the display set in Journal. Desktop composition by Platinum Manuscript Services Manufacturing by Quebecor Fairfield Book design by BTD/Sabrina Bowers

LIBRARY OF CONGRESS CATALOGING-IN-PUBLICATION DATA

Pasick, Patricia.
    Almost grown : launching your child from high school to college / Patricia Pasick.
      p.   cm.
    Includes index.
    ISBN 0-393-31710-2 (pbk.)
    1. College student orientation—United States. 2. Education—Parent participation—United States. 3. Adolescent psychology—United States. 4. Parent and teenager—United States. 5. Parents—United States—Psychology. I. Title.
LB2343.32.P37   1998
378.1'98—dc21   97-37065
                                                                              CIP

W. W. Norton & Company, Inc.
500 Fifth Avenue, New York, N.Y. 10110
www.wwnorton.com

W. W. Norton & Company Ltd.
Castle House, 75/76 Wells Street, London W1T 3QT

3 4 5 6 7 8 9 0

To my parents, Jean and Ted Carino,
who launched me with love

CONTENTS

Acknowledgments

Writing a book is a communal effort. I am deeply grateful to many people who entrusted their stories to me and gave support and guidance to this project. My husband Robert Pasick lent one of his many creative sparks to ignite the book, and then quietly provided the domestic and co-parenting support I needed to take it to completion. He brought me countless capaccinos and never-failing encouragement and good cheer, even in the wee hours of the morning. Our sons Adam and Dan were really the inspiration. I am very appreciative of their willingness to let me reflect with them, and about them, as they began the leaving home process. Adam, the first to launch, handled my deliberate scrutiny of his senior year with his usual grace, ease, and sharp humor, and the contributions from his journal were invaluable to me. Dan endured my questions and crazy-making writer-mother life with patience and interest. He never failed to ask how it was all going, and his experiences in high school lent an important perspective.

The rich and thoughtful stories of many unnamed clients, unknown Internet users, and my friends—both younger (almost grown) and older (always growing)—are the spine of this book. Their important contributions about the leaving home process shaped and anchored *Almost Grown*. The Gordon, Wilson-Tobin, Freund-Ross, Plunkett, Heys, Simon, Axelrod-Peraino, Quinn, Cook-Krabbenhoft, Dickinson, Ufer, Dubin, Wiss, Hopkins, Augustyn, Pryor, Long, Hoover-Marshall, Holz, Rinker, and Soebbing families generously allowed me interviews. A set of young people graciously shared their experiences around our kitchen table, with the help of chocolate chip cookies: David Heys, Nora and Jessie Gordon, Carrie Holmes, Karin Lutter, Toby Freund,

Leah Plunkett, Jon Holz, Nate Phiney, Andy Jacoby, Alex Clay, and Peter Rinker.

So much of the transition of college occurs in the teem and throb of high school hallways and classrooms. I especially want to acknowledge the invaluable guidance and information from a set of high school counselors: Richard Tobin of the Greenhills School, Pat Manley of Huron High School, Bruce Munro from Evanston Township High School, and the entire counseling staff at Pioneer High School. Judith Dwoskin and her class at Community High School contributed a whole writing assignment.

The colleges and universities are the receiving end of the leaving home process. At the University of Michigan I particularly thank Penni Reed and Jennifer Cross, who granted me their time and thoughts. College deans around the country lent me their ideas for this book: Dan Walls (Emory), Mike Sexton (Lewis and Clark), Christopher Guttentag (Duke), Rick Shaw (Yale), Tom Parker (Williams), and Jane Reynolds (Amherst). Students and faculty from the Fielding Institute, especially my cluster of students in Ann Arbor, and particularly Nancy Hansen, Ruthellen Josselson, Marcia Hunter, Williams Simons, and Charles Felton, lent their support and stories, which I warmly appreciate.

This book would not have launched without the expert research assistance of my friend Lynn Olson, who came through at crucial moments with just the right citation, article, reference, or fact. Carrie Holmes, another assistant, took valuable time from her senior year to help with research. The staff at Ann Arbor Center for the Family, Chris Pearson and Nancy Yonkman, and Angie Killian good-naturedly tolerated my last-minute urgent requests for help.

To my tireless and creative writing group, Donna Freund, Sandy Simon, and Betty Ann Gilliland, as well as Karen Dickinson, Beth Melampy, and Mary Stock, I owe many thanks. At several anxious spots in this project, they provided encouragement, important feedback, great humor, and a continual warm hum of support. Artist-friend Sue Heys generously helped me launch one phase of this project at a summer retreat. Colleagues at Ann Arbor Center for the Family were another source of positive energy. I'm especially thankful to Jo Allen for her enduring sparkle, mentorship, and guidance, and appreciate the feedback on specific topics from Moira Hubbard, Paul Estenson, Mary Whiteside, and Judi Kleinman.

I am indebted to my editor, Susan Munro, who was encouraging of this project from its earliest inception. She, along with Selena Leary and Casey Ruble, helped my writing expand and contract. Together we shaped a book that maintained its energy and vision. Thanks as well to Barbara Moulton and Marilyn Mason for early support and guidance.

Finally, I so appreciate the loving attention and steady stream of confidence from my parents, siblings, in-laws, and extended kin, as well as the continual sustenance from Barry and Eileen Gordon, who, like my family, knew me when "writing" was a far-off dream and this book was just one morning's idea.

Introduction

This book was born early one morning in Ann Arbor, the summer before our older son Adam began his senior year of high school. I was constructing a "To Do" list befitting a mid-life psychologist and mother with two teenagers: check my answering service, schedule Adam's senior pictures and a college tour in Minnesota, make notes for a meeting of family therapists, send Dan some socks at camp, call Donna to schedule our writing group.

From the radio in the kitchen I heard a warm, thoughtful voice. Novelist Anne Lamott was describing her book *Operating Instructions*, a diary of her son's first year. As she read selected passages, I found myself drawn deeply to this moving and humorous narrative, yet resisting it at the same time. Hearing Lamott's loving angst about her newborn and emerging motherhood, I felt uncomfortably stirred.

After a few minutes, I knew why: Lamott's book chronicles the first year of daily life with her son. In the coming fall I would begin the last full year of living with my own son. Time drew me backward to 1976, his birth year, and then catapulted me into the future, to his leaving our home for college. As I thought of Adam and then Dan away at college, their rooms standing empty, a strong wave of sadness tinged with relief washed over me. I understood the confusion and inevitability that poet Adrienne Rich described: "Things look at you doubly / and you must look back / and let them happen."

My husband Rob saw that my reactions to the radio interview were quickly turning to mild anguish, and he suggested that I write about the coming year. I had recorded Adam's milestones in a Baby's First Year book, he reminded me. Why not a book about Baby's Last Year?—even though this surely would not be our last year of parenting Adam, and our "baby" was now nearly grown, with a car, computer, and electric razor.

I began to keep a journal about my own experience of Adam's college transition years, and the journal gradually expanded. I initiated research about adolescent psychology and parenting. I listened to the stories of over one hundred generous adults and young people in focus groups, in high school corridors, in ivory tower college offices, and on the sidelines of sports events. I went on-line to gather information from parenting bulletin boards. *Almost Grown* contains a choice selection of those stories, some with names and details changed to protect privacy.

My keen interest in this project gathered energy when I found few useful and substantive books about parenting adolescents, especially in the transition to early adulthood. To my dismay, only one or two seemed useful. As a baby boomer, I was used to parenthood buttressed by the usual stack of parenting guides (I once bought a book about how to buy children's books). I soon discovered I wasn't the only one searching for a book to fill that gap. Everyone—from the father who found me at his son's tennis match to the mothers group that joined me at a local deli, from the plaintive students who E-mailed me to the serious group of counselors at Dan's high school—seemed eager for solutions to the maze of college-related decisions and challenges ahead for families.

I concluded that parents wanted not only information about the college search process but also sound guidance as their children sped toward independence. It was also clear that some parents were eager to understand possible reasons for their own emotional reactions to this transition.

I chose to write a book that was practical, psychologically grounded, and celebratory of adolescents and families living in a rapidly expanding and challenging culture. *Almost Grown* is filled to the brim with information from all quarters about the transition to college: developmental and family psychology, parenting education, secondary schools, and the colleges themselves. It is intended to be a useful guide for parents of late adolescents who are trying to understand many things simultaneously:

◆ How to find a sane and healthy way through the maze and haze of voluminous information about the college search

◆ How to understand what is happening psychologically with their sons and daughters

◆ How to understand the emotional developmental changes within themselves and their families

◆ How to parent toward both independence and connection, and educate teenagers about living in today's world

The voices of teenagers, parents, siblings, teachers, psychologists, poets, high school counselors, college officials, and dormitory advisors are all here. Together they address how adolescents think and feel about themselves and what support and guidance they especially need from their parents.

I learned that there is no right formula for the exciting and intense process of going to college. Instead, parents and students find themselves at varying points on a wide continuum. For some, the college search is well underway by tenth grade; for others, the process does not catch fire until senior year. Some adolescents are enthusiastically leading the charge to match themselves with a college. An equal number seem overwhelmed by the whole idea of going to college, let alone the involved process of searching and applying. It can be an exhausting and emotionally charged time for some parents and kids, while a few wonder what the fuss is about.

As a psychologist, I have long been convinced that the years before and after the end of high school mark a key developmental point for parents as well as adolescents. One mother said, "Facing the large stack of applications for colleges and financial aid on our dining table, I have competing urges to hire a consultant, put my head down and cry about Brad leaving us, and give myself a gold medal for helping him get to this place."

Little has been written about the powerful impact on parents and families when young people go away—or grow away—from home. Like several of my friends and clients, I felt confused and emotional about this phase of parenting, especially as it converged with my own mid-life.

This book addresses that intersection and those challenges of mothers and fathers in their forties and fifties whose lives are simultaneously filling and emptying.

One way I filled the space made by Adam's departure for college was to begin writing in earnest. That passion, and my own heart, is found in the journal entries scattered throughout *Almost Grown*. Writing down my experiences—from the mundane to the mind-blowing—prompted daily reflections about myself, my sons, and our family. On paper I began to consciously reflect how life and parenthood was changing before my eyes as Adam applied to colleges, then left for the University of Wisconsin-Madison, and his brother Dan began this whole process again.

Adam likes to write as well. Parts of his journal, with his blessing, are included with my own. This was never side-by-side writing. On the contrary, we didn't read each other's entries until the end of his senior year in high school. Reading about his own process was a privilege. So were the conversations with Dan and my sons' friends. This generation wants very much to be heard. Their early entry into an adult world of pressure, competition, and danger can leave them reeling, as their stories reveal. These young people are reminiscent of the teenagers of my own Age of Aquarius generation. They are excited (when not overwhelmed) by a seemingly endless array of choices, self-actualized beyond their years, intensely connected to their peers and peer culture, and striving for societal change.

Going to college is a major step toward adulthood. Watch closely on move-in day. As many sons and daughters stride into the dormitory, they will look over one shoulder, wanting to keep their changing parents and changing families in view as long as possible. My hope is that *Almost Grown* will support all the various journeys and changes, while honoring the family roots that sustain them.

Almost Grown

Launching Your Child from High School to College

CHAPTER ONE

Adolescents from High School to College

Pat / November 6

> *Adam often stares up with a barely tolerant look that says, "I can't wait until I get out of here." This is how it should be, I guess. As a senior, he should be eager to leave home. I once worried that we have made it all so nice for him here. It's been a bountiful room and board. We hardly ask him to help out with anything more than leaf-raking, snow-shoveling, room-straightening, dish-doing, and poop-scooping. We're pleasant. We're not crazy, alcoholic, or argumentative. We like his jokes. His brother is not the obnoxious, jealous sort. We have a great dog. And, most important, we have great videos and CDs. Why leave surrounds like these?*

Adam / January 8

> *Yesterday was my eighteenth birthday. The folks gave me my first birthday present over breakfast at Angelo's Restaurant. It was some sheet music for the jazz piano. Cool. I did the whole gratitude thing. Then they handed me another envelope with the words "From Your Uncle" on the front. I figured it was my token whatever from my Uncle Peter or Phil, but it was my notice from Selective Service. I had thirty days to register for the draft or face criminal prosecution. What a sick and twisted thing for my parents to do. I'm so proud of them.*

Launching an adolescent from high school to college raises big and little questions about growth and development. A major parenting task during this transition is to assess your adolescent's readiness to cope with a wider world, a new set of relationships, and increased independence.

But isn't it too late? parents ask. Isn't my child already launched? The answer is a complex "no." True, much about your child's personality is well-formed by now. But there is ample evidence that parenting adolescents actively and consciously, particularly as they begin leaving home, makes a positive difference in later adult life. This chapter will address the set of competencies needed by adolescents who are almost grown and leaving home for the first time.

SPECIAL CHALLENGES OF LEAVING HOME IN THE '90S

I remember—actually remember *only*—the beginnings and endings of my parents' sentences when they lectured me as a teenager:

- ◆ Your generation has no . . . and so the answer is *no*.
- ◆ Your grandparents never let me . . . so don't think you can get away with *that*.
- ◆ I wasn't born yesterday . . . so I *know* what you're up to.

When I catch myself feeling aghast at the lifestyle of our almost grown sons, and start to compare my generation to theirs, I'm in an odd time warp, merged with my parents. Is the pathway to adulthood so very different for young people today? Absolutely, many of us would answer.

Like most of my female baby boomer peers, I was home-bound and fairly protected in my early adolescence. Social life consisted of slumber parties, a few school dances, and Saturday afternoon gatherings at the drugstore. These were the times captured by *Happy Days*. By high school I went to an occasional—mainly dry—party, played some innocent pranks at football games, and had a few low-key romances. I rarely had access to the family car. And, for me and most of my friends, college choices were preordained by location, cost, or tradition; only a quarter of my senior class went on to higher education. When I left home for the University of Michigan, I had spent little time away from my parents, my two younger brothers, and our suburban home.

Consider the contrast with our own children. Adolescence has expanded in time and meaning way beyond the 1960s, when the Beatles song character silently closed the bedroom door, leaving a note that she hoped would say more. Adolescence begins much earlier than we once thought. For some kids it starts as early as nine to eleven years old and continues until they are financially independent and living in places of their own. That means adolescence may stretch across fifteen years.

When parents aren't groaning at the thought of a long adolescence, we're debating which sex is harder to raise. In the 1990s we have seen many challenges to the way we think about female and male adolescent development. In the years between the publication of Carol Gilligan's *In a Different Voice* and Mary Pipher's *Reviving Ophelia* there has been a groundswell of interest in encouraging adolescent girls to remain vocal and achievement-oriented through high school. In response, sociologists and psychologists have focused new attention on the affective and relational needs of male adolescents. Books like Olga Silverstein's *The Courage to Raise Good Men* and Ann Caron's *Strong Mothers, Strong Sons* urge parents to fight the male gender role stereotype that encourages almost grown men to be staunchly self-sufficient and extremely competitive at the expense of their relationships with others.

By the time they leave home for college, many middle-class young people will have traveled to distant places, achieved modest or major athletic, artistic, or scholastic goals, held a paying job, lived away from family, and learned a different language. Some sixteen- to eighteen-year-olds have covered more ground by car and computer than their parents did by age twenty-six or twenty-eight.

This astonishing pace and abundance have a sobering side. With a wider, more accessible world has come a set of realities once thought to affect only adults:

Danger: Drug use, alcohol consumption, and sexual intercourse are now commonplace among middle to older adolescents and such high-risk behavior among younger teens is rising sharply.

Pressure: A typical high schooler has a busy life balancing a host of competing activities. Sixteen-hour days are not uncommon for some adolescents striving to balance homework, a job, sports, artistic endeavors, friendships, family responsibilities and chores. The pressure for an attractive college profile begins on average in the eighth grade and continues non-stop almost to high school graduation.

Competition: Intense worrying about grades and scores, college applications, class rank, and making the cut are typical in young people looking anxiously toward college and career. As Kendall Lott of Radford University notes, "Kids are like ducks on a pond. They look cool, but underneath, they're paddling like crazy."

Adolescents in the '90s are living in a far more diverse environment than many of their baby boomer parents. The traditional family of two parents and their children is no longer the norm. A recent Census Bureau report indicated that only twenty-five percent of the nation's households took the form of a married couple and one or more children under age eighteen. Living in a stepfamily or in two separate family units is commonplace for teenagers. Further proof of increased diversity is found in a 1996 figure that at colleges and universities one in four students, on average, belongs to a minority group.

Parenting adolescents in today's world means readying them for a fast-paced, increasingly complex, and diverse environment, one that offers an immense array of choices and challenges. Now more than ever, adolescents need that preparation to grow into healthy, happy, and productive adults.

IDENTITY: DON'T LEAVE HOME WITHOUT IT

Living with adolescents who are about to leave home is like trying to catch fireflies on a hot summer eve. By nature's design, a firefly's phosphorescent glow is intermittent. The only way to catch one is to follow its dark form carefully and watch for its light, that wonderful yellow flash. Adolescents can have that same glow—and that same elusiveness. They flit away from us, making it difficult to know all the complex changes happening inside them. But we particularly sense their agony and ecstasy as they struggle with issues of identity, self-esteem, and independent thinking.

Pat / May 26

> *Is the Adam I saw this morning—on the last day of his senior year—an unshaven boy tearing out of the house with nary a good-bye, a stale bagel in one hand, a jumble of clothes and books in the other—is this a glimpse of Adam the adult? Or is it true, as Donna said today over coffee, that I can't really predict his future identity? Adam's birth as an infant took several long hours, but his birth as an adult will take years. Just like in pregnancy, who knows how he'll turn out?*

The words "adolescence" and "identity" are almost synonymous. One father, cynical and sarcastic about his son's unpredictability, answers the telephone with, "Sorry, he's not at home. He's finding himself." Our younger son Dan spent his early adolescence worshiping and trying to emulate sports heroes, spent tenth grade obsessed with rock artists, and now as a high school senior is passionately interested in reading about the gang behavior of urban teenagers.

For many young people, the years from fifteen to twenty are infused with experiments in identity. These excursions to the new and unfamiliar are often bewildering to parents. And when these explorations seem too dangerous or different, they are distressing. One mother, Judith, a petite, remarried mother of two who works as a bank manager, expressed despair and frustration at her older daughter's many changes:

> *I don't know Elissa anymore. She used to care about how she looked. We wore the same clothes. I helped her with her hair. Now she shops in used clothing stores and delights in looking like a homeless person! "What happened to the skirts and hair scrunchies?" I ask her. "That's not me anymore," she says. All she wants to do is paint and draw and be with her theater friends. After working hard to make the swim team, she announced yesterday that she's quit. She's not even sure she wants to go to college right*

away. When her dad (my ex) and I challenge her on this decision, she is adamant that we accept her for who she is. I'm trying, and he's trying too, but it's just not like her to act this way.

As parents we try to reassure ourselves that many of these changes are explorations and not, as Elissa's mother fears, permanent transformations. These experiments in identity are pathways our children follow to discover what makes them unique and special. This is a time of questioning:

- Who am I?
- Where do I belong?
- What are my roots?

Adolescents are discovering what values are important to them. Researchers have shown that teenagers privately ask profound questions of themselves:

- What do I believe in?
- What and who are important to me?
- Is there a God? What about good and evil?

Throughout this stage of development, young people are constantly evaluating themselves in relation to the physical, intellectual, and social aspects of selfhood:

- Do I like my body?
- Am I smart and creative?
- Am I popular?
- What do I feel passionate about?

If these questions sound familiar, perhaps you remember asking them during your own adolescence. (Or, if you're in a mid-life searching mode, you may have asked them this morning.) What do you think your son or daughter is thinking and feeling about these questions? The answers will guide your child's leaving home and his or her behavior when entering college and young adulthood.

Research also tells us that not all adolescents move through identity formation in the same way and at the same pace. Some young people, like Elissa, come through several crisis-ridden explorations on their way to some consistent sense of self. Very few settle on an identity by the time they depart for college. Many actively explore different identities before they leave home for the first time.

Others seem to have the whole identity process on hold, perhaps waiting to experiment until they are out from under their parents' watchful eyes. They float through high school unattached, it seems, to any distinct way of being and believing. Consider Sean, a neat, sandy-haired boy with an inclination for flannel shirts, khakis, and chewing gum. He had a reputation among his friends for being "easygoing." He rarely took a stand about anything, never expressed a passionate interest, and was happy to go along with whatever the group did or felt. Once away from home, Sean found his way to friends and activities defined by a love of jazz. He found a niche in a small college band, and decided to major in communication. On parents weekend, his folks walked into his dorm room to find him clad in torn blue jeans, a black T-shirt, and an earring, his room lined with music posters.

For still others, adolescence causes hardly a ripple. These young people settle on an identity very early. Often they mirror their parents' interests and values, or some particular religious or ethnic culture. Parents, pleased at the way these youngsters have "turned out," are secure and happy. The pathway for these adolescents is not always so smooth, however, once they enter a college environment very different from their home. The diversity of beliefs may shake them to the core and, away from the secure base of home, they may become initially quite homesick and unhappy. This describes Janine, an earnest African-American young woman. With a close group of friends at church and high school, she followed a straight path of good grades, community service, and excellent work habits. Her parents, both doctors, were important role models for her. She seemed older than her years and was well-liked by the more mature white and African-American adolescents at her high school. She chose a large university in a nearby state, and was assigned to a freshman suite of four roommates: two white women, an Asian, and an African-American. Janine's minority suitemates quickly joined Black and Asian student caucuses, became involved in some campus-wide political actions, and pressured her to do the same. Her roommates challenged her mainstream values and appealed to her identity as an African-American. She resisted her peers, only to find herself somewhat ostracized by them. By Thanksgiving, Janine was unhappy, less sure of herself, overwhelmed with the weight of difficult freshman classes, and talking about transferring. "I thought I knew who I was," she said to her distressed parents. "Now I don't know."

When students leave high school and the community where they reside, they carry within them a "presenting culture," as psychiatrist Vincenzo DiNicola calls it. My mind conjures up a brown leather "cultural" suitcase held by a fresh-faced eighteen-year-old awaiting the train that will take him or her to new places. But DiNicola's "presenting culture" is neither so specific nor so static. Culture is a sense of who you are within the context of a changing family history and set of ever-evolving family roots. It is about ideas, meanings, and rules. It programs behavior, world views, and emotional experiences like leaving home.

Ethnic and racial minority students heading to college will face extra challenges to identity that white students may escape. No white student will ever have to prove his or her "whiteness" to a peer group, the way many African-American or Hispanic students are asked to demonstrate their solidarity with their own racial groups. Nor do white students have to "live down" the myth that they are out to skew the class curves, the way that some high-achieving Asian students must do.

The good news is that for an overwhelming majority of students going to college involves identity-searching and identity-changing. More so today than ever before, young adults are challenged to "learn about others, their experiences and their perspectives, their blind spots and their prejudices," says Edgar Beckham of the Ford Foundation's Campus Diversity Initiative. For this generation of students, who will be living and working in a world community, this kind of other- and self-understanding is critical.

Is there any comfort for parents during adolescents' search for identity? Yes. Psychologists who study adolescents are in consensus about a number of issues:

◆ Developing an identity is what makes separation, independence, and becoming a unique individual possible.

- A firm identity also lays the groundwork for future intimacy. If you don't know who you are, you may more easily become what someone else wants you to be.
- Our children's identity tends to come from all sources, not just peers but also the family. An adolescent who tries on a lifestyle 180 degrees from his or her family's tends not to maintain that difference over time. Family continues to be the main source of values and code of behavior.
- Identity is not superglued at the magic age of eighteen or twenty-one. Developmental change continues across the lifespan and is always subject to influence.

That's not to say that living with our children is easy as they struggle to explore identity. In high school, multiple earrings and neon hair may be the banners for who students are and who they're not. In college, young people may come home for summer vacation sporting a new religion, political ideology, or a barely disguised scorn for their parents' lifestyle. I remember coming home after my first year away and tackling my father hard on issues of prejudice, for example. Adolescents have a way of pushing parents' comfort zones:

- We may not like the identity that we see our children developing.
- We worry when they appear to be rejecting family values.
- We worry about strong influences, especially the "wrong" ones.
- We don't like being criticized or de-idealized as parents.
- We tend not to see an emerging individuality; instead, we see rebellion and peer conformity.

Parenting a rapidly growing and changing adolescent during the transition from high school to college means accepting a certain lack of control and a fair degree of uncertainty. If only we could heed the lines in a Margaret Mead poem, which begins, "You must be free to take a path / whose end I feel no need to know."

Ideally, parents and teenagers negotiate a balance between separation and connection, built upon the emergence of new identities and roles. One mother, herself a student in graduate school, aptly describes this kind of positive process:

> *My daughter has woven her sense of self through both disavowing and assimilating parts of me. Her rejection of my values, my "style," and me was more painful than my intellectual knowing had prepared me for. . . . Her leaving home and my own identity process as a mid-life student have allowed me to be open to the possibility that my child is actually a unique person in her own right. . . . At her core she is more like than unlike her parents . . . for better or worse! . . . I don't completely know my child these days, and I don't always like the identities or clothes that my daughter is trying on, but I'm sure that she will emerge from her identity process as a woman I will respect.*

IDENTITY ISSUES

WHAT PARENTS CAN DO

Give your adolescent permission to explore interests, even if those interests seem worlds apart from your own.

Introduce your teenager to a diverse array of adults who have a variety of jobs and careers, and who come from differing cultures.

Curb your own fears when your child is trying on identities. Often these identities are temporary.

Encourage discussion about ethics, morality, government, and culture. The day's news is a good jumping-off place.

Remember your own adolescence and the ways you did and did not identify with your parents.

See what you can learn from your emerging adult. The metamorphosis underway can enliven and broaden your own life.

SELF-ESTEEM: THE INNER ROOMMATE

A young man named Brian wrote me from his freshman dormitory: "I really can't stand my roommate. He's from the put-down school of being a guy and always finding ways to criticize me. Like he made fun of my clothes, my music, my hair. At first, it got to me; I was really down for a while. Then I thought, 'Well, *I* like the way I am, even if he doesn't.' I have my own roommate—the person I've gotten to be and like."

Brian has enough self-esteem to override teasing. For most eighteen-year-olds, liking yourself is linked to feeling well-liked and accepted by peers. Yet what drives self-esteem most in adolescents is the knowledge that important adults in their lives are genuinely proud of their accomplishments, competencies, and forward progress.

What are the signs of good self-esteem? We have only peeks into our teenagers' inner lives, so how can we judge their self-esteem? And it can vary maddeningly from day to day. Self-esteem takes many forms: personal, social, physical, sexual, intellectual, and creative self-esteem. Ask yourself:

Is my child generally happy? On average, do positive moods supersede blue or angry times? Despite the mood swings that characterize adolescence, a more or less happy young person tends to feel the self-value that comes with a high personal self-esteem.

Is my adolescent able to follow his or her heart at times, and not the will of a valued peer or group of friends? This is a marker that your child's social self-esteem is becoming firmer, readier for the onslaught of the many different codes of behavior found in college life.

Does my teenager seem to like his or her body and have a sense of physical competence? We accept that young people at this age are focused intently on how they look compared to everyone else, including the actors and models displayed in the media. One hair out of place, jeans or shoes that do not conform, or a facial blemish makes an enormous difference to teenagers. And we know that emerging sexuality takes up a lot of an adolescent's fantasy life. Young people forever wonder, "Am I attractive? Are my sexual feelings normal?"

Adolescents of either sex with a good dose of physical self-esteem tend not to make an inordinate number of self-deprecating remarks about their bodies. Nor do they spend copious amounts of time, at the expense of other areas of development, trying to mold their bodies into an ideal image.

Does your child feel adequate intellectually and creatively? For adolescents heading to college, it's a toss-up between which kind of self-esteem will best carry them forward: social competence or academic talent. Doing reasonably well in school and feeling rewarded for accomplishments is a major source of self-esteem for young people. In America, what you *achieve* is often synonymous with who you *are*. Good grades, however, do not ensure that an adolescent has positive self-esteem. Some young people with outstanding academic records feel quite inadequate, even in the face of a transcript laced with *A*s and *B*s. Very high demands from parents and teachers may feed adolescents' fears of "not being good enough."

It's not easy to balance unconditional positive regard, which may inadvertently reward mediocre effort, and conditional regard, given only for excellence. With college ahead, a set of *realistic* goals, agreed upon *together* by parents, kids, teachers, and coaches, is a firm foundation for continued growth in self-esteem. It is important to make sure that your child has some experience in an activity that offers him or her sure success. If you are concerned that your child has self-esteem problems, you can be helpful in some specific ways outlined in the accompanying box.

SELF-ESTEEM
WHAT PARENTS CAN DO

Try to understand the source of negative self-esteem. What dimension appears to be suffering—friendships, schoolwork, body image? Making a reasonable guess takes some observation and a little careful probing; an adolescent may not be completely frank. After all, he or she has an "image" to maintain, even with a parent. Don't *insist* that your son or daughter has a self-esteem problem. Instead watch, listen, and ask gentle questions: Is there some part of your life that isn't going very well right now? Is your confidence down about something? Do you wish something were going better?

Help by being comforter and advisor. By middle or late adolescence most self-esteem concerns are about things outside of the family: a best friend who has suddenly turned cold, a new difficulty with academic work, passing comments by friends about body shape. Parents help best by offering their ears, their understanding, and, if requested, their advice. This is not the time to go to bat for your teenager to solve relationship problems, except in extreme situations (like prejudice or harassment). Your teenager needs your support to help him or herself.

Talk about yourself. As adolescents begin to leave home, they increasingly appreciate stories about how parents felt about themselves in adolescence. Share the positive *and* the negative stories. It will be comforting for your child to know that you were, for example, very unsure of yourself academically when you left for college or that you worried a great deal about making new friends.

Don't panic if your college-bound child begins to show self-doubt. Adolescents often have a resurgence of insecure feelings about themselves right before departure from home. A once-solid sense of self-esteem may temporarily melt in the face of a new, scary-looking situation.

Seek help if your child seems withdrawn, sad, and upset more days than not and does not respond to parental support. Problems of this kind are best dealt with *before* your child leaves home for college. Are there other key adults in your child's life who can get to the sources of the problem? A relative, minister or rabbi, coach, or teacher? The parents of a best friend? If your concerns mount, talk to high school guidance personnel or a physician for a referral to counseling. Ask your teenager if he or she would like to consult someone outside of the family. If your child is missing a lot of school, if sleep patterns seem very disrupted (too much or too little sleep), if you hear even vague mention of suicide, insist upon professional intervention.

INDEPENDENT THINKING:
CRITICAL ANALYSIS 101

Sprinkled through the chats in bleachers and grocery stores are the mild complaints of many parents. Do these statements sound familiar?

- Suddenly, everything is an argument.
- Everything I say and do as a parent is wrong or stupid.
- She's always catching me in some inconsistency.
- He thinks only of himself.

These despairing statements may sound like complaints you have muttered about your adolescent, but take heart. Most likely, they are signs that your child's cognitive development is on target.

Remember when your child was just learning to walk, and then would want to walk, and walk, and walk? As adolescents begin to realize their capacity for being good thinkers, some want to argue, and argue, and argue. By middle adolescence, teenagers have developed the ability to reflect upon themselves, others, and society. By the time they leave for college, most have become abstract, flexible thinkers. Regardless of their differing achievement levels, they now critically analyze their own thinking—and yours. In childhood, "Do your homework" was a rule, to be either followed or broken. By adolescence, the homework rule—for that matter, *any* rule—is something to be scrutinized, reflected upon, and perhaps challenged. As one parent noted, by her daughter's senior year she was worn out from arguments about school assignments:

- Why should I do homework every night if I don't have any?
- Why do it now when it's not due until next week?
- The homework assignment doesn't teach me anything, so what's the point in doing it?

We may not be used to being challenged in this way, and on so many issues. It threatens to undercut our authority and our values and can seem rebellious and affrontive. Moreover, adolescents, especially younger ones, seem to live in a world peopled only by themselves and their friends. Some of this behavior is about separation, a kind of cognitive leaving home that young people practice before the actual event.

Of course, when adolescents' behavior is extreme, parents may find it intolerable.

New levels of thinking, or questioning, should not be confused with the adoption of a permanent belief system. Some parents panic when they hear their offspring argue for ideas that are in direct opposition to the family's values. They imagine that these passionate rantings portend the kind of adults their kids will become. Not necessarily so. A teenager who argues for the legalization of marijuana does not necessarily turn to a life of drugs.

Similarly, a high school senior who argues for College A one weekend because of its strong engineering program may well turn around and argue the next weekend for College B because its students take only one course at a time. Then, after a particularly dreary week of disappointing grades or three new essay assignments, the adolescent may argue forcibly in favor of taking a year off before starting college.

The ability to make well-reasoned arguments, a skill we should encourage in young people, is not to be confused with winning arguments. Parents do best if they listen respectfully to their adolescents' points of view, express their own, and then make a decision appropriate to their children's level of maturity. Moreover, arguing isn't the same as disrespectful or abusive accusation. Forming and defending their own ideas and defending them are important skills for college-bound adolescents. Learning how to manipulate or bully to get their own way is not.

INDEPENDENT THINKING
WHAT PARENTS CAN DO

See some of your adolescent's challenges as signs that he or she is growing, not necessarily rebelling or rejecting your values.

Look at the positive side of arguing. The young man or woman who can argue rationally and convincingly will be able to stand up for beliefs later on in life, and be able to tolerate a wider diversity of views.

To short-circuit some arguments, turn the tables. Ask your child to make a good argument for and against the position he or she is taking about schoolwork, curfew, time management, or other responsibilities.

Help the adolescent whose arguments with you look more like outbursts to state a position calmly and logically. Then listen, compromise if possible, and, even if you feel you must take a firm stand on an issue, praise your child for his or her part in the discussion.

If your adolescent seems particularly compliant or passive in the face of adult demands and requests, encourage him or her to speak up. Your son or daughter may be disagreeing with you in silence.

RESPONSIBILITY: THE FIRST SURVIVAL TOOL

"I know I shouldn't be doing this," said a friend, Jan, on her portable phone, "but at this very moment I'm cleaning up Karin's desk looking for her application to Northwestern. I don't know how she can tell what's in this mess. You won't believe it, but I found three parking tickets, two overdue library fines, and her driver's license! She's driving around illegally, she owes the city money, and she expects to survive at a college next fall!"

Is your adolescent ready to shoulder the responsibilities of independent living? Can she manage her own money? Can he get himself to school and work on time without you? Does she handle long-term projects well? Does he plan and follow through? How well can he remember to carry out important tasks without your reminders? Can she keep track of personal belongings without the aid of a Persistent Parent Organizer? (Note: Persistent Parent Organizers should keep in mind their adolescent's new emotional need for privacy. Is finding those parking tickets in your child's desk necessarily worth the argument that might ensue?)

Working parents of adolescents in today's culture are used to having their children spend a significant amount of time on their own. Like their parents, many high school students have multiple major responsibilities to juggle: school, work, child care for younger siblings, home chores, lessons, team sports, performances. This generation of high school students is so used to managing myriad tasks that, for some, college living may actually be simpler.

The major difference, however, between a busy, responsible high school senior and a similarly active college freshman is that the high school senior has a safety net. The college student doesn't. In high school, when a well-organized, conscientious adolescent gets overwhelmed by details or forgets something important, a parent can usually step in to help. Our younger son had difficulty with car keys in his junior year of high school. We bailed him out once after he locked them in the car, and then a second time after he lost them altogether. Then we stopped helping. In college, that back-up will be missing, and he is likely to find that a jolt.

Matt, a new student at a community college, decided to treat his two-year college experience as if he were living in another city away from his mother, even though he was in an apartment across town. Accordingly, he called just once a week and tried to resist stopping at home or checking out a course decision with his mother. "I didn't realize how hard that would be," he related. "Last year I made most of my own decisions, but I knew my mom was always around to catch mistakes or do things I forgot to do. This year, since I'm trying to be entirely on my own, it's pretty hard."

Your child will be handling some areas of responsibility, like money and personal health, for the first time (see chapter 7). In these areas, parents naturally find it much harder to take a "hands-off" position, but letting go is much easier if children have had some experience with things like bank cards and thermometers.

What is a reasonable set of responsibilities for a high school junior or senior getting ready to leave for college? Most college advisory personnel suggest that both male and female students be able to:

- Get up on time, and plan bedtime with the next morning's schedule in mind.
- Budget time reasonably well and keep a calendar that notes classes, appointments, and deadlines.

- Manage a checkbook, credit card, simple budget, and telephone calling card.
- Keep track of important papers and belongings.
- Know when medical attention is necessary.
- Do laundry.
- Make simple meals and eat healthily.
- Budget academic responsibilities against an active social life.
- Ask for help when overwhelmed.
- Know how to plan ahead.

Don't despair if your teenager still lacks these competencies. Even if your child is heading to college this fall, it's not too late (see chapter 6). One mother whose daughter was a Wesleyan freshman spent the last hour on drop-off day explaining how to balance a checkbook against a monthly statement.

Decision Making: What to Do, When, and How

Part of being responsible is making good decisions. Choosing a college or deciding whether to attend college right after high school may be the biggest life decision of teenagers' lives. That choice (if they are given a choice) is difficult for most teens, particularly if they have had little prior practice in decision making. How many decisions does your son or daughter make right now? In what areas? Are there certain kinds of decisions you worry about? What successful decisions has your child made?

As an adolescent's world expands, so do the choices. Some are comparatively simple: What homework to put first and last? What kind of language or science to tackle? Work at a paid job or not? Try out for a team or orchestra position? Buy this shirt or that jacket?

How does your adolescent handle these decisions? Logically or impulsively? Is your child reasonably decisive? Does he or she seek out needed information and consult others appropriately?

Other decisions are hidden from parents and have more to do with risk taking. Here we hope for the best. We hope that our teenagers gauge situations accurately and use their heads. We hope that our words of stern caution ring in their ears, but know that they don't. We want to shout the right answers to our teenagers' inner questions

(Should I drive even though I've had a beer? Should I skip class to leave early for a concert?).

Some answers seem obvious to us as parents, but do we really know what good decisions are for our children all the time? After two weeks of class, our younger son, Dan, suddenly decided to drop chemistry from his eleventh grade academic load. The course required solid algebra skills, not his area of strength, so he decided to delay chemistry until after he had another year of math. Rob and I inwardly and outwardly groaned. Wasn't he giving up too early? Shouldn't he get extra help and push on? Dan argued that he couldn't risk a deflated grade point average—he'd take chemistry as a senior after he'd already applied to the college of his choice—he'd risk that he'd be better equipped in a year. We nodded our approval; his arguments were sound and the risk was moderate. But privately we worried.

Sometimes we forget that an adolescent's task, particularly in the final years of high school and first years of college, is to find his or her own way, even when that means taking risks.

Risk Taking

Sandy, the normally unshakable parent of a college senior, offered this story about responsibility and risk:

> Within days of her eighteenth birthday, Sarah informed us that she was now eighteen and no longer required our signature to learn to skydive. As a lifelong acrophobic, I thought this sounded like a greater than acceptable risk, so my mind searched for reasons to forbid her to skydive. But she was right: I could not really forbid her, since she was over eighteen. Finally I decided to give the issue over to her father. After her first jump, Sarah described every detail of the experience and gave us the vicarious thrill of flying. Three years later, she is a fully certified skydiver and proudly displays her skydiving certificate in her rooms both at college and at home.

More than any single achievement, or accolade, or accomplishment, parents want their children to be safe. Because infants rely on their caregivers for an extended period of time before they can survive on their own, we are quite used to assuming responsibility for our children's health and welfare. In their late adolescence we must turn that job over to our children themselves, and it isn't easy. Adolescents lack judgment and experience, we say collectively as wiser and older adults.

Not necessarily. Some researchers point out that on average adolescents are no more risk taking than a typical thirty-year-old. Most young people *are* making decisions from some logical, albeit inexperienced, place, not acting solely on a whim. And in all honesty, mid-life adults take some high risks themselves: Can you say that as an adult you never drank alcohol and then drove? Have you never risked pregnancy through lack of birth control? Or invested far too much money in an iffy stock? In fact, risk taking is an important part of many serious adult careers.

Clearly, the basis for some adolescent decisions is flawed. Researchers speculate that some bad decisions are due less to impulse than to lack of knowledge and experience. Other risky behaviors are driven by curiosity, group contagion, sheer fun, or peer pressure. We know this as parents, and as Anne Roiphe describes in her book *Fruitful: A Real Mother in a Modern World,* it's awkward and painful to let adolescents go:

> *I know I can't help, solve, sooth, remind, caution, protect, save. I can't follow them into their room, into their journals, into their days. I am full of self-pity. I feel wronged, innocent, awkward. Sometimes I am like a detective, lurking in their shadows, picking up matchbook covers to see where they've been and rifling drawers looking for signs of sex, drugs, love. I know I am not the only mother keeping this vigil. That is small comfort. I feel like an exile in my own home.*

In my clinical practice, I ask adolescents "caught" in dangerous acts to describe the reasoning behind their risk taking gone awry. Sometimes hopelessness makes "Why not?" the guiding force behind decisions: "It doesn't matter if I get kicked out of school or get pregnant; I'm too stupid for college, anyway." Often sheer misinformation and inexperience have been at work:

- ◆ I thought you could get three speeding tickets without losing your license.

- Marijuana doesn't impair your judgment, and it isn't addictive.
- My period is so irregular, I probably won't get pregnant very easily.

We do want adolescents to have the self-confidence to take reasonable risks in areas where it makes sense: take the chance to display artwork at a local gallery, try out for a highly competitive team or orchestra, submit an essay to a writing contest, try to get a job working for the city engineer, call a new friend, apply to a highly selective college or university, or take a year off and travel before starting college. You may have a child who needs a gentle push to take more risks, especially if he or she is living close to home. The trick is to actively help adolescents explore without inviting danger and to monitor them closely enough to spot risk taking that has serious long-term consequences.

Do you believe that your son or daughter takes too many dangerous risks or too few reasonable risks? Parents *can* influence risk taking.

RISK TAKING

WHAT PARENTS CAN DO

Give your adolescent many opportunities to make decisions, and be generous with praise for those that work out positively.

Talk to your teenager about how he or she estimates the benefits and costs of certain behaviors. How does your teenager handle peer pressure? These conversations may reveal some important gaps in knowledge about high-risk behaviors like drinking and drug use, sexual intercourse, and reckless driving.

Help your teen to develop a sense of "other": seeing things from another person's point of view, how other families and culture see behaviors, why laws exist, how one person's actions affect others, the value of empathy and caring. This is what moral teaching is about.

When you can, help your adolescent to recognize and prepare for high-risk situations.

Problem Solving

Adam / October 30

> *Today was truly the pits. There wasn't any real reason for it but I felt depressed and sad all day. I think I need to spend all night working on school work, with no distractions, and then break a good sweat on the bike. Clean that old system right out like a bucket of jalepeños. But I think I'd rather wallow in my own miserable misery for a while. I'm in the mood for discussing existentialism over espresso with people in tight-fitting black turtlenecks. Everyone will have names like Andre and Isabella and we'll all be ironically detached from life.*

Mild mood shifts are part of adolescence. Leaving home will test any adolescent's capacity for effective problem solving and healthy coping. A larger world, bigger responsibilities, and more relationships mean that our children will have to thread their way through dilemmas big and small in college:

- My roommate is driving me crazy.
- It's so noisy in the dorm at night.
- I'm failing chemistry!
- Where did all my money go?
- My girlfriend back home is losing interest in me.
- What should I major in?
- I might be pregnant.
- Should I transfer?
- I just feel like quitting.

How does your child typically cope with problems? Most adolescents who are adjusting well to leaving home strike some balance among three strategies: figure it out myself, talk to my friends (including siblings), and talk to my parents (or other authority figures). Think of how your child balances the resources of self, peers, and adults when a problem arises. His or her method may be different from, but as effective as, your own. It may change depending on the circumstances and it will certainly continue to evolve away from home. There is no ready formula, and there are pluses and minuses to each style:

- The adolescent who relies most on her or himself to cope with problems may function very well away from home *or* may let a difficult problem smolder too long.
- One who is heavily reliant on peers may easily transfer that coping strategy to newly made friends at college *or* feel a gap in coping with the daily absence of high school friends.
- The older teen who tended in high school to lean heavily on parents for help with problems may reap the benefit of their steady counsel and go on to be a good problem-solver in college *or* feel inadequate to cope away from home.

The parenting trick is to respect your child's own coping style *and* assess whether any of the three resources—self, peers, and adults—needs some new emphasis. Most important, make sure that your almost grown child has ample opportunity to make his or her own decisions, large or small. Weave the words *decision, problem solving,* and *coping* into conversations:

- What is your decision about (preparing for the SAT or ACT, drinking after prom, your summer job)?
- How will you solve this problem of (a low grade in calculus, too few or many college choices)?
- How are you coping with (pressure to do well on your AP tests, saying good-bye to friends, uncertainties about your college choice)?

Clearly, some coping strategies create problems of their own. The young person who solves problems by putting them out of mind or, in the case of drug and alcohol use, *altering* mind finds that unsolved problems grow instead of disappear. Conversely, a high schooler who overfocuses on problems and becomes very anxious tends not to find solutions either. Some adolescents minimize, fabricate, and manipulate in the face of difficulties. Those who have learned to lie and charm their way out of difficult situations will find less sympathy among adults and peers in a college environment.

If your adolescent copes in any of these ways, look homeward first. Whether we like it or not, our children borrow heavily from our own styles of solving problems.

PROBLEM SOLVING
WHAT PARENTS CAN DO

Help your adolescent develop new problem-solving strategies by assessing your own ways of coping as a parent.

Keep steady but gentle pressure on a son or daughter who is avoiding a problem or difficult decision (e.g., to keep or get a job, to look at colleges, to plan a summer).

Give an anxious, ambivalent adolescent some structure and time limits for problem solving.

Stay the course and be stricter with a teen who is trying to wriggle out of a problem by being a fast talker or a minimizer.

Keep in mind that it's not too late to help your child begin to turn around old habits.

ADOLESCENT SEXUALITY: DON'T LEAVE WELL ENOUGH ALONE

"It was supposed to go better with the baby boomer generation," I thought glumly after trying to talk with Adam about birth control. After all, I came of age in the sexual revolution, basking in the glow of Woodstock. Many of us had tried to cast off our parents' prudish, Victorian attitudes and the heavy guilt and fear that came with them. As parents, we had used the anatomically accurate words for genitalia. When our children asked about sex, we were frank and forthright. We headed into their adolescence with an open and educated attitude, that teenagers should feel positive and proud of their bodies, including their sexuality.

But "the talk" with my son Adam had been an awkward, one-sided affair. Like most parents of teenagers (and more like our own parents than I wanted to admit), Rob and I unconsciously took a "let sleeping dogs lie" stance and only dared to broach the subject when the need to do so was all too clear. We "fit the data" of research on parents' treatment of adolescent sexuality:

- Unfortunately, most parent-adolescent discussions about sex occur *after* a teenager has clearly initiated sexual activity.
- Parents often lack accurate information and are uncertain themselves about sexuality.
- Fathers, even fathers of boys, are dismayingly uninvolved in their teenager's sexual education.
- Parents' underlying fears are that talking about sex will stimulate more activity and that adolescents are sexually crazed, promiscuous, and irresponsible.
- An adolescent's sexuality almost always triggers memories of parents' own days as sexually active young adults, and the reactions to those memories shape our parenting beliefs and behavior.

Adolescence, particularly the ages of eighteen to twenty-two, is a time when young people consolidate gender role identity (how masculine, how feminine), sexual self-esteem, self-perception of sexual attractiveness, and sexual orientation. College gives almost grown teenagers the space for this developmental task. Young people are very likely to engage in sexual practices during college. By age twenty, eighty percent of men and seventy percent of women have engaged in sexual intercourse.

For parents, the task of sexual education and socialization as children move from high school to college is complicated. As a society, we have sanctioned an enormous early exposure to sexual violence—for example, through the media—but we have little knowledge about how to process that exposure in the family. I once "handled" the frank portrayal of a brutal rape on television by simply turning the television off and saying to a set of stunned teenagers, "You aren't going to watch that here." End of discussion.

Why didn't I take the opportunity the movie presented? The bottom line, described by an expert in the field, is that "Adults do not seem to know how to deal with adolescent sexuality any better than adolescents know how to deal with it themselves." In hindsight, I could have used the movie to launch a discussion with my son about his reaction to the scene. We know that many sexual behaviors are dangerous and destructive to individuals and to the society at large: unprotected casual sex, sex under the influence of substances, early and unwanted pregnancy, sexual harassment, and rape. As adolescence has begun earlier and ended later, we have faced increased concerns about unprotected sexual intercourse and the sexual relationships among very early teens. HIV/AIDS, the rise of other sexually transmitted diseases (STDs), and teenage parenthood are now sociobiological problems of immense proportions.

Our tasks as parents regarding adolescent sexuality are complicated by the fact that young people have many "scripts" from which they take their cues: gender, family of origin, peer subculture, class, ethnicity and race, religion, and the society at large. A white Irish-Catholic boy living in middle-class rural America is likely to think and behave differently about sexuality than a Hispanic teenage boy living in San Diego, or an East Asian Hindi girl recently immigrated from New Delhi, or an African-American Muslim girl from New York City.

What should parents know about today's adolescents and sexuality? As much as possible. A study reported in 1985 described the sexual practices of adolescents, ages thirteen through eighteen (the picture in 1998 is not likely to be vastly different). Erotic fantasies are frequent in over seventy percent of both boys and girls. Fantasies, sometimes accompanied by soft porn magazines, are used for arousal, sexual substitution, and sexual self-knowledge. Masturbation is relatively common, more for boys (forty-six percent) than girls (twenty-four percent). A certain amount of guilt and shame still exists about masturbation, although social condemnation has faded.

Recent studies of sexual practices between heterosexual adolescents reveal that by tenth to twelfth grade, nearly half have had sexual intercourse. By ages seventeen to eighteen, fifty-eight percent of girls and sixty-five percent of boys have engaged in vaginal intercourse. Oral sex is fairly common among adolescents of both genders by senior year of high school (twenty-six percent). Some engage in this practice from the fear of pregnancy and HIV; others to protect virginity. (Teenagers must be told that they can contract HIV/AIDS or other STDs through oral sex, just as through intercourse, if they do not use a condom or dental dam.)

Homosexual encounters for most adolescents are transient and exploratory. The growing (at a snail's pace) social acceptance of a gay or lesbian orientation has meant an increase in homosexual experimentation in some high schools, provoking alarm among adults who regard homosexuality as sinful, deviant, or morally corrupt. Openly gay teenagers continue to face negative reactions from some parents and friends. In one study, thirty percent of gay teens reported physical assaults and fifty-five percent reported verbal abuse related to sexual preference.

Homosexual teens and straight adolescents with gay or lesbian parents are very likely to encounter prejudice and harassment from high school peers. These young people may need an extra nudge to "come and talk when you get comments." A few, but not most, heterosexual teens of gay and lesbian parents become very active sexually as a way to "prove" their straightness to themselves and peers. Most, however, are ahead of the game in confronting their own sexual identity and preference.

A 1995 report by the National Commission on Adolescent Sexual Health noted that a healthy sexual relationship, whether gay or straight, boils down to five words: consensual, non-exploitive, honest, pleasurable, and protected.

SEXUALITY

WHAT PARENTS CAN DO

If you haven't already, begin to accept your almost grown child as a sexual being who has normal sexual longings, curiosities, and behaviors. Accept that your adolescent may make different choices than you made as an adolescent. These choices are embedded in culture and are not necessarily signs of a character defect or abnormality.

Invite adolescents to talk with you well before you sense that they are actively experimenting with sex.

If you think that your son or daughter is engaging in sexual intercourse, ask about protection and be open to talking about it. If you can't provide them with education about protection, arrange for them to talk with a physician, nurse, or Planned Parenthood counselor.

Allow yourself to remember your own emerging adolescent sexuality. Talk about that time with a trusted partner or friend to sort out the particularly strong reactions you may have to your own teenager. Are any of your past experiences shaping your parenting in extreme ways?

Don't believe the myth that talking about sex with teenagers makes them more likely to try it. Stay educated about sexual practices among adolescents. Stay informed about birth control and methods of sexual protection and dare to have an open and frank discussion with your son or daughter about what's available. Let him or her know what your opinions are, even if you expect disagreement.

Stress the importance of *choice* in sexuality. Sons particularly need education about sexual harassment, rape, and other kinds of sexually intimidating and violent behavior, especially regarding the role of disinhibiting substances like alcohol and cocaine. Daughters especially need education about the power aspects of sexuality: the loss of power that results from combining substance abuse and sex, and ways to handle sexual coercion.

If you think your child is trying to tell you he or she is gay or lesbian or if he or she has announced a homosexual orientation, work toward an accepting attitude and give your adolescent support. These young people are facing enormous prejudice in our society, and it helps them a great deal if their parents are accepting.

EATING DISORDERS: FOOD NOT FOR THOUGHT

Crash dieting, punishing exercise, and an obsession with body shape are regular features of Western culture, as any parent of an adolescent girl well knows. This atmosphere has given rise to serious eating disorders among three to five percent of the teenage girl population. Anorexia (extreme weight loss) and bulimia (bingeing and purging) are primarily adolescent disorders and claim many more women than men. The causes of both patterns are not fully known. However, it is generally agreed that they represent emotional problems rooted in low self-esteem, a high need for control, and a culture that promotes a very thin body-image, particularly for females. Anorexic young people, who are often high achieving and socially withdrawn, are sometimes found to be struggling with growing up and with their emerging sexuality. They have an intense, irrational fear of becoming fat. Adolescents with bulimia tend to be more extroverted and appear well-adjusted. They ride an emotional roller coaster, according to Lawrence Steinberg, wildly vacillating between self-loathing when they binge and elation or relief when they purge by vomiting or taking laxatives or engage in extreme exercise.

Both disorders require treatment and, particularly in the case of anorexia, can be life-threatening. Adolescents with signs of anorexia and bulimia often resist treatment and must be coaxed—or taken—by parents and friends for help. If you suspect your daughter or son has the signs of either problem, be aggressive about seeking help before your teenager leaves home. The current college environment may, both directly and indirectly, facilitate and foster the occurrence of eating disorders in vulnerable students. High personal and interpersonal stress is commonplace in the first year, college social life can be out of control or isolating, and there is ample room to hide a disorder. Most colleges are aware of these problems and are increasing medical and psychological counseling for students.

SUBSTANCE ABUSE: EVERY PARENT'S BIG WORRY

Like many parents, I read the statistics about drug and alcohol use in high school and college, and—after absorbing the shock of the numbers—feel a deep, sorrowful discouragement. The main reasons adolescents use substances (in decreasing order of influence) are social pressures ("It's what most of my friends do when we hang out"), family and societal role models ("Why can't I do it? My parents and every adult around me does"), hedonistic purposes ("I do it to have fun"), disinhibition ("I loosen up when I get drunk"), and as a coping mechanism for covering feelings and coping with stress ("I feel better").

Not surprisingly, these are also the main reasons why adults use alcohol and drugs. Our entire Western culture is, according to psychologist Joseph Nowinski, pro-chemical and anti-dysphoric:

> . . . we have become, collectively, a society that is phobic of anxiety, grief, or any dysphoric emotion, just as we've become preoccupied with enhancing and sustaining euphoria. The power of this cultural ethic on youths can't be overestimated.

Comparatively few teenagers choose a course of abstinence as they move toward adulthood. Most are moderate users; others are binge drinkers and smokers with serious addictions by middle to late adolescence. There is little comfort even if your child is in the "moderate" group:

- ◆ Judgment is impaired as soon as alcohol or drugs are in the bloodstream. In the bodies of inexperienced, risk-taking adolescents, that can mean car accidents, violence, and unwanted or forced sex.
- ◆ The use of alcohol in adolescence may lead to increased risk for using marijuana and other drugs. There continues to be both support for and criticism of this stepping-stone theory of substance use—that is, the use of alcohol leads to marijuana, which leads to harder drugs. In fact, most adolescents who experiment with alcohol and marijuana don't go on to harder drugs. However, almost all cocaine users have a background of drinking and pot-smoking.
- ◆ Drinking patterns established in high school often persist during college (with a threefold risk for high school binge drinkers).

You may already have had to confront this issue head on. You may have dealt with an arrest, an out-of-control teenager, or a drunken party in your home. You may have seen the frank signs of heavy drug and alcohol use by your adolescent or, more tragically, the loss of life or function in someone you love.

Or you may be just skirting the issue. "I'm just crossing my fingers that nothing happens to my daughter out there," said one mother, who then reached down to knock on wood. "When she gets to a college campus I'll be relieved that she has little access to a car. That's *my* big worry about drinking. We've been lucky so far, in part because Shelley doesn't drink that much, mainly on the occasional weekend when there's a party."

With the ample supply of marijuana in the United States, "weed" is the drug of choice at many high schools. Baby boomers who remember their own pot-smoking days can no longer afford to shrug their shoulders at their kids' use of marijuana. Today's adolescents who use pot smoke it more often and smoke much stronger marijuana. In 1995 a University of Michigan study of national high schools reported that nearly one in twenty high school seniors is a daily marijuana user, with thirty-five percent using it at abuse levels. "It takes me five minutes to find weed at my school," says a typical high school student.

Marijuana is a particularly insidious drug, a substance that for a time allows steady users to function. One depressed young woman I saw in my practice, an honors medical student, smoked marijuana every day of her college career and was continuing to smoke in medical school. She was making *A*s but could not see any connection between her depression and pot use. I attributed this level of denial to her probable addiction to marijuana.

The good news is that the rate of alcohol use nationwide among teenagers in senior high school has fallen somewhat. Many young people are using good judgment about their usage or have escaped addiction. One young woman, Carrie, made such a commitment to herself in high school:

I just decided that I wanted to experience my life fully, not through the haze of drugs and alcohol. Why ruin fun that way, or a

close moment with a friend or a team? It has meant that I have a
smaller circle of friends, most of whom feel as I do. I also have been
in the difficult role of "mother" and "designated driver," watching
over my friends who drink and smoke pot.

The bad news: the use of alcohol has risen steeply in middle school, especially among girls.

A Crash Course in Drug Education

The typical progression of substance use by those adolescents who go on to become serious addicts is as follows:

- Nonuse (as few as twenty-five percent of eighth graders are in this group)
- Nonproblematic alcohol use
- Marijuana use
- Problematic alcohol use (abuse)
- Use of hallucinogens, amphetamines, and other pills
- Use of cocaine
- Use of heroin

The motivational stages of substance use and abuse by adolescents, according to Nowinski, are:

- Experimental (motivated by curiosity)
- Social (motivated by "fitting in")
- Instrumental (motivated by altering emotions or behavior)
- Habitual (users do not feel "normal" when they are straight)
- Compulsive (life is increasingly organized around substance taking)

Instrumental use can easily lead to addictive use. Although those recovering from marijuana addiction do not suffer from the physical withdrawal symptoms of alcoholics, it is a substance that produces negative physical changes in the body and becomes psychologically addictive over time.

Adolescents who are depressed and/or have attentional problems in school are particularly susceptible to using substances regularly. Note: Adolescents taking antidepressant medication or Ritalin are usually advised not to drink alcohol. Multiple Ritalin pills mixed with alcohol is a common home-brewed "buzz," and mixing alcohol (a depressant) with antidepressants defeats the purpose. A few of the antidepressants (MAOIs) are not safe with alcohol.

Women, as a general rule, tolerate less alcohol than men because of their lower body weight and normally higher proportion of body fat (fat tissue is not effective in alcohol metabolism).

Substance Use and Abuse in College

Leaving home brings substance abuse into clearer focus. Obviously, not every college student uses substances abusively, and some refrain altogether. *But the overwhelming odds are that, even if individual adolescents choose abstinence or moderation, they encounter alcohol and marijuana regularly in their social lives during high school, and those odds increase dramatically during college.* Away from parental supervision, your adolescent will make his or her own decisions about usage. College officials, with the help of some student groups, are trying to reduce substance abuse through legal measures and social pressure. But most efforts touch only the tip of the iceberg. Asked if drinking, pot, and other drugs were as rampant on campus as people think they are, one college official admitted, "It's all true and even worse than you think."

The information gathered about college alcohol use in 1993 by the Harvard School of Public Health and the Robert Wood Johnson Foundation is very—forgive the pun—sobering. The survey of 17,600 students at 140 four-year colleges and universities reveals that:

- ♦ Forty-four percent of U.S. college students engaged in binge drinking during the two weeks prior to the survey (for men, binge drinking is five or more drinks in a row; for women, four or more drinks in a row).
- ♦ While there was wide variation among colleges (from one to

seventy percent), at almost one-third of the colleges more than half the students had an episode of binge drinking during the past two weeks.

- Being white, involved in athletics, or a resident of a fraternity or sorority increased the odds that a student would be a binge drinker.

- Very few students—even those who binge drank three or more times during the past two weeks—said they had a problem with alcohol at the time of the survey.

- About half the binge drinkers (one in five students overall) were *frequent* binge drinkers—that is, they had been binge drinking three or more times in the past two weeks. The consequences: drunken driving, missing class, falling behind in school work, engaging in unplanned and unprotected sex, getting into trouble with campus police, damaging property, or being injured.

SUBSTANCE ABUSE
WHAT PARENTS CAN DO

Educate yourself and your children thoroughly about drugs and alcohol through written material, tapes, and discussion, even if adolescents resist. (One up-to-date written source of drug and alcohol information is *Buzzed*, a book by Cynthia Kuhn, Scott Swartzwelder, and Wilkie Wilson.) It's not enough to say "It's bad for you." Be informed about physiological and psychological changes wrought by substances. Point out to early adolescents the subtle ways drug and alcohol use is marketed in the media.

Refrain from heavy use of alcohol and drugs yourself while your children live at home. Adolescents are much more likely to abuse substances when their parents do.

Take a firm position about alcohol and drug use. For some parents, this is a zero-tolerance position; for others, the stance is no drinking and driving, or no in-home use, or no hard drugs, or some other middle-ground position.

Talk to your adolescent about how he or she copes with peer pressure, and what kinds of resistance or avoidance behavior might be necessary to avoid substance use and abuse.

Talk to other parents and school personnel about patterns of use among your adolescent's peer group.

Be watchful, even in the college years.

Seek help for adolescents who demonstrate patterns of repeated abuse (including bingeing), heavy use, or addiction.

CHAPTER TWO

Surviving the College Search

Adam / December 1

> *I'm counting the days until my acceptance letter comes. I can't bear
> to think of the alternative. I know I'm setting myself up for a mon-
> ster fall, but I just can't help it. I daydream about walking out to
> the mailbox and pulling out the envelope. I open it with shaking
> hands and let out a primal scream of joy and triumph that brings
> the neighbors out. "Who is that madman out there? Oh, it's just
> the Pasick boy, knew he'd snap sooner or later." Then I pass out in
> the road, a dazed look of happiness on my face.*

Pat / October 23

> *I will be happy when this school year is over, in the same way I
> would be glad to have a cast taken off, or a debt gone, or be out of a
> bad job. The weight of responsibility on parents with college-bound
> kids in high school is huge. The irrational inclination to bring final
> judgment on your parenting is more enormous still. Have we done
> right by him? Should we have sent him to private school? Will he
> get into a college that is a good match for him? Trust your instincts,
> I tell my clients, particularly the women. Yet in this march toward
> college, I don't trust my own.*

My sense in the journal that our family was on a "march" begs the
question, "For how long?" The shortest distance between two points—
say, high school and college—is a straight line. Gaining admittance to a
college can be as easy as taking the SAT *or* ACT (four hours for either

test), picking *one* affordable institution which will very likely accept you (maximum one day in the college literature), filling out *the* college application (four hours), and getting a parent or two to complete *the* financial aid forms (four hours). That's two days' time over the course of two years.

Few students and their parents make it that simple. Many families spend tens of hours in the college search process, from the spring of the sophomore year (PSAT time) to the spring of the senior year. The college search becomes an ongoing course of its own, complete with a syllabus, schedule, and homework assignments. Parents and teachers prod college-bound teenagers to:

- ◆ Plan test-taking strategies and appropriate coursework.
- ◆ Enrich their college resumés with extracurricular activities and community service.
- ◆ Establish a relationship with teachers who can write recommendations.
- ◆ Calculate grade point averages and class rank.
- ◆ Make a target list of institutions.
- ◆ Send for college brochures.
- ◆ Make campus visits.
- ◆ Write a dazzling college application and interesting essay.
- ◆ On average, complete anywhere from three to nine college applications.

As parents we devour material and maps, huddle over the family budget (where *will* $1,000–2,000 a month come from?), and scrutinize the tax return of the previous year (panic—did we make too much money last year to qualify for loans?). We puzzle over what kind of college seems best for our almost grown kids: big or small school? public or private? far away or close? university or college? liberal arts or pre-professional? homogeneous or diverse? Calendars fill with deadlines for the PSAT, ACT, SAT, Achievement Tests, APs, and applications. We go from table to table on college night, and we make college visits. Meanwhile, everyone has a life to lead.

Some other issues may never receive serious consideration in the bustle. Bruce Munro, student activities director at Evanston Township

High School in Illinois, has a daring idea for parents: ask your children to consider an alternative to college after high school. "If college wasn't a choice, ask them what they would do instead." The answers may hold a lot of information about your student's passions.

Whether the college search takes twelve hours or twelve weeks or twelve months, it goes best when parents find a mind-set to guide them through the process.

WHAT IS COLLEGE FOR?

What are you drawn to in the college brochures? The pictures of kids chatting seriously in small classes about big topics or the statistics on the numbers of students getting into graduate school? In my interviews about this question, I found that most parents tend to fall into one of two broad categories: those for whom the beginning of college represents *year one of adulthood*, the time to get your first foothold on a career ladder, and those who believe that college is *year thirteen of growing up*. Even for parents who seek a blend of the two approaches, the college search process is often guided by how strongly parents lean toward one stance or the other.

College as Year One of Adulthood

Many parents believe the main reason that students enter a college campus should be to figure out what to do before they leave it. This is a college-as-career-preparation philosophy. Those with this mind-set hear themselves saying (or silently thinking) statements like:

- College is the first door to a career.
- College is a stepping stone on the pathway to . . .
- Childhood is over; it's time to grow up and be serious.

The cost of tuition, particularly at top-tier schools, leads some parents to be quite career-minded about their children's college education.

"They want more value for their dollar," as one college admissions dean put it, "and value is more visible in a pre-professional college track." The overall economy is another major player in this mind-set. When parents and students believe that jobs will be scarce and highly competitive, they are likely to define higher education as job skills training.

To be sure, the statistics are sobering. One recent large-scale study (over 10,000 students) reported in 1996 that forty-three percent of college students sampled the year after graduation (1993) were "under-employed," defined as jobs that were part-time, did not require a college degree, or had no career potential. On the other hand, the era of downsizing may have created a boom in jobs for college graduates with business-related majors (administration, economics, finance, marketing, etc.). Some families have the financial resources and commitment to support postgraduates. Others do not, particularly those who are sending someone to college for the first time. A few may be expecting the new college graduate to begin supporting another sibling's education or contribute financially to the family at large.

Where students go to college matters a great deal to College as Year One families. They want a school with a good track record for the particular career interest the student chooses, or a reputation as an easy "ticket" to graduate school or work. Some want a prestigious, highly ranked school. These parents and students do careful, early research, and the college search process tends to be deliberate and focused. Both the quality of academic programs and opportunities for pre-career internships and experience are highly important.

"I'm not going to spend a lot of money just so my son can have a good time and meet new people," one mother said. She was scowling over college literature with glossy pictures of kids white-water rafting and walking through a rainforest. Parents with this mind-set for college are not enthusiastic about institutions that mainly market an interesting four years. (Colleges themselves assume they must appeal first to the students and second to the parents. Often they try to sell themselves through photos as places where young people will first and foremost have fun, and save the career preparation information for the text and graphs that parents will read.)

Note that at most colleges and universities, curricula oriented toward a particular career beginning the freshman year are rare (exceptions are engineering, music, and nursing schools). You can expect that your child will be in a liberal arts program *designed to avoid a career focus* for the first two years.

A college search philosophy that emphasizes career preparation by graduation has certain advantages:

- The match between student interests and college strengths tends to be easier. The choices are immediately narrowed if a student's strong interest is marine biology, for example.
- Parents feel more justified in spending tuition dollars that won't be "wasted" on directionless pursuits.
- Students who have a strong career interest by year one and have matched it carefully with a college or university may be more satisfied and motivated in their academic work. After college, these students may more easily move to internships, graduate schools, or jobs in their chosen fields.

There are disadvantages as well to a careerist philosophy. Some college counselors worry about students who make career choices by high school's end. Says college preparatory counselor Richard Tobin of the Greenhills School in Ann Arbor:

> *The kids who are one hundred percent certain of their career paths scare me a little. At age seventeen, how well do they know themselves? On what basis can they make that judgment? Have they internalized some parental expectation? They may not have a clue about whether they'd be happy in that career.*

Other counselors point to the danger in selecting schools based solely on career-related criteria. If you *like* your school, for example, you are more motivated to work hard. Factors like location, size, diversity of the student body, and the variety of athletic, intellectual, and creative stimulation contribute to a student's overall satisfaction and enrichment at college.

Remember Dustin Hoffman's Ben in *The Graduate*? Cornered by

Mr. Robinson about his career choice (or lack thereof), Ben found himself nodding numbly to the suggestion "Plastics." A clear career path to guide the college search should come from a careful, internal assessment of a student's strengths and interests, *not* from a student's desire to please or pacify adults. Many students will invent a career direction under pressure from their parents. The student who enthusiastically says "Finance" when pressed about his or her future may mean "I don't really know, but to get you off my back, I'll say 'finance.'" Career explorations take work and maturity well beyond the experience of most high school seniors. Parents who pressure their children to make career choices this early may do so because of their own anxiety.

What happens when career-oriented students choose a "specialty" school, tackle its core courses, and then decide they are ill-suited for the work? All of a sudden, often after disappointing freshman grades, they begin to dislike a particular career track. Panic may set in. While academic struggles in the freshman year are normal, they are worse when it seems that a future career, even a career start, is at stake. One high school honors student saw her Year One of Adulthood get off to a rocky start:

> *I chose a Midwestern school for its great engineering school. When I nearly failed my freshman calculus class, I became really depressed. Not only was my career choice doubtful all of a sudden, but I got worried about letting down my parents. They had been so proud of my accomplishments in high school, and so thrilled that I got into this school.*

Even students who excel in college programs narrowly oriented to particular careers can discover later, as they begin jobs or graduate work, that their career/college choice was premature or off the mark. On the other hand, when the match between college and career feels good from the beginning and that enthusiasm continues, students clearly have a head start on Year One of Life. Said one senior from Indiana:

> *I'm really grateful to my parents for encouraging me to develop my talents for music early in my high school years, and to have a*

clear focus. By the time I was a high school sophomore I knew the three places where I could envision going to college, and geared everything in those directions. I was accepted early to my first-choice school, and by freshman year of college I was already second chair flute in the top symphony. For this summer I'm interviewing with many major arts festivals around the country, and I hope to be in graduate school next fall at a pretty big music school.

College as Year Thirteen of Growing Up

This philosophy toward the college search is typified by a father who had this to say about the process:

I don't want my son settling too early on a career and tracking himself into a college program that doesn't allow him ample room to explore himself fully. That was my mistake. I decided on a business major, put the blinders on, and headed into corporate life right from college. Later I discovered that, not only was it not for me, I didn't even know me.

The philosophy is captured in the following kinds of expansionist statements made to adolescents:

- ◆ College years are the best years of your life—so enjoy them.
- ◆ This is a time to explore to the hilt—expand yourself!
- ◆ College is a continuation of learning and growing.
- ◆ It's a wonderful opportunity to open your mind, not make up your mind.
- ◆ Pursue your interests, not your career, in college.

College for these families is the last stop before the train leaves for Serious Life. Perhaps in wistful nostalgia, some parents want their children to enjoy freedom from the responsibilities of full adulthood. Many hope their students choose a college or university that has a strong liberal arts tradition; they may have had that type of education themselves. These parents are not necessarily less zealous about the college search than the Year One group, and the choice of college often matters just as much. They do, however, tend to let their children lead the college search, as part of the growth process. Their mind-set toward college has some distinct advantages:

- There is less pressure to find exactly the "right" school for a particular career, although they want the "right" school for other reasons.
- Students feel free to search for a college that fits their learning style, geographic preference, and a wide range of interests.
- Young people are encouraged to explore a variety of academic and creative pursuits without early pressure to choose a career. When they reach some tentative goal through declaring their major in the sophomore year, it's a decision founded on a more realistic assessment of interests and strengths.

Doctors who were music majors, accountants who focused on psychology, lawyers who studied theater—the college history of professionals is more varied with every generation. College and university officials earnestly hope that students use their undergraduate education to broaden themselves and not commit themselves to a narrow pathway. They point out convincingly that meaningful paid work in many careers doesn't usually come until after graduate or internship-type training. Even the student planning to be a physician or investment banker is, from the perspective of many graduate schools, best off in an undergraduate liberal arts program, provided that the graduate program prerequisites have been satisfied.

On the other hand, it's disconcerting to parents to see their children wait tables or work in video stores the first year out of college. Students who lack a career focus upon college graduation may need a fifth year of unpaid career exploration to find a direction. Parents worry that the open-your-mind philosophy toward college education does not open enough doors to career opportunities. And a growing number of parents find it hard to justify spending as much as $20,000 a year or more just to enable their late adolescents to continue self-exploration and self-expansion, especially if the family is making considerable sacrifices to afford tuition.

The Problem Philosophies

A few mind-sets about kids and college are fraught with problems:

"Getting In" as a measure of self-worth. Every year school counselors, particularly those in communities where parents are highly educated and achieving, get ready for an anxious group of students—and parents—who seem nearly desperate for admission into a particular institution. These are kids who tend to attach self-identity and self-worth to Getting In. The application becomes the embodiment of everything they are. Usually the college is a highly selective one. Sometimes it is the school that has educated the family for generations. Sometimes these adolescents are the first to go to college in their families or come from families recently immigrated—or wanting to immigrate—to the United States, and being accepted or rejected has political consequences.

Christopher Guttentag, an admissions officer at Duke University, has seen both positive and negative changes in late adolescents:

> While students applying to colleges are more accomplished and more sophisticated than ever before, and make many more informed decisions, some see college acceptance as a referendum on their qualities as a person or a student. They are concerned with creating a resumé that looks good, as opposed to one that really tells us who they are. Combine that with normal adolescent insecurity, and you have real pressure. Sometimes their parents contribute to that pressure, believing that getting into a highly selective and prestigious school is the culmination of everything they have worked for, validation that they've done it right.

Parents, particularly those with children who have high expectations, are warned not to use language like "We'll be so proud of you if you get in" or "We know you can do it" or "Keep your goals high and in sight." Those statements only perpetuate the myth that sheer achievement will get an adolescent into a highly selective college. In fact, great effort and innate ability don't ensure anyone admission to top-ranked schools. Harvard University turns away about eighty-eight percent of its applicants; the percentage of *all* applicants who could do the work (that is, those who have the requisite high scores and grades and fine essays) is about eighty-five percent.

Parents who take personal ownership of and pride in the college admittance process are problematic. "I always worry when parents come to me and say, '*We're* really interested in your college,'" says Mike Sexton, the Dean of Admissions at Lewis and Clark. "These parents are often vicariously involved in the college search, and while I applaud a certain consumerism attitude toward this process, overinvolved parents often set the stage for adolescents who fear disappointing them and who may be ill-equipped to manage their affairs at school."

Personal pride issues among parents, while problematic, are understandable. When their students are accepted to selective, prestigious schools, parents may feel a sense of personal accomplishment themselves. In truth, the public accolades from our parent peer group can feel very gratifying. The myth is alive and well in Western society that good parents invariably have good children who go to good schools, thereby ensuring a good life.

Conversely, if your child has struggled in school, has fewer options than other students, and attends a low-ranked college, you may feel that you have failed somehow. You may worry that others will judge your parenting negatively. Friends' reactions even to admissions at selective schools are indeed noticed.

Pat / April 22

> *Our whole family gathered in a good friend's kitchen, eager to tell him of Adam's decision. Although Adam scarcely noticed, our friend was clearly disappointed. In Adam? In us? It wasn't clear. He forced a smile and said, "Oh . . . really?" when Adam proudly presented the news. Adam didn't notice the slight, but I did.*
>
> *What I wanted from this friend was what I think any senior and his family wants after a college acceptance and decision: hearty congratulations and exuberant pride. Instead this high-achieving friend reacted like someone who, millennia ago, after the hunt, might have*

> *said, "I see your son did not shoot the biggest elk."*
> *I will try to forget our friend's thin enthusiasm. And proudly*
> *cook the elk my son has brought back to the tribe.*

College as the fulfillment of parents' dreams. Few parents can honestly say that their hopes for their children's future have no relationship to their own past, especially if that past has held some major disappointments. W. B. Yeats's poem speaks poignantly to this connection:

> *But I, being poor, have only my dreams;*
> *I have spread my dreams under your feet;*
> *Tread softly because you tread on my dreams*
>   *—"He Wishes for the Cloths of Heaven"*

When our son casually mentioned that he might apply to my alma mater, I lurched into instant hope and nostalgia.

Pat / August 20

> *Adam asks me to drop him off at the Student Services Building for*
> *an application to the University of Michigan. In an instant it's*
> *1968, and I'm back in my own senior year at U.M., wearing a char-*
> *treuse cape and mini-skirt. I'm charging up to the desk in that same*
> *building, looking for a work-study job. Is that same grouchy lady*
> *still there? I see myself cross the street to the Union to pick up*
> *lunch before walking to Angell Hall. Will Adam cross this same*
> *street next fall? Sit in the same desk? This is sheer delight, the pos-*
> *sible continuity from my life to his life, and sheer madness that I'm*
> *so enthusiastic about it.*

Parents who want the best for their children often look back at their own early adulthood, picking and choosing through the experiences they want their children to repeat or not. In hindsight, I wished I had taken my writing more seriously in college; so I found myself dropping hints to my older son that he should consider a career in journalism, *my* old dream. As our younger son, who is athletically, socially, and creatively talented, applies to college, I hope that he continues to pursue those skills, unlike my brothers who pushed aside some of their dreams to pursue more practical careers.

Unfortunately, our own dreams as adults cannot be wholly satisfied by our children. They have dreams of their own. If you always wanted to be a doctor or teacher or musician, and didn't have the support or the resources for those accomplishments, your children will not fare well if they feel the conflicting pulls to gratify their own passions *and* their parents' old passions. When parents' and children's dreams are *similar,* that's joyous. When they're linked ("I want you to accomplish what I never could"), that's a set-up for failure.

College as the ticket to success. More than once I have heard myself and other parents say that getting into College A is a real "ticket," a free Advance To Go card, like the ones we used to draw from Chance and Community Chest playing Monopoly.

But ticket to what? College pamphlets would have us believe that *their* institutions lead directly to a happy and successful adulthood. The pictures are of exuberantly smiling, active, and dedicated students, equally competent with frisbees, friendships, and final exams. As one college handbook cautions, parents may believe that some colleges represent utopia, that a "good" college will lead to a "good" life.

In fact, some parents turn their children's high school careers into a marketing campaign, shaping an image and building a resumé that with top grades and scores will seem to ensure a place at a highly ranked institution. College admission deans like Dean Thomas A. Parker of Williams College, an institution that floats easily to the top of many magazine ratings, has concerns about parents who create what he calls "designer kids":

> *These adolescents have been on a fast track since birth. The sheer level of accomplishment in both academic and non-academic areas is incredible. So is parent involvement and pressure. If a student does not achieve across the board, in all subjects, in all activities, then something must be wrong, from these parents' perspectives. They forget that late adolescence is a time of explosive cognitive and*

personal growth, not just a series of successes. By the time students get here they need time for dreaming and reflecting, time to read whatever they choose and follow their interests. In fact, I urge students to take a year off between high school and college to follow a quirky path.

Parker distinguishes between "pressure," which is a constant push for excellence, and "expectations," a quiet and deep confidence communicated to the student as "You can do it."

What is missing in the college-as-ticket philosophy is the reality that college is only a resource, one that different students will use differently. A diploma from a prestigious college may open some doors, but not if a student hasn't grown in identity and life purpose or developed any real competencies to apply in the work world. Conversely, a diploma from an institution ranked low by *U.S. News and World Report* or *Newsweek* may be gold in the hands of a graduate who achieved high honors and has exemplary skills to present to a future employer.

A college for Mom, a college for Dad. Occasionally, parents are deeply and openly divided about the college search process. Each has a favorite school or kind of school. One may want an adolescent to be aggressive in the application process, while the other is adamant about a no-pressure philosophy. All college-educated parents have had different encounters with college life and want to impart the good and bad aspects of those experiences to their child. But some parents become hostile and openly split. Students are then caught in a no-win loyalty battle and must finesse the process. Some may withdraw from the college search process altogether; others may try to please both parents by applying to where Mom wants and where Dad wants. Either finesse leads adolescents away from their own desires and choices and can sour an otherwise exciting process.

The college search process may throw divorced parents, even those with shared physical custody, together for the first time since the separation. Unless some sort of family trust or special savings account exists for college, divorced parents and their students are strongly urged to jointly agree upon a list of colleges and how to pay for each.

In the best-case scenario, almost grown adolescents get strong support during the college search from both divorced parents. If divorced partners have worked cooperatively during their children's upbringing, college talks are just another set of conversations about their best interests in this crucial transition from adolescence to adulthood. If there has been ongoing animosity, it's not too late to forge a temporary alliance to help launch adolescents to college.

FINDING A COLLEGE
SEARCH PHILOSOPHY
WHAT PARENTS CAN DO

Reflect privately and then with the student and family on the question, What is college for? Do you lean more toward a careerist philosophy or an expansionist one?

If you and another parent or stepparent are split about college philosophies and choices, find a way to keep your child out of a triangle. One way is to support the student being in the lead, without any pressure to please parents. Another way is to avoid taking an absolutist, black-white position. Compromise is the solution, not winning your point.

If you have very strong feelings that your child attend a certain school, or type of school, ask yourself why. If the answer is more about your own pride than about your child's gain, consider ways you can accomplish new goals for yourself as an adult.

Be clear about your working definition of a successful college experience, and then be open to discussing (as opposed to selling) these ideas with your college-bound student.

Work toward reassuring your child that the college acceptance is not about self-acceptance or his or her worth in your eyes.

COACH OR FAN? PARENTS' ROLE IN THE COLLEGE SEARCH

College guidance counselors are in wholehearted agreement that the responsibility for the college search and applications should be *mostly* in the hands of the students, with parents providing support, interest, and assistance as needed. Not everyone is comfortable with this sounding-board, respected counselor role. It's no wonder. What to do after high school is usually the biggest decision of an adolescent's life. Some very naturally take on the job of planning a future after graduation; some would rather their parents do it for them. Most teenagers are in between those two poles. With adults gently nudging them toward the lead and overseeing the process, most adolescents begin more or less to accept this responsibility and, by senior year, make the college decision by themselves.

If you have been very active in your child's education, putting your child in charge of the college search may be a difficult change: As our first son entered his junior year (only two years from college!), I shifted abruptly into parental high gear, the way I always did when some major phase in our children's life appeared on the horizon. When they were ready for preschool, I researched, I rehearsed, I ruminated until we found the right place. Then I got them ready for the change. Same for middle school, same for high school, so why not for college?

"Because it is time for you to let go and downshift into a support position," a wise friend gently told me. "If you control this process, either your kids will start to avoid *it* and *you*, or they will get lazy and let you do all the work for them. Either way, they will tend to select a school based on what *you* want, and then resent it and you later in life. Or, worse, they may drop out or refuse to attend college at all."

I only partially listened. The college guides, college literature, maps, and forms filled my desk and a whole file drawer. I tried to simply "encourage" and not "push," and to keep my internal cheerleading squad under tight control (I wanted to yell, "It's a *great* school. It's *perfect* for you!"). A low-keyed role wasn't perfect for someone like me who likes a lot of control, and I played it imperfectly. It felt unnatural, almost irresponsible, and it was clearly anxiety-provoking to stand back as an ardent fan and watch our older son take himself through the process. Many parents report similar feelings and question whether the less active role is realistic:

- After all, aren't adolescents impulsive and impressionable?
- How can they logically and objectively make such a huge decision on their own?
- There's so much information to absorb; how do they have the time to do all the tedious research?
- What if my child makes the wrong decision? Isn't there a lot at stake, including money?
- I think by now I know my child better than she knows herself.

Richard Tobin, college preparatory counselor at the Greenhills School, offers parents several comforting thoughts when their anxiety grows during the junior and senior years. First, a student's college choice is an educated guess, at best. This is true, no matter how many people become involved, even if the group includes a professional college counselor. All the many *numbers,* like ratings, rankings, grades, and scores, imply that college admission is an objective process. It isn't. "It's a messy process," says Tobin, "one in which parents or kids will never find out everything they want to know or be absolutely clear about a college/student match."

Even when a match seems nearly perfect, the decision can be made—or unmade—by gut instinct. Tobin tells the story of a young man who made a painstaking search through the college literature and campus visits. On the way home from a family vacation, he and his family casually stopped at a "non-matched" college and the student instantly bonded with the place. He turned to his father and said earnestly, "Dad, this place just feels so right for me. I want to go here." And he did.

Jane Reynolds of Amherst College advises parents to trust their children's instincts when it comes to selecting a school that is challenging, but not daunting, intellectually. "They know what the pecking order is, they understand when a school feels right to them. I have never received a call from a student, though I get lots from parents, about why he or she was not admitted here."

Parents need not—should not—stay too far in the background during the college search. Like any good fan or assistant coach, they need to know the way the game is played. Do help your son or daughter gather information about colleges and financial aid. Talk to other parents. Read through all the literature and make note of due dates and requirements. Take advantage of natural opportunities for discussions: for example, your school's College Night or visits from friends and relatives who have recently attended a particular college (emphasis on recently—colleges and universities change dramatically in one generation).

Students benefit from parental assistance in anticipating special challenges they may face in college. For example, if your child will be in a minority at college—by race, class, disability, or sexual preference—you can help him or her by exploring expectations, concerns, and coping strategies. One African-American woman spoke poignantly and painfully of her first year away at school:

> *I grew up in an almost exclusively Black, Southern community where I was a really good student. My parents couldn't afford the kind of travel or summer study that would have let me live day to day in racially mixed groups. We were thrilled that I was accepted to a Northern college, at a school that was very academically challenging.*
>
> *That was all short-lived. It was predominantly white, and once I got there, I was subject to remarks and innuendo I had never heard before. It was a terrible year. After I found a group of other African-Americans, it got better. My parents did their best, but I wish I had been more prepared for what happened to me.*

Marginalization, stereotyping, frank prejudice—some minority adolescents appear to have already successfully negotiated these attitudes and behaviors. However, entering a new, uncertain system may generate significant worries and fears. Parents of minority students can help by trying to surface the issue of difference in college setting, perhaps by sharing their own personal stories of prejudice.

In college, issues of racial identity can arise with members of one's own race. Sylvia Jones, an African-American faculty member at Eastern Michigan University, advises students of color who are often faced with pressures to choose between being either Black or white, with no middle ground.

> *There are degrees of racial identification in young people, which arise from their family and home community. When they get to college, they are thrown in with other African-American young adults who vary in their identification with the Black culture. And this can be hard, for example, on someone who has both African-American and white friends. For example, some Black students, working themselves to make a stronger racial identity, look askance at someone from their race who dates a non-Black student.*

Minority students now comprise twenty-five percent of college students. Colleges will continue to increase their enrollment of minority students and become more sensitive to the needs of diverse students. Many institutions are quite serious about addressing issues of difference and promote a real learning environment. Others pay only lip service to their responsibilities as a diverse setting, and the atmosphere is one of separation and isolation.

Pioneering students who are the first in their family to enter college have three big tasks ahead of them. The first is like any student's goal: gaining admittance to colleges of their choice and financial aid that will sustain them. But the other two jobs make the college search more complicated: these students must learn the ropes of college admittance without the benefit of their parents' past experiences; and often they are faced with educating a parent—sometimes a foreign-born parent—about the process. As a young man from Korea, a senior in an urban American high school, described:

> *My parents, who never went to university, sent me to the States for high school because they wanted the best for me. I stayed with friends of relatives, learned English, and worked very hard in school. I am applying to college now, though it is difficult because I must teach my parents how to fill out the financial aid forms. Also,*

they do not understand why I want to leave New York City, where there is a Korean community, to go to the University of Texas. They will agree, I'm sure, but I spend a lot of time in letters convincing them. As soon as I earn enough money as an engineer, I will bring the whole family over from Seoul, including a younger brother and grandmother.

Parents who have no experience with college themselves often find it helpful to use their student's high school counselor as a guide through the college search process. The many choices, forms, tests, and interviews make this a daunting and often intimidating process for parents who are unfamiliar with college and/or American colleges.

MINORITY STUDENTS
WHAT PARENTS CAN DO

During college search or orientation, ask direct questions of college professionals about how the institution supports minority student life and services and helps students deal with prejudice.

Work toward understanding the difference between concerns or values that come from your own experience and those that are clearly part of your adolescent's struggle as a minority student. For example, you may have your heart set on your child's attending a historically Black or Hispanic college, while your student wants a more diverse college—or vice versa.

Encourage your student to talk about the challenges he or she believes lie ahead in college and the coping strategies that tend to be helpful. For example, how does your daughter or son think that a minority status will affect social relationships with peers?

WHAT ABOUT MONEY?

"Rising College Costs Imperil the Nation" and "With College Costs Sky High, It's Time for a Savings Plan." The headlines are enough to send any parent into instant panic, or at least in search of a second job or second mortgage. With few exceptions, parents are anxious about college tuition and aghast at the steep rise in college costs. This is aptly termed sticker shock by author Neale S. Godfrey, who watches parents become paralyzed when they see total college costs and then do nothing.

Godfrey and others emphasize the multitude of grants, loans, and scholarships available for most students, at most institutions. Such financial aid commonly breaks down into four types:

Scholarships: Awards to students based on merit or merit plus need. Available through educational institutions, private foundations, service alumnae groups, and governmental agencies.

Grants: Awards based on financial need that do not require repayment. Available through educational institutions, the federal government (Pell, Perkins), and state agencies.

Loans: The most common are government-guaranteed, low interest (8.25 to 9 percent) loans to students (Stafford) and parents (PLUS). These are offered by private lending institutions or colleges. There are no upper limits on how much parents with good credit ratings can borrow for PLUS loans; however, students must first reach the limit on their Stafford loans before parents can receive PLUS loans. That limit in 1997 was $2,626 the first year; $3,500 the second; $550 for the third and subsequent years; and $8,500 for each year of graduate school.

Work-study programs: Jobs that allow students to earn money while they are enrolled in school.

Even though there is money available, college is still a very costly item in most household budgets. Paying for tuition may mean one parent working an additional job, an after-school or weekend job for the teenagers, and family cost-cutting and sacrifice in vacations, weekend recreation, and toys. Having two children simultaneously in college will add over $25,000 to our annual budget; this has forced us to look at our financial strengths (the ability to earn money) and liabilities (failing to save, eating out too much, and traveling on credit).

Some of the panic is unfounded. Parents can take comfort in at least three realities:

1. Financial aid is no longer just for the poor, and scholarships are not just for the very top students. If families are willing to borrow, college is still affordable. Middle- and lower-income students need not rule out an expensive college or university, and even higher-income qualified students can obtain aid if they are especially sought by some institutions. For example, forty-one percent of all students and sixty percent of students at private four-year colleges receive financial aid.
2. The soaring tuition stories apply mostly to the approximately thirty-five mainly private colleges and universities charging $20,000 or more for tuition and fees. In 1997 the average tuition and fees for the 11.1 million students attending public institutions was over $3,000 a year. The 2.9 million students who attended private four-year colleges paid an average of about $12,000 a year in tuition and fees, with only two percent paying $20,000 a year or more. (Of course, at both private and public institutions, room and board are also major expenses for families of students living away from home, hiking overall costs at public and private universities to more than $10,000 and $21,000 respectively.)
3. Congress has passed a series of tax credits beginning in 1998 to help ease the burdens of college costs for single and married parents with adjusted gross incomes of up to $150,000 a year.

Finding college money is difficult for most families, but finding a workable mind-set about money is something everyone can do. Two myths surround money issues. One myth is that education is a commodity, like a home or car or major appliance, in which price reflects value. An expensive college doesn't mean that it is necessarily the best institution for your student. Each year the popular magazines list schools that are high in quality and relatively low in cost.

The second misconception is that a school's tuition reflects how well your son or daughter will be educated. As Richard Tobin of the Greenhills School notes, the school is not the education. A student who takes the initiative can get a fine education almost anywhere. Conversely, at a fine school, a young man or woman who is unhappy or unmotivated may devalue the education by failing to take advantage of the institution's resources.

Part of developing a good mind-set about money is being clear about what your family can afford for college costs. Be realistic and open with your student about:

- How much money is available for college from savings and other sources
- What aspects of higher education (name? size? specialty?) you're willing to spend money on
- How much debt you are willing and able to shoulder
- The realities of after-college debt (e.g., monthly payments) resulting from student loans
- What is expected from the student in return for tuition and room and board (working? finishing in four years? repayment? a certain grade point average?)

Dean Mike Sexton, of Lewis and Clark, says:

> *Parents owe their students a clear sense of the present reality about money. I get dozens and dozens of sad letters from accepted students who decline because their parents have let them apply without the family's financial commitment behind the application. I just read a letter today: "Dear Dean Sexton, I regret to decline my admission despite the fact that I would very much like to come. My father can only afford part of the tuition and will not support my coming."*

Understandably, many parents are squeamish about divulging financial information to their children. Bringing up the topic of Our Family's Money may seem more *verboten* than talking about sex. Others choose to stay in their own denial about what's affordable until the acceptances roll in. Some fear that their soon-to-be college students will feel "guilt tripped" if they talk realistically about what they can afford. True, it is not helpful to *open* a money discussion with a long list of what you have had to sacrifice or will sacrifice for your child's college education. However, confronting money realities with your adolescent and handling this issue *early* in the college search process have some distinct advantages:

- ◆ Your child steps closer to the adult world, where money comes from hard work and good money management.
- ◆ You avoid the very difficult situation of giving thumbs-down to a college choice after acceptance.
- ◆ Being clear about what you can afford makes it easier for your student to bargain with colleges and universities about a financial aid package.

There are some clear "don'ts" when it comes to a partnership with your student about money issues. *Don't* avoid financial realities and put off the hard talk about which colleges may be out of the ballpark because they are likely to be too expensive. True, for excellent students a college may offer a handsome financial aid package. But your student should know what *your* bottom line is. As high school counselor Pat Manley notes, "The strategy of 'Well, we'll wait to see if you get in and then assess whether we can afford it' sometimes backfires. When students work hard to be accepted to a particular college only to find it is totally unaffordable, even with some financial aid, they are angrily disappointed and feel set up."

Don't use money as a way to steer your child toward certain schools and away from others. If you have concerns about a particular institution because of its location, orientation, or offerings, say so; don't say "It's too expensive." And *don't* forget to factor in the cost of transportation to and from home as a real college cost. In fact, it's probably safe to add a hefty miscellaneous category to the college budget to cover unanticipated costs.

MONEY

WHAT PARENTS CAN DO

Don't throw your arms up in despair at college sticker prices. While every family has some bottom affordability line, explore all the options for financial aid. *Apply for aid even if you don't think you will qualify.* With your student, learn about the four types of financial assistance. High schools, The College Board (which brings you the SAT), and any of a number of web sites have easily accessed information.

Read and fill out the *current-year* FAFSA (Free Application for Federal Student Aid) early in the college application process. This form is used by most colleges and universities to determine your EFC (Estimated Family Contribution). In order to be eligible for any of the federal loan programs (e.g., Pell, Perkins, PLUS, Stafford), families must complete this form. Unlike IRS forms, the FAFSA is not difficult to fill out. It's available from colleges, high schools, and off the Internet. If a parent refuses or neglects to fill out the FAFSA, the student is likely to be ineligible for financial aid.

Keep track of financial aid deadlines (sometimes different from application deadlines) and enrollment requirements. Some financial aid grants require full-time attendance; if part-time enrollment is acceptable, a certain number of credit hours is required.

Challenge the mind-set that the published tuition rate for a given school is a fixed figure. Increasingly, filling a college class is like filling an airplane. In order to fill it, people are recruited at different prices. At one small school, the 1,227 undergraduates were paying 755 prices to attend. Tuition discounting (through grants), especially at smaller, less prestigious schools, is fairly common for less affluent, more able applicants who are attractive to the school.

Forget the idea that tuition can be drastically lowered by declaring your student independent of parental support. Among the guidelines from the federal government are the requirements that the student be age twenty-four or older, or married, or have a child before independent status will be recognized.

Should your financial status change significantly at any time during the application/enrollment process, notify the financial aid administrator at the college.

Keep in mind that federal student aid is dependent on maintaining satisfactory academic progress once in school.

Divorced parents: Federal guidelines direct that the custodial parent is responsible for college costs. The custodial parent is the parent the student lived with most during the past twelve months OR, if student didn't live with a parent, the parent who provided the most financial support during the previous twelve months. If a custodial parent is remarried, the stepparent's income is also considered. Some colleges will examine the divorce decree to support the required obligations.

College-bound students from divorced families may become involved in a difficult and dismaying parental struggle about college money. Unless college tuition, room and board, and living expenses are part of the divorce agreement (rare), or there is another substantial source of money for college, such as money from grandparents or full scholarships (also rare), divorced parents ideally come to some agreement about financial responsibility for college costs. Do not count on colleges to sympathize with individual situations. Custodial parents, unless there is some other specified legal obligation, are responsible for college costs.

A substantial number of divorced parents, particularly absent, nearly absent, and non-custodial fathers do not pay for college. Judith Wallerstein's long-term study of children of divorce revealed a startling statistic: Of sixty middle-class, college-educated divorced parents followed for twenty-five years, barely half sent their children to a two-year or four-year college. And of those children attending college, only one in ten received financial support from one or both parents. Sadly, only one-third of college students received money from their fathers, who, by some accounts, felt their financial obligations were over after age eighteen. Lower- or middle-income single parents who have the full responsibility for their students usually qualify for financial aid. Mothers with primary custody of their adolescents, however, were often living on a shoestring budget to cover basic survival needs.

For divorced parents with joint responsibility for children, the college search process will almost always bring increased contact with ex-husbands and ex-wives. This is not usually easy. For a still-angry-after-all-these-years ex-couple, old issues about power, control, money, and respect may arise, pitting one parent against another. When this happens teenagers are swept up into painful triangles and conflicts as their parents take positions to "win" arguments about college and defend against being controlled. (Of course, these problems can as easily arise between contentious married partners!)

In one divorced family seen in my practice, a divorce agreement made during the children's college years, while covering the low in-state tuition, did not address any room and board costs, which were half of the total college bill. The high-income father made a monthly deposit to the tuition account but refused to pay for housing, books, transportation, and other living costs. The middle-income mother was left so financially strapped by these expenses that it affected her children's college plans considerably. The older daughter moved out of state and enrolled in a less expensive college. The younger son, who became estranged from his father during the divorce, took eight years to finish an undergraduate education.

Another client whose parents divorced when she was very young found herself uncomfortably begging a distant father each semester for tuition checks. Her parents, who no longer spoke to one another, never agreed upon a fair financial plan for their daughter's college education. She took six years to obtain her undergraduate degree. Without a secure financial base in college, many young adults like my client have to work full-time jobs to afford housing and tuition, sometimes alternating semesters in college with semesters working full-time.

WHAT DIVORCED PARENTS CAN DO

Talk with your ex as a parenting partner as early as possible in the college search process. Be as clear as you can about your visions, your resources, and your concerns. Try not to ask your child to play ambassador.

Remember that, for an adolescent feeling vulnerable about leaving home for college, the surest route to poor adjustment is to leave behind two arguing parents and feel responsible for their misery. This is not a time to take a rigid position with your ex. Ask yourself: "What is in our child's best interest?"

Get support from family, friends, or professionals who can coach you when you're feeling particularly angry and upset at your ex.

If you are in the divorce process as your child is planning to leave home for college, make financial responsibilities for *all* college bills (including room and board) clear in the financial settlement. If funding for college is simply not available, be honest about that and actively help your son or daughter to find other sources of college funding.

CHAPTER THREE

Finding a College Search Process That Works

If you are on the brink of your student's college search process, consider this advice from a set of high school seniors:

- Before convincing a school that he has some worth, a student must first convince himself. For this reason I advise parents to be patient.
- Parents should be extremely supportive throughout the application process. It is very hard and agonizing and takes a lot of time. We try as hard as we can to do our best.
- Create the least possible stress at home.
- Parents put a lot of pressure on kids to do well. To do well in life means going to college. If kids don't accomplish this, they feel horrible and think they have failed their parents and themselves.
- It may seem as though giving your child the final decision for college is the right thing. But the stress might be devastating. They might want to impress the world and make you proud of them, and so choose some fancy institution. But I warn you: they will also feel an overwhelming sense of guilt that can blind them from seeing what the right decision might be.
- Keep the fridge stocked with ice cream sandwiches.

Doesn't this phase of parenting come with an instruction booklet? Well, no—every family invents a unique process based on the family's and student's particular characteristics, resources, and strengths. But the experiences of other parents and the advice from high school and college counselors can be very helpful in the process. They offer some clear messages about *what to avoid* if you want this experience to be growth-producing and positive.

First, don't get way ahead of your son or daughter in the actual search and application process. If your child resists taking the lead, *at least* stay on the same page. Don't make all the phone calls, don't set up the visits for your student, and, above all, don't fill out the applications (just proof-read the essay). And don't cajole, pester, yell. . . . Instead, lend your support and wisdom (rehearse the phone call, consult on the visits and forms, etc.). Above all, don't call the admissions office yourself and try to gain acceptance for your student. If you have previously attended the school and have been a regular financial donor that will be clear to the college without your shouting it from the rooftop of the alumni club.

Second, even if you lean toward the philosophy that college should be career preparation, don't *demand* that your student know clearly what he or she will adopt as a career or even what to major in. With few exceptions, your child will probably make something up just to please you. Students who prematurely and erroneously commit to a career path begin to feel terrible about letting their parents down if the choice becomes a poor fit for their abilities and interests. Or they may continue to pursue careers that ultimately make them miserable.

Third, try to resist going straight to the college literature to find the schools where your student "can get in." That is clearly the tail wagging the dog. Invite your child to reflect on his or her own qualities, personal style, and interests—then and only then turn to the possible matches.

Fourth, resist the myth that there are only some 200 good schools in the United States, and the rest are for academically less talented students. As author Thomas Haydn notes, having only a high school diploma gains admission to 700 junior and community colleges and 130 four-year colleges. A *C* average is acceptable to another 1,000 colleges and universities, while a *B* average allows most students to attend all but about 200 institutions. Students with average academic records in high school need special encouragement to look past the selective schools on the lists of their more academically oriented peers and see the ample group of schools that are likely to welcome them.

Fifth, while you may become frustrated in the college search process, try to avoid questions that imply some judgment, like "If you can't decide on a college, how are you going to make even bigger decisions later on?" Straightforward inquiries are more helpful: "What are you thinking about college?" Even if your student doesn't really engage with you, your questions may register later.

Finally, don't let the college search process become another achievement, something else to accomplish. Choosing a college is just that: The student chooses a place that will serve some general goals and interests. Making the application process one in which everyone becomes very anxious about whether or not the student will be chosen misses the point. Colleges are resources, not judgments about who will or will not be successful in life. Parents may have to bend over backward to make the point to their students, because our Western achievement-oriented culture works against that grain, as our son's reaction points out.

Adam / December 17

Well, I got the news today. Deferred. No matter how you look at it, it's like our good friends at the admissions office have said, "Sorry, big guy, you're not good enough right now. But we'll throw you in the pool again, where the competition is much harder. That way you'll have absolutely no chance of getting in here."

Every time the phone rang today after I opened the dreaded letter, I raced over, picked it up. I expected to hear the voice of the director saying, "I'm terribly sorry, we've made a mistake on your application. Please come to our school on a full scholarship." I'd let him wait for a few beats, and then say, "I'll have to get back to you."

MAKING THE RIGHT MATCH

Most students who feel like they've chosen the right place say the school connects with a core aspect of who they are. Call it soul, self, or spirit—it's about something on the inside.

Not every late adolescent has the inclination and opportunity to begin knowing about "self" at this level. Parents can be helpful to this process, especially if they approach their students with a genuine curiosity and respect for their developing identities.

The following questions can spark students' self-assessment, not just about which school but about which *kind* of school might be a good fit:

What would you like to have a chance to expand on, given what you're doing in school and out of school? If met by a quizzical look, you can prompt, "Think about all that you do in any given week or month. Is there anything you do that really makes you happy? Is there anything you're curious about?" If *that* draws a blank, encourage your adolescent to work with a guidance counselor at school, who will lead him or her through some standardized interest surveys for secondary school students. Or use some of the quicker self-assessments found in some of the college guides.

What do you find yourself daydreaming about in the future? Is there anyone whose work or lifestyle appeals to you? Not all young people are comfortable sharing their private thoughts about the future with their parents, particularly if they are worried about negative reactions. However, parents can stimulate those thoughts. Whenever possible, find ways for your son or daughter to have conversations and/or experiences with various adults whose work is even remotely interesting to him or her. Don't insist on coming along; simply try to facilitate the connections if your child agrees.

What is your learning style? Do you like to work independently, figuring things out for yourself (implication: larger school)? Do you feel that it's important to have a good working relationship with your teacher and other classmates (implication: smaller school)?

What kinds of people do you like or not like being around? Are they like you? Not like you?

How far away from home do you want to continue your education?
Caution: The answer "As far away as possible" should be taken with a
grain of salt. Students who feel overcontrolled often correlate distance
from home with amount of freedom. Even a commuting student can
control the amount of time spent with parents once at college. Some
students want to be able to come home any weekend they wish; others
want to make that less likely but still be within striking distance should
they feel like being home.

TENTH GRADE

College becomes an active player in kids' lives from the spring of the
sophomore year, when the first PSAT scores are reported to colleges
searching for the best and the brightest. Tenth graders wonder: Will I
be able to go to college? Which one will take me? What if I can't get in
to a "good" one? Will I disappoint my parents? How will I compare to
my friends? Nora, a sophomore from Cleveland, writes: "It can get
stressful to work so hard in school now for something so far away.
Sometimes it's better to set short-term goals and think of doing the best
I can for the moment."

For many sophomores like Nora college is still a distant possibility,
just an approaching warm or cold front on the horizon. Mothers and
fathers, looking through their special set of parenting binoculars, see
college coming. But their adolescents are still adjusting to the day-to-
day excitement of high school. A parent who plops down a book like
College Comes Sooner Than You Think, as I did, is likely to be met by
rolling eyes and shrugging shoulders. College is no competition for
staying ahead in geometry, a state track meet, friends meeting at the
beach or bistro after school, the first day behind the wheel, next Fri-
day's rock concert, or a twenty-page essay due next week.

A student's grade point average is the most hallowed number in high
school. Most college-bound sophomores focus on their G.P.A.
Whether you endorse it or not, in many communities high school

becomes a scoreboard: G.P.A., class rank (another Important Number), SAT/ACT scores, Achievement Tests, and AP exams. Even athletics and extracurricular activities may take most of their meaning from how they enhance a student's college resumé. Most educators regret this heavy emphasis on the future for adolescents, who are naturally focused on the present. It becomes a war between having a life and planning a life. Or, as one mother wryly put it, "The rat race begins at puberty, not at college graduation."

For some students the pressure for top grades, whether self-inflicted or parent-inflicted, is extreme. Consider these E-mail messages from distressed honors students:

I'm just a freshman in high school, but I'm still worried about my future. . . . I take honors classes and have a 4.17 G.P.A., but the highest is 4.67. Should I be so worried now? School isn't so hard for me, but the SATs scare the heck outta me. I read in a magazine that it's easier to get a perfect score now. Is that true?

I really want to attend Columbia University. My grades are okay: 4.2. I have all honors classes. My SATs were scary: 610V/720M. Here is the super-scary part: my class rank is 56/570. I'm only in the tenth grade. Will colleges understand how competitive my high school is?

WHAT PARENTS OF SOPHOMORES CAN DO

Try a low-key approach to PSAT scores if your son or daughter takes them in the tenth grade. Since the test gets returned to the high school, encourage your student to see the results as information about gaps in learning. A low score is not a clear sign of his or her capacity as a future college student.

Exploring interests, widening a base of experience with a whole range of subjects and activities, should be the focus in the sophomore year. This is the time for students not only to test academic ability but to explore values and enjoy new friends, new freedoms, social events, and extracurricular activities.

If your child scored rather high on the PSAT, you may be receiving a mountain of college literature. A laid-back approach is best. Have fun reading it, then file it away until next year. The sophomore year tends not to be the best year to begin a target list of schools.

Keep grades in perspective. Sure, grades count toward an overall grade point average. But most colleges and universities look at the whole academic record over three or four years. Dismal performance in a class or two or even three will not seal your student's fate.

ELEVENTH GRADE

Focus on grades often peaks in the junior year, especially now that many colleges encourage students to submit their applications just as they are becoming seniors. But juniors have other agendas as well. This is also the year when they are earnestly and happily living more independently of their parents. Almost all juniors are driving, many have their own money from jobs, peer groups are solid, romances may be flourishing, athletic and artistic accomplishments are solidifying. Many juniors don't want to think about college, even though most are worried about grades.

This is the year to step back and let your teenager be more in charge of course selection for senior year. Said a father, Barry, "I really tried to let my daughter sort through the pros and cons of her classes, even though I had to bite my tongue a few times to hold back my advice. In no time at all, she'll be doing this herself for college, and we won't be there."

College seems more real in the junior year, but life as an adult is still an abstraction. Few juniors have a clear sense of which careers they want to pursue. Most don't want to be nudged out of their secure high school nests to talk about The Future. As one of my son's friends put it: "The only time I think about college is when my parents make me."

Ferris, a New York City mother of a junior, struggled to accept that some of her son's activities are not intended to be college-enhancing:

> While the primary occupation in junior year is supposed to be about grades, SATs, and college stuff, Isaac has specific interests in conflict with the college agenda. It's a delicate balance to support him in all his areas of interest, especially when there's no obvious accomplishment to stick in the college folder: like listening to jungle music or making graffiti drawings or reading about living in the desert.

Some students have vague attractions to different colleges, mainly acquired from what friends or siblings have told them. A few make what seem to be clear statements about what they want and don't want ("There's no way I'm going to school in this state"), driving family anxiety higher. To their parents' despair, some adolescents aspire to attend certain colleges for a variety of supremely superficial reasons. My friends and I once swapped examples of the worst reasons to go to a particular school, straight from the mouths of our adolescent babes:

- ♦ It's got a great basketball team.
- ♦ There's a lake nearby for sailing.
- ♦ I hear the food is half-way decent.
- ♦ During Greek week, all the girls dress up in these fabulous formals and line the walkway to the houses.
- ♦ Madonna went there.

Some parents of juniors are several steps ahead of their children. (Warning: If you are too far ahead of your student, this will be your project, not your student's.) ACT or SAT testing and test preparation, along with college tours during spring break, bring college discussions to the fore.

Parents are often frustrated in their efforts to get college talks going. The only way we could get Adam into conversation about college was to make an appointment with him. By the end of the junior year, most teenagers are confronting their strengths and weaknesses as high school students. Our son Dan returned from school one day during his junior year. "I made my grade point goal by .014 points," he announced. Self-evaluation is positive and can lead to realistic decisions about college. But sometimes a look into the academic mirror is unsettling for adolescents and their parents, particularly if performance goals have not been met.

WHAT PARENTS OF JUNIORS CAN DO

If by mid-year your son or daughter has not begun to talk about college, begin to broach the subject. Students planning to apply to college early in the fall of the senior year get busy by the junior year. (In fact, most students take the SAT or ACT in the spring of junior year, and both tests have application dates—check the counseling office.)

Even if kids are not yet focused, parents should find a mind-set for the college search and begin to educate themselves about loans, scholarships, financial aid packages, and college testing. Divorced parents should begin talking with one another about the coming changes.

The junior year can be full of stress and anxiety about grades, scores, and college applications, or it can be the beginning of a positive adventure. Some families use school vacations in the junior year to visit colleges and travel at the same time. Cruising the Internet together for college information is another parent-student project.

Above all, continue to remind your student that you are interested in and proud of his or her activities and achievements. Try not to let anxiety over grades and test scores or the college search dominate the family landscape. As John Lennon sang so well, "Life is what happens while you're busy making other plans."

TWELFTH GRADE

By senior year, college is no longer at the horizon's edge. Instead, as one senior put it, "It's right overhead, hovering over me." The future may feel very positive, exciting, and full of adventure. But at least until the college admissions process is over, it may loom large and scary as well.

Anxiety at school and home grows in proportion to the sheer number and selectivity of colleges to which students are applying. "I lose sleep over practically everything," said one senior.

Parents are often nudging (and nagging!) their children to make decisions and fill out forms. If there are differences in the family about college, they are sure to emerge this year. Many seniors have had a few productive discussions with their parents, tentatively thought out what they want to pursue in college and which institutions are a good match. Others avoid the whole topic, especially if they know the conversations will lead to a clash of opinions about college.

The scene at school is only slightly less intense. "It's all we talked about in the fall," said Megan, a senior at a large high school in Ann Arbor. "By January we were all so sick of the topic it was banned from conversation." Students report competing urges to apply to the popular schools their friends have chosen *or* follow their parents' advice *or* go with their own instincts. Competition can be fierce among students in affluent communities. One counselor told me about two students in a Southern private school who conspired against a third honors student by writing a phony, negative letter of recommendation to a college to which they were all applying. Non-college-bound students or those enrolling in community colleges may feel a cold blast of snobbery from kids applying to four-year schools.

Being a junior means evaluating one's strengths and weaknesses as a student. Being a senior going away to college the next year means facing fears about acceptance versus rejection and separation versus connection. Whether your student is being expressive or not about these kinds of feelings, you can bet that they hover somewhere in day-to-day life. Some will block out the college application process by procrastinating or through other kinds of avoidance behavior like losing things or chronic indecision.

This kind of behavior usually drives parents crazy. One mother—a high school teacher, no less—described the outcome of her daughter's artful dodging. All her attempts to get her daughter focused on college choices were in vain until the midnight month of December when Rayna finally picked up a college guide: "She ultimately applied to Bates and Bowdoin, and then Vassar and Wesleyan only because they were near the front and back of the book, and she didn't have time to read about schools from the middle part of the alphabet." Last-minute applications will send parents screaming into the night.

Pat / December 4

Can one seventeen-year-old and one supportive, if overresponsible, middle-aged mother turn out five college applications in one sunny Sunday afternoon? What if the teenager has just broken up with his girlfriend? What if his physical therapist has just expressed doubt that his back will be ready for the tennis team in the spring? What if we don't own a typewriter anymore?

As the applications sit like so many stone slabs in the blue file box, I see we have failed him in at least one huge respect. We have taught him that sheer will, determination, and coffee can make up for procrastination. Who knows what this will lead to in life: running out of gas on a freeway, frenzied income tax calculations every April 14, pulling leaves out of roof gutters during a blizzard?

Increasing numbers of colleges and universities are offering application options: *rolling admissions* (colleges consider each application as soon as all materials are in and notify the student as soon as possible), *early decision* (students apply by some date in the fall and must sign a letter of commitment if accepted), and *early action* (like early decision, but without requiring a commitment).

These options have both intensified and relaxed the senior year. Early decision and early action mean that students need to know where they want to apply in the first semester of the senior year and complete their applications in early to middle fall. Applying early also means that students can't use their senior year academic record to boost their college resumé. On the other hand, many seniors who have the college decision out of the way by mid-December say they enjoy their senior year more thoroughly. Quite a few seniors combine early and regular applications, and find that the whole search process works better when they know that at least one college has already accepted them.

At the other end of the continuum, taking a year off from school may make a great deal of sense for some students, counselor Bruce Munro notes. It can be a time to build confidence or skills, experience another culture, or explore an interest. An increasing number of books and "time out" placement services are addressing this need. Some students take a year off by deferring a college admission, and an increasing number of colleges and universities welcome this option. Other young people defer the application process itself. Most colleges and universities feel that able students are stronger academically when they begin college if they've taken a year off first, despite parents' fears that momentum for continuing education may be lost. The advantages, if parents support the plan, are threefold:

- ◆ For a student who is burned out from four hard years of high school work, it provides a badly needed change of pace.
- ◆ After a year of exploration, students tend to be clearer about career goals.
- ◆ An extra year before college is another year of growth and maturity.

The disadvantages to delayed application or enrollment to college are: (1) students may lose some precious momentum for academic life and find it hard to re-engage in the college search; (2) taking a year off may only postpone facing some underlying issues, like low self-esteem; and (3) a delay, which looks attractive to a high school senior, may be sorely regretted once peers have gone in different directions. There is some research indicating that students who delayed their entry to college took longer to complete their degree once they began. (This outcome might be due in part to lack of money to both start "on time" and keep going in a steady stream of semesters.)

WHAT PARENTS OF
SENIORS CAN DO

Keep the instrumental tasks of the college search distinct from the emotional tasks of separating and letting go. There is enough emotional energy in the family of one senior to light a whole village. Whenever the usually positive college search process is getting emotional, ask yourself if there aren't some other uncomfortable things going on for you or your adolescent: saying good-bye, plain old being scared, fatigue, stress.

Expect some up-and-down times, and a lot of uncertainty, even old childhood behavior. One father described how his usually fiercely independent daughter, a senior awaiting a college decision, insisted that both parents sit right next to her while she wrote an English paper. Our eldest son began putting fluorescent stars over his bed, just like the ones he loved when he was a toddler.

Don't assume the college search is the biggest thing on your adolescent's mind, even if it seems to preoccupy you.

After the application process is finally over, acquiesce if your child declares a moratorium on college talk until all the letters arrive in the mail. Everyone needs a break from the future and a chance to savor the last few months of high school.

Seniors Who Get Stuck

If your college-bound senior is resistant to talking with you and doesn't appear to be making any forward progress on the college search, ask your adolescent what he or she thinks the problem is. If that doesn't yield any understanding, and it's still very difficult to discuss college within the family, encourage your student to work with a college counselor. Call the counselor first to alert the school system that your student may be feeling "stuck."

Second, you can invite another adult to open up the conversation about college: an older sibling, a favored aunt or uncle, a family friend, even another parent. Ask your student what adult knows him or her pretty well and encourage a conversation between them. Sometimes parents are not the only or even the best adults to help adolescents reveal what is important to them. The alternatives include someone who is qualified and expert, such as a paid professional college counselor. And any number of excellent books and computer programs help to provide a structure for self-assessment and college planning.

COLLEGE VISITS

No experience is more interesting or more stirring than visiting colleges with your student. For parents of first-borns heading to college, these visits are like a Leaving Home 101 class. One senior, Leah, described how her father began dealing with the coming separation while they were on a college visit:

> My Dad was regressing a little. He started holding my arm as we were crossing a busy street, and giving me exact directions how to find a bookstore that was in plain view across the street. The last straw (but I loved it): he dashed into a shop and bought a Kermit puppet for me.

True, after a few college tours, the institutions can seem all about the same, and the rhetoric, well, rhetorical. However, college visits are educational not only about certain institutions and cities but about college life in the '90s. And, like it or not, it's a chance for parents to gauge just how much we have aged and just how conservative or liberal our values have become. Our pediatrician once paraphrased Winston Churchill when I told him how my own drug behavior as a college student left me confused about what stance to take with our children: "If you're a college student and you're not liberal, you have no heart. If you're an adult and you're not conservative, you have no brain."

There's nothing like the shock of the first college visit to jar one's comfortable values. At Columbia University, the site of my first tour as a parent, my eyes widened when I walked past an armed security guard at the campus gate, and grew wider still during a dormitory visit. The newly mopped corridors were strewn with white three-by-five cards fallen from a wall-mounted holder. Soon we parents were peeling them off our shoes. They were instructions about how to use a condom and dental dam, with accompanying pictures.

The trick with college visits is to drink in the general ambience without a great deal of investment and romanticization, as a friend found:

The campus was picture-perfect. It fulfilled my fantasy of college life. The fall day, the golden carpet of leaves, the sun playing off the colors on the trees, a small intimate campus, the ivory tower of academia, a quaint inn across the street—I was definitely ready to enroll. With Toby at a dormitory with a weekend host, I attended a warm parent coffee, heard an earnest provost speak, went on a group night tour with an English professor holding forth about the town's ghost tales. After a lovely night at the inn, I couldn't imagine how anyone could possibly not want to attend this wonderful school.

Toby wasn't sure. After spending the night with a quiet kid who preferred TV to his hallmates, after several uninspiring meals and a visit to a very basic introductory English class, he wondered if a small college was too restrictive. He had also nursed a bad cold when he was there. Did his impressions hinge on whimsical things? Could he have had a totally different experience with a different host, his cold gone, the food better? Possibly. This is where luck comes in.

FINDING THE RIGHT COLLEGE FOR THE STUDENT WITH A DISABILITY

Graduating high school students with learning and attentional disabilities visit colleges with an eye less to ambience and more to resources. One student, Nate, about to begin his senior year, anticipated the challenges he will face in college:

> *College will definitely be more challenging than high school because I won't have as much help from professors as I've had from teachers and teacher consultants. And it'll be harder to concentrate because other things will compete for my time: friends, activities, sports. One positive is that I think I'll compare myself less to other students because there are so many of them and everyone is taking different classes. I plan to use study groups to help me in ways that my consultant did in high school. And my parents and I are looking for a college that has a good resource center to help with learning disabilities.*

If your adolescent has demonstrated physical disabilities, including attention deficit disorder (ADD or ADHD), learning disabilities (LD), a sensory disability, or a psychological disability, you may want and need to play a more active role in the college search process. It's a delicate business, however, one requiring parents to walk a fine line. On one hand, taking the lead as a parent seems prudent. A disorganized or impaired student may become easily overwhelmed with the level of detail and tenacity required in a college search. And a student with a spotty academic record and special needs is likely to need extra reassurance about applying to schools, especially if it means leaving a familiar support system. On the other hand, the hour is near when an adolescent with special learning needs will have to organize and seek support without parents or an assigned resource teacher. Giving up any part of the support role is not easy for parents who have been central in their children's learning, but it's important that they relinquish some of that job to their almost grown children.

As our younger son, an above-average student with learning disabilities and ADD, began to think about college in his junior year, I had fears that he would simply avoid the whole process by setting his sights on the school most likely to admit him. Except for English and social studies, school has not been wholly interesting for Dan. His talents are more in the social realm, in what Daniel Goleman has called "emotional intelligence," and in both athletic and creative areas. To his credit, Dan has decided he will lead his own college search process. We will help with organization, due dates, and gathering important information. He has begun to target schools that seem to have a structured program for students like him.

Clearly, there are some additional questions that need attention when adolescents with disabilities are applying to colleges and universities:

Will the student apply as a disabled student? More than nine percent of college freshmen (over 140,000 students) report having a disability. In 1994 the number with learning disabilities for example, rose to close to 50,000.

The good news: Under Public Law 94-142, Section 504 of the 1973 Rehabilitation Act, and the newer 1993 Americans with Disabilities Act, no qualified individual with a disability can be denied access to or participation in services, programs, and activities at the college. Having a disability does not ensure admission, but hundreds of colleges and universities do assess applications from students with disabilities in a flexible manner if students choose to reveal the problem. (If students do not wish to reveal their disability, they need not do so; colleges and universities cannot inquire in their application about the presence of a disability.)

The bad news: Most college administrators have had very little experience with the laws and accommodations for disabilities. Some faculty still believe that learning disabilities are just excuses made by students with little intelligence or motivation for academic work. And according to one specialist and author, "the climate appears to be making a U-turn back to being less sensitive, more skeptical and less agreeable to giving students accommodations for LD."

What kinds of academic support are available at the college? Colleges are required to provide academic accommodations to students with documented health, emotional, and learning disabilities. These include: additional time to complete tests, coursework, or graduation; substitution of non-essential courses for degree requirements; adaptation of course instruction; tape-recording of classes; and modification of test taking/performance evaluations. Institutions may also provide auxiliary aids such as note-takers, readers, taped texts, and scribes.

What kinds of documentation for disability are required to obtain an admissions review and services? While individual schools vary in their requirements, most want some formal documentation of the disability *accrued throughout the high school career* (not just documented right before college applications are filled out). Check with the college to learn what is required to validate a particular disability.

HANDLING ACCEPTANCE AND REJECTION

Try as we might to convince students otherwise, a college acceptance or rejection will have some personal meaning to our adolescents. We try the usual arguments:

- It's not you but the application that was rejected.
- You were among a pool of many qualified applicants.
- It was a very competitive field.

When college rejection feels like personal failure, some vulnerable students can become deeply despondent, particularly if their whole high school career has been oriented toward a particular college admittance. One California newspaper reported during the acceptance/rejection season that a senior high school student in an affluent community committed suicide the day after receiving a rejection letter from a prestigious university. Her resumé was reported in the obituary: National Merit Scholar, president of her class, co-captain of the swimming team, award-winning flutist.

College admissions offices get hundreds and hundreds of calls every

April from baffled and distressed students. Dan Walls of Emory University says:

> *The rejection is particularly difficult for some students. They have worked very hard and done so well in so many areas. This is the first experience perhaps of someone saying "no," maybe the only time they haven't succeeded. They want to know what they did wrong, and our attempts to describe the kind of competition they faced don't always seem to help.*

College counselors *strongly* advise students to apply to schools that are more likely to accept the application ("safety" schools), as well as a more selective institution (a "reach" school). A second-choice school should be a real choice, one the student has some excitement about, cautions Richard Tobin of the Greenhills School. Our son applied to a set of three very selective schools, in addition to several "safety" schools. His philosophy, borrowed from the father of a friend, was: "If you don't get rejected somewhere, you didn't reach high enough." And rejected he was. Despite the statistic that ninety-two percent of all college applicants get into their first- or second-choice schools, our son's application was rejected by his top three schools. It was a very difficult few hours on the day all the rejection letters arrived, but thankfully it was short-lived.

Pat / December 17

> *In the family room where Adam was stretched out on the couch, even the back of his head looked discouraged. A pile of mail lay toppled over. As I walked into the room, my heart—and now I know where this cliché comes from—my heart sank for him as he held up several white rectangular shapes over his head without facing me.*

My reassurance was probably thin and ill-timed, but I tried: These college rejection letters were about the loss of a dream, the loss of a certain vision of the future. But, I told our son, you have still the rest of your senior year, and a whole as yet undiscovered future.

Parents' reactions to a college rejection can determine whether a student remains glum and unmotivated or moves past the disappointment. Foremost, parents should not take the rejection as a sign that *they* have somehow failed the student. And, in spite of your dismay, try not to give the impression that your adolescent has failed or disappointed you somehow. As one author notes, your child "wants to come through for you. He wants you to be proud of him. Even beyond pleasing the family, he probably looks forward to letters as proof that his or her qualities are appreciated by society at large."

The key word here is "proud." Deeply disappointed young people need reassurance from family members that they are proud that the student reached high and took the risk of rejection. Support also needs to extend to students who risk the mild dismay of friends and turn down college offers. Carrie is one of those students:

> *I applied to five big schools away from home, places with good reputations. As I began getting accepted I realized that I hadn't researched well and that I wasn't prepared to move across the country. So, instead, I've decided to attend the local community college for a year and then transfer to a new college. The most difficult part of this plan is the criticism I face from others. But I'm confident about my decision.*

Parents and counselors can help students whose applications are rejected by their first-choice colleges by getting them excited about another college. The list of schools should include a really good second or third choice, which can step forward and produce enthusiasm. We visited one of the Other Schools with our son in the crowded April month he had to make his decision. That college visit had a special intensity to it.

Pat / April 19

> *I wandered the streets of Madison and the University of Wisconsin campus, knowing that I was in new emotional territory. I began to let newness turn to familiarity, like an acid solution turning basic before my eyes. I walked State Street over and over, looking at the same buildings not once but three and four times. I began assem-*

bling images and sounds and smells, the feel of the wind coming across Lake Mendota, the smell of the coffee houses, the flash of colorful banners on the central campus.

I know he'll choose this school; I can see it in his eyes, in the way he holds his head when he talks about it. It's a great place, I begin to tell myself. The people look interesting and on the gentle side. It's a fine university, a beautiful campus. I'm lost in my own emotional scramble, wanting to know things about U.W. at a crazy level of detail. I want to know the size of the English department, which dorms have the most freshmen, and where exactly the airport shuttle pulls up in front of the union. No one but me seems the least interested in these things. Maybe it's a mother's thing.

I feel a strong pull of sadness that I won't be part of Adam's daily life anymore. We are sitting on a concrete bench, resting. The air belongs to Spring, the almost green grass belongs to students throwing frisbees, playing guitars, lying with books propped under their elbows. The sheer energy of it all, the whole promise of the coming year and a new generation, helps my sadness to drift away across the lake.

CHAPTER FOUR

Parents' Experience of the Transition Years

Pat / August 23

I awoke this morning to hear Adam's accident-pocked Oldsmobile roar into gear. As on many mornings as a mother, I forced myself awake. Did he remember his packet of materials for school registration? (Jolt: His senior year.) Yup, the packet on the table was gone, and Adam gone as well. Outside a cloud of dust lingered where his car had churned down our dirt road. Head back to bed.

But first, a glance into his room. (Big sigh.) A huge tumble of sheets and damp towels on the bed. Teetering piles of papers and notebooks from last year on his desk. T-shirts and tennis shoes strewn about. Cellophane CD wrappers glistening on the floor.

And something new: a large cardboard box of college applications next to the bed. Adam had been filing them neatly into bright blue folders long into the night. (Delight.)

I was suddenly very still, a leftover animal instinct saved for times when something potentially alarming is very near. And in an instant I found it, a little stabbing thought: This is Adam's last year of living at home. I leaned against his doorway. (Tears.)

Adam / November 22

Writing college applications certainly makes it easier to deal with the folks. Every time one of them gets ready to yell or have me do some heinous task like taking the garbage out, I see their thoughts parade across their faces like a teleprompter: "He won't be here a year from now and I'll miss him, so I'd better not yell at him. He'll never call me from school, and then fall in with the wrong crowd and join some cult and generally behave like I did in college."

The sad parent, the sardonic adolescent—the contrast in images is only part of living with an almost grown teen who is sharply focused on friends, fun, and the future. What is it like for *parents* living with an adolescent getting ready to leave home? I put this question to several parents interviewed for this book. Many images emerged:

I find I'm in a time warp going fast forward, but also in reverse. With my daughter I get to reexperience the real excitements of my youth: falling in love, getting excited about ideas, discovering a book which I think will change my life.

We feel like we're groping in the dark, struggling to find our daughter, who has silently disappeared from view.

It's as if we're all on a trip to an unknown destination, and so there is adventure. But my wife and I are forever getting lost, and even if we found some direction, we're uncertain if we're on the right road.

Any attempt to nudge our son toward college fails. It's like moving a huge boulder with a teaspoon.

I feel life is like the Fourth of July spread out over two years. The fireworks can be beautiful, but they come with loud noises.

Children's leaving home tends to spark a series of changes in parents as the years from high school to college unfold:

- We begin to actively separate from our adolescents (usually with their generous help), bringing both loss and positive change.
- The more time they spend away from us, the more memories we have of our own adolescent separation from home. Flashes from our children's younger years begin to dot our thoughts and feelings.
- The phrase "empty nest" makes sense at times—and then it doesn't.
- We feel sad and stunned at odd moments.

- ◆ We catch ourselves dreaming, not just of the past, but of the future, imagining what our children will be like as adults, and what we'll be like in the next stage of life.
- ◆ Time with our adolescents in the present begins to feel precious, as we celebrate special moments, accomplishments, and achievements with them. At the same time, as college begins to loom, we begin to anticipate relief from the intensity and anxiety surrounding life with older adolescents.

THE ACHE AND JOY OF SEPARATING

On a hot, dusty Saturday afternoon a youthful father, David, sought me out at a tennis tournament where our sons Dan and Evan were playing a key match. Someone had told him I was writing a book about children leaving home, he said. Was it done, and could he read it? His older son Ben was leaving for college in eight weeks, and he had been thunderstruck by the impact of Ben's near departure: "I've never before had such back to back strong feelings of both great joy and great sadness."

Are you ready—or, like David, not quite ready—to separate from your college-bound child? Even though leaving home is probably a lifelong process, it comes into sharp focus during the year, months, or weeks in which your adolescent prepares to leave for college. How well that transition goes depends both on your child's personality and level of independence *and* on your own capacity as a parent for letting go and separating. Our growth and our children's growth are intertwined. The more mature our children seem, the easier it is to let them go. And the more we let go, the more opportunities adolescents have for learning to live on their own.

The day will come when you say good-bye to your child in his residence hall, at the edge of some college campus, or as she drives to her first day of class. How will you know when you're ready for this big separation? I asked a group of mothers whose children recently graduated from high school to list the telltale signs of readiness:

When Melissa's friends called to ask where she was, and I didn't know or worry that I didn't know.

When Aaron left for a camp counseling job for five weeks, and I was happier for him than sad for me.

When I actually looked forward to Kate's leaving for spring break. It wasn't just the serenity I needed; it was not having to wonder where she was.

When I realized that I had stopped keeping track of Jamie's schoolwork, lessons, and weekend job. She was doing it—and with her own appointment book to boot!

Remember when your child was five years old? You held that small hand as your son or daughter came upon something awesome or overwhelming: a busy playground, a crowd of new children, a roaring ocean. Your interlocked hands tightened. After a few moments one of you loosened the grip, a sign that it was time to let go. Soon your hands unlocked. You bent down with some words of encouragement and guidance. Your child went off in search of adventure while you stood ready to troubleshoot. The connection was still there, even while you separated.

If, out of your fear, you held on too tightly and too long, your child struggled to get free from you. If you let go too quickly, you found your child lingering anxiously by your side or dashing off before you could give your instructions.

Separating, then, is a two-way process. In adolescence, holding your child's hand is mainly symbolic. Your job is to create an environment or base that is loving, predictable, and safe. Your child's job is to explore the larger world. By the end of high school, most adolescents are ready to pull free from their parents; if separation has occurred gradually and gently, most parents are ready to let them go.

In *Necessary Losses* Judith Viorst laments:

> *. . . they still must leave and we still must let them go, hoping that we have equipped them for their journey. Hoping that they will*

wear their boots in the snow. Hoping that when they fall down,
they can get up again. Hoping.

There are many individual differences in the ways adults and adolescents choose to separate. How well do you usually cope with major
separations? Are you someone who handles big good-byes rather per-
functorily, or are they emotionally wrenching for you? Do you react at
the moment of departure, or later?

Some people make little fuss, accepting fully that separation is
inevitable, a natural part of living in a family. Letting go and saying
good-bye are not terribly powerful for them; there is no backwash or
rush of great feeling. "I don't understand why you're so sad," my husband offered gently after our son Adam left for camp the summer
before he went to college. "This is natural. This is good for him. I'm
happy, not sad."

Others become very anxious about separation. They don't like it,
they avoid thinking about it, and they feel quite awful before and after
a major good-bye. Some adults feel the emotional impact of a separation *before* the event; other individuals are more affected *afterward*.
Depending on your culture, your personality, and your own family patterns and values, separation rituals (for example, good-bye parties or
dinners; cards, notes, or gifts) will be more or less helpful to the
process. The point is that separation affects everyone differently.
Knowing your own style will help you anticipate how to cope as your
adolescent leaves for college.

SEPARATION
WHAT PARENTS CAN DO

Anticipate what separating will be like as your adolescent
goes off to college. Recall how other separations have been. You
are likely to repeat the pattern, unless you consciously work to
change it.

If you are still "holding on" to your child, practice letting go.

Get support for yourself from your partner, other family members, or friends.

If you feel you have prematurely separated or disconnected from your adolescent, try to understand why and then work toward closing some of the distance.

Remember that your child is very likely to stay in good touch while in college, by E-mail, phone calls, letters, and visits.

Try to understand what separation will mean to you in the context of gender, family form, and culture.

Mothers from Apples, Fathers from Oranges

Mothers and fathers, in general, tend to differ in how they react to their children's leaving home. The differences lie well beyond the usual characterization of mothers as emotionally aware and expressive and fathers as nonreflective and private.

Mothers, socialized and rewarded for paying close attention to relationships, tend to focus on the leaving home process earlier than fathers, and therefore begin coping with the emotional change gradually. Fathers, attending more to the outward signs of their children's growing up (like having a job or driving a car), do less of that early adjusting. As their children leave home, they may have delayed reactions compared to mothers, who have been anticipating the change for years.

Mothers, if they have spent more time with their children, have a stronger sense of the parent-child relationship: what it is and isn't, what it means, when to work on it and how. Fathers, if they have spent relatively less time with their adolescents, may struggle with strong feelings of sadness and guilt as children get closer to leaving home. They may have missed out on a meaningful relationship, and now, with college around the corner, it seems too late.

Even fathers who have "been there" for their children during their childhood and adolescence may have not felt truly connected to them. Larry, a self-assured father of four, sat with a group of men exploring issues about men at mid-life. When it was his turn, he offered a story:

Three of my children have already left home. One day recently I passed by the ballfield where I used to practice with my son—I was there for nearly every game, that kind of dad. But, you know, I can't remember being there. I mean, I have no memory of any specific game, any of my son's at-bats or fielding plays, any special moments. I was there but, given my distractions about my work, I wasn't there. And that saddens me.

Mothers are more likely to react to this major separation as both the loss of a child and the loss of a role, making the sadness greater. Fathers may also anticipate missing their children but, unless they have had significant caretaking roles in the family, some are actually preparing to step into a more central, career-advising role with their almost grown children. Fathers who come onto the parenting scene late in their children's lives produce bittersweet reactions in some mothers, as this father in a traditional family noted:

I can understand my wife's reactions to the kids' coming to me now with career questions. She's been the one in their daily lives, doing all that unappreciated work, and now they're turning to me. She's on the sidelines, thinking, "What about me?"

Some mothers are able to identify acute feelings of sadness as their children get ready to leave home. A poet, Sharon Olds, writes movingly about this stage of motherhood in her poem "The Lady Bug":

the first days of our daughter's life
when I bent double over her cradle
as she slept, my tears odd, wild,
tropical spots on the cot-sheet
I swore to her I'd raise her until in her
strength she could leave me.

Some fathers have more difficulty recognizing and expressing the emotions that come with separation. They may express sadness as irritation or withdrawal. Worry and uncertainty about their children may appear in the guise of increased attention to work, rigid parenting, or increased alcohol use. At mid-life, a flagging career and the feared physical signs of aging may add other stresses. Painful feelings of loss in fathers are complicated by gender role socialization, patterns that make coping more difficult. Men are socialized to be logical, deny their feelings, and keep things to themselves. And, unlike mothers, fathers tend not to seek out direct support from other fathers going through a similar process. In "Rites of Passage" poet Lucien Stryk described a father's separation from his son:

> *we brush by. I follow down the path*
> *we've loved for years. We try to*
>   *lose ourselves,*
>
> *yet there's the river, churning south.*
> *I muse on what I've given,*
>   *all I can't.*
>
> *My son moves toward the bank, then turns*
> *I stop myself from grasping at his hand.*

Gender differences, however, are far less black and white than they appear. Some working mothers also feel a sense of having missed out on their children's adolescence and more than a few feel isolated from other women during this life change. Some fathers have enjoyed the brotherhood of other men and have a keen sense of their fatherhood.

Sons Leave, Daughters Are Forever: Fact or Fiction?

Is that old adage part of your current belief system? For centuries, females in many Western cultures were socialized to stay closely connected to home while males were told to go out and work (or play). This distinction tends to have different meanings within different cultures, of course, but the myth still has a toehold in the 1990s. Generally, males tend to be nudged from a warm, safe, and supportive nest earlier and more consciously than females. They are sent from home to become independent, ambitious, and competitive. Females tend to stay more emotionally connected to mothers (and sometimes fathers), are more protected by both parents, and are socialized to domestic life, even as their parents dream of daughters with challenging careers.

Debate rages among feminists, educators, psychologists, sociologists, and biologists about whether these socialization patterns are natural or merely a product of acculturation, and whether they are healthy or harmful. We are finding new ways of raising stronger, more autonomous girls and more sensitive, relationship-oriented boys. Social revolutions of this kind take place over several generations, and change is slower than many of us want. In the meantime, as parents launching daughters and sons into adulthood, what do differences between girls and boys mean about separation?

- A rapidly changing parent-son relationship may be harder to monitor than a parent-daughter bond.
- Girls may find it easier to be expressive of their apprehensions about separation, enabling parents to be supportive. A similar set of feelings in boys may go unnoticed or be disguised as indifference or distance.
- In the absence of emotional cues, parents of boys may have a false sense of security that the changes surrounding leaving home are not deeply stirring for their sons.
- The world is more dangerous for girls than for boys, leading parents to be more protective and more anxious about daughters' leaving home.
- Parents of girls leaving home may have a harder time separating from them, but assume their daughters will stay connected to the family.
- Separation from sons may be less intense, but parents may fear that sons will become permanently disconnected from the family.

Home Is Where the Heart Is: Divorced Parents

In many ways divorced parents are experts about how to cope with separation, losses of many kinds, and change. First, the nest has been reinvented once before, proof that it can happen again. Second, if you are divorced you may be already used to spending significant time away from your son or daughter. Sharing physical custody of your adolescent has meant that periodically the child is out of sight. Unlike parents whose children live with them every day, you may already have had ample practice separating and reconnecting. Third, the tremendous personal and family change required of many parents in the divorce process may have turned you into a more self-aware adult and a more conscious and present parent.

Yet, divorced parents may find other aspects of the leaving home process especially difficult. Single, divorced fathers and mothers who have been the primary caregivers for their children may find separation very difficult. The strong daily, domestic partnerships that can arise between a single parent and child may resist the coming change. And if a single mother or father has come to lean on a child for primary emotional support, the college separation will be difficult for both. Moreover, an unpartnered single parent may lack support and a sounding board during the separation difficulties.

Dana, a teacher and single mother of a seventeen-year-old daughter, spoke of her strong ambivalence: "I will miss her terribly, but I am so eager to get her launched, because I'm running out of parenting steam. That means I'm turning into a big nag to get her to grow up quickly, and I react very negatively to any sign that she's still young and unequipped to be independent."

Her daughter Alena is equally unsure about the coming separation: "I love her; I'm all she has. And she's all I have, which is why I hate it when she leaves town. But I can't stand her smothering kind of mothering. I hope she has a boyfriend by the time I leave for college."

This mother and daughter pair are caught in a push-pull cycle common in single-parent families with adolescents: Any sign of independence from either is both welcome and worrying, while dependence is comforting but resisted. This family resolved their problems by conscious efforts to change. Alena grew to become more responsible, and her mother became more patient about her growing up.

Most divorced parents report that the launching stage stirs up feelings about the former marriage. Emotions and conflicts that seemed resolved may surface and memories of a child in younger years emerge. Sadness, anger, bitterness, regret—all of these feelings may be experienced as the departure for college nears.

For the remarried family, especially a recently formed one, a child's departure for college may feel premature. New connections with step-family members and family rituals might still be forming. Stepparents who have worked hard to develop good relationships with their step-kids report an odd mix of relief and loss. Said one father:

> *No doubt about it, when Jason leaves for school, my relationship with him as stepfather will probably improve, and his mother and I will get some much-needed time together. But I'm also pretty unsettled: Just when Jason and I were finally learning to get along with one another and find that we both love jazz, he's leaving. I worry that we haven't had enough time together to cement our connection.*

This fear is probably unfounded if the stepparent-child relationship has had some positive footing. As children leave the nest, issues around authority tend to fade with all parents and parental figures, opening space for more egalitarian relationships.

Letting Go as a Minority Parent

Clearly, cultural differences about separation exist: Factors like the time of immigration, regional differences, and levels of intermarriage and acculturation affect a family's reaction to adolescent separation. Yet, some anxieties are common to almost all minority parents:

- ◆ How will my child fit in academically and socially without feeling marginalized?
- ◆ What if my child "fits in" too well and forgets his roots and identity?
- ◆ How will my child cope away from the supports in her home community?
- ◆ Will my child neglect his family in an attempt to "belong" at college?

It helps immensely for minority families to trust that family and eth-nic ties will endure. It is also useful to have contact with other families whose adolescents are going to the same college or university. Some institutions will provide families with the names of local students. A network of connections that includes students and counselors is avail-able in most higher education settings once a freshman begins school and residence.

FLASHBACKS: REMEMBERING YOUR OWN SEPARATION

If anything about parenthood is true for all parents, it is this: Watch-ing our children grow and develop evokes memories of our own child-hood and upbringing. Memories resurface with even greater frequency when our offspring become adolescents. Most of us remember clearly what adolescence was like, even if younger childhood years are fuzzy and vague. We recall the highs and lows, the struggles and accomplish-ments. We remember the days that surrounded our departure from home. Some of us left for college; others left home for military service, a job, or marriage.

I resisted thinking about my own separation story for many months while our son's senior year rolled inevitably forward. Finally, I had to return to that time; I knew that I was getting stuck in too much sadness, for some long-ago reason. One confusing day, I tried to figure it out in my journal:

Pat / November 3

> *My own leaving home happened quite gradually, but not without some anguish as I wrenched away from the strict rules and roles my parents had imposed in high school. I lived at home during a two-year, junior college stint, then left home more sharply for the Uni-versity of Michigan at age nineteen. I remember my mother buying me towels, making me a robe, and folding new sweater sets into a green American Tourister suitcase.*

I couldn't remember details of the actual college departure day, only the giddy feeling of complete, impending freedom. (In fact, this is a common report from college students today. Parents and younger siblings can recall that day in great detail; the freshmen remember only the feelings.) My parents sent me a little money, cookies, and letters, and in exchange I sent them good grades and innocent pictures of four girls in hair rollers vacuuming an apartment. My folks thought my living situation, an apartment with some conservative high school friends, was a safe harbor.

But this was 1967. A sexual, social, and political revolution was brewing at the University of Michigan—and elsewhere. I tried unsuccessfully to keep that hidden from home, along with the artifacts of that culture: birth control pills, cigarettes, peace signs, and the new music of the Jefferson Airplane, the Beatles, and Rolling Stones. My own leaving home was gradual but culturally dramatic.

As our son left home, it helped to recount that time, especially the separate, clandestine life I created for myself away at college. Our son, I reminded myself, will find his own pathway to a distinct identity. Remembering the past to make sense of the present is often very helpful. But going back in time to our own adolescence can lead us to face issues of honesty and privacy. Are there some painful or embarrassing aspects of leaving home that you'd rather your children not hear about? Drinking and drugs? Depression? A bad college choice, or huge disappointment? A too-hasty romance? Failing a class? Fights with roommates? Some of us in the baby boomer generation now launching kids to college were deep into a social revolution as young people. Do we tell our children about that time? Sharon, a youthful mother who left college after two semesters of a free-wheeling life style would vote "no": "I don't want Jason to know the kind of trouble I had in college. I don't want him to follow in my footsteps, or get the idea that it's okay to party and not study."

Family therapists are agreed that secrecy about parents' own adolescence and early adulthood does *not* protect their children. Ironically, the *less* our children know about our experiences coming of age, the *more* likely they are to repeat them. And sharing your life experiences after high school frankly and openly makes it more likely that your teenager will seek out your guidance and protection should problems arise.

REMEMBERING YOUR CHILD IN YOUNGER YEARS

> *. . . It seems no time since I would help him to put on his sleeper*
> *guide his calves into the gold interior,*
> *zip him up and toss him up and*
> *catch his weight. I cannot imagine him*
> *no longer a child, and I know I must get ready,*
> *get over my fear of men now my son*
> *is going to be one.*
> —from "My Son the Man" by Sharon Olds

Your trips to the past may also include remembering when your almost grown child was younger. This is not sentimentality. Major life transitions, like children leaving home, often trigger flashbacks to earlier times. Our hearts and minds are searching for continuity, for clues that the choices we are guiding our child toward are good ones, and for comfort in memories of good times. Jamie told this story of his daughter's senior year:

> *One Sunday, while we were waiting to hear about Leah's early decision application to Harvard, I came across a journal I kept during her first five years of life. I wasn't sure whether or not to read it; we were all trying to keep our anxieties at bay at home. But there they were, stories of her as an infant and toddler. After ten minutes of reading, I rushed upstairs to the kitchen where Leah was eating her lunch, sat down, and started to read her these vignettes. After a few minutes she stopped me and said, "Dad, you're having a hard time with this, aren't you?"*
> *I was. I was thinking of her growing up and going away. For a moment, I wanted to hold on and remember her as a small child.*

During these moments of parenting review, all the tedious aspects of caregiving may recede—the schedules of lessons, recitals, and games, the doctor and dental visits, the food preparation, the laundry, the constant tidying of toys and books, the late-night vigils over homework. What may come into focus instead is an odd assortment of mainly pleasant memories. In "First Formal" Sharon Olds captures this strange collision of present and past:

> *She rises up above the strapless, her dewy*
> *flesh like a soul half out of a body.*
> *It makes me remember her one week old,*
> *soft, elegant, startled, alone.*

Adolescents themselves occasionally get into the "remember when" act. Two small steps backward are sometimes helpful before a giant leap forward. Our son took a drive through our old neighborhood the spring of his senior year of high school and peeked into his first, early backyard, which bordered a woods. Later he recounted the many hours he spent flying around our court on his Big Wheel and reminisced about the upstairs dormer bedroom where he and his brother used to sleep. One young adult woman, Selena, had a good explanation for this behavior: "We *feel* grown up at some point, so we don't have to prove it anymore. Nostalgia goes wild."

At times an adolescent's departure for college means remembering the people who used to be part of their lives. Remembering the death of a cherished grandparent or the premature death of a parent may be part of the emotional context for a child leaving home for college.

Parents, too, may reexperience past losses as their children leave for college. One mother, Donna, whose husband died six years prior to her son's graduation from high school, commented on the extra sadness she expects to feel at her son's departure from home: "Saying good-bye to Toby will be like losing Bruce again, partly because Toby is so much like his father."

MEMORIES GOOD AND BAD
WHAT PARENTS CAN DO

Remember your own story of going off to college or leaving home. What part of that process do you hope is repeated—or not repeated—with your child?

Try to understand the separation and leaving home *patterns* in your extended family. Is the process usually positive for the adolescents and adults? Is it different for males and females?

Share these stories—even some difficult ones—with your children as they move toward leaving home. They will listen best if you make these personal recollections, rather than lessons or expectations.

Indulge the urge to time travel back into the past. Even though they can trigger sadness, pleasant memories can be soothing reminders of happy times with your child. If you begin to wish for those days again, remember the tedious moments as a daily parent or start dreaming of the many joys yet to come.

THE MYTH OF THE EMPTY NEST

As parents we have absorbed many cultural messages that influence how we understand our feelings. The standard piece of pop psychology directed to (usually) a mother who sighs sadly about her children leaving home is that she must be experiencing "empty nest" syndrome.

When I first heard the words *empty nest*, I remembered a childhood friend's mother. A short, lively, and beaming woman, Mrs. S. had a small nervous breakdown when the youngest of her three daughters left home. The cure prescribed by their family doctor in 1969 was to foster children and fill the nest again. When I visited on a college break it looked like odd therapy after her twenty-seven years of parenting. Their house was littered with cribs and bibs, and Mrs. S. seemed to have deeper, not lighter, shadows under her eyes.

Parents who have two or more children will still have a pretty full plate of responsibilities after launching the first child to college. Siblings who are second- or third-born shift their positions in the family after the oldest leaves home. Some come forward with needs they have kept patiently on hold or begin to develop and shine in new ways. Our younger son, Dan, grew into a more serious student and tennis player after his brother left home. Much of our "emptying nest" time went happily to supporting his school interests and athletic career. And while our nest was less full of children, we still had a strong sense of family.

Even one adolescent is demanding on time, energy, and parenting know-how. "Kids of any age or stage living at home are open files on our hard drives," said one engineer mother of three. "It's not until they all leave home that we can close those files." Even then, they return intermittently. There is firm evidence that most late adolescents leave home gradually. College students often return home for brief stays until they achieve financial independence.

Does empty nest have to mean emptiness? The answer from most parents, after the shock of a quieter house, is a resounding "No!" We have always had *more* than plenty to do. As children leave home, the nest may still be filled with work and community projects or caretaking older relatives.

For many mothers and fathers, an emptying nest means, above all, more time and space for themselves. No wonder that at times we roll around the emptier—ergo lighter and roomier—nest with glee and abandon. Most parents have balanced multiple responsibilities and roles and deferred many of their own interests and passions. The new nest stands ready to welcome a host of hobbies and interests, dreams deferred for the sake of childrearing. I turned my attention to a new career in academia, exercise, writing, and reconnecting with old friends. My husband rekindled an interest in poetry and began a new business venture.

An adolescent leaving home for college sets the stage for changes in identity for everyone in the family. Parents renew or begin intimate relationships, find new work projects, create new homes and living spaces, pursue new education or training, get off the mommy and daddy track in their companies or move up the ladder, become athletes. A few turn a serious hobby into a new career. From an on-line bulletin board entitled "Empty Nest" come these positive thoughts from women:

> *My husband and I are trying to rediscover ourselves and put our relationship on another level. So far we walk together and plan small travel jaunts . . . college is a budget buster, so we just try to share our moments together.*

> *I'm so glad that I was able to give my children the self-confidence to become independent. Yes, it's lonely at times, but I've gained more than I lost when the last one left, not to mention my car keys, phone, and a whole new closet. I didn't get fired from motherhood—the job description changed.*

> *After twenty-six years of being a stay-at-home mom, it dawned on me that now I could truly be myself for myself by myself.*

For most parents, the transition is a mixed picture of positives and negatives, as two full-time homemaker mothers anticipate:

> *What do you do after so many years always being there for the kids? I was always the mom in the stands at the swim meets, football and softball games, team mom. So right now I find myself working a lot . . . and trying to remember the things I used to like to do. It's hard remembering who you were, and the house seems so quiet.*

> *Now that I'm facing the empty nest after raising six children to adulthood, I know that there will be sad spaces in this rambling house. I've thought about a job, going back to school, but they represent being tied down, just like it was with the kids. As much as I loved that role, I want to break out by traveling and doing as I please with my day.*

A blissfully emptier nest is not without a residue of uncomfortable feelings for parents. Most of these emotions are about confusion and transitions:

> *I feel so lost and never dreamed I would ever feel like this. I always knew where I was going, what I was doing, and what had to be done.*

> *The worst part of not having the kids home is the boredom. There was always something going on, someplace to go, someone to talk to, especially with a year-round athlete who actually wanted us at her games.*

> *So much of my life, actually* most *of my life, has been defined by being "Mom," even though I have always had a career. I'm finding it difficult to redefine who I am and feeling a little lost . . . and I miss my "babies."*

Fathers are not immune to these feelings. For a significant and increasing number of men, fatherhood has meant playing a key nurturing and socializing role for their children. Some fathers have spent extended time with their children as single, divorced dads, or while their wives have worked outside of the home. As an article in the *Boston Globe* recently detailed, the empty nest is now also a male phenomenon:

> *. . . because so many baby boomer fathers were deeply involved in child-rearing, the empty nest syndrome has become a common male affliction. . . . In contrast to previous generations, many frequently put quality time with their children ahead of advancing their careers. Few regret the choice, but some are now discovering the closeness and bonding that makes parting that much harder.*

Some mothers and fathers report a nagging guilt. Partly the guilt is about feeling happy or relieved that our children are leaving us. If we love them, aren't we supposed to feel awful as they get ready to leave us? The answer, of course, is yes and no. Yes, our feelings of loss are testimony to the close bonds between our children and ourselves. But, as every new parent recognizes after that first night out without a clinging infant, it's a good feeling to reclaim yourself even partly from the serious, demanding role of parenthood.

Another form of guilt can beset parents who have had full-time jobs outside of their homes. In hushed tones around the office snack area, working parents—even those who have always felt confident in their decision to pursue a full-time career—describe a backlash of guilt about having spent large amounts of time away from their children. Multiple roles may have given us some immunity from intense loss as the nest empties, but not from guilt.

As first a graduate student, then a psychologist and teacher, I have always spent time away from our two sons since they were infants. Our first son's leave-taking for college meant a resurgence of regret that I hadn't given him more of my time. I sensed there were cracks that had developed from the strains of our dual-career home. In his last year at home, I tried eagerly to patch them before he left.

Pat / September 21

> We are an odd lot, we mothers who have seniors. Those working moms among us who are trying to spend more time at home are an especially sorry sight. Having parked our feminism in some storage bin, we frenzy about the kitchen desperately trying to attend to these large bird babies before they leave the nest. We clutch college applications in one hand, cookbooks in the other, and checkbooks between our teeth. We follow our seniors around trying to lasso a few minutes of time, in which we ask limp questions like "How are you?" and "How's school?" A directive like, "Clean up the garage" goes right down the toilet as soon as we get THE LOOK. THE LOOK means, "Are you kidding? Next year, I'm outta here."

EMPTY NEST

WHAT PARENTS CAN DO

Try to understand what the phrase "empty nest" means to you. Less parenting? Different parenting? As your first, middle, or last child leaves home, what will it mean for you, your partner, and your family? Discuss your thoughts with significant people in your life.

Trace the empty nest experiences in your own family of origin. What followed your own leaving home: good times? difficult times? How did you wish it had gone for you and your family when you left the nest? Are there cultural, racial, or ethnic stories about leaving home that will add to the personal meanings of an empty nest?

How do you imagine you will manage emotions that may arise from the empty nest?

SWEET SADNESS

Some parents will have feelings akin to grief as their children prepare to leave home for college. How intense the sadness is or how long it lasts depends on a long list of factors. One mother described this as a strong physical feeling, like "waves of longing that nearly bring me to my knees." Another said, "It was like a death. Things would never be the same after my daughter left for college."

At the start of our son's senior year of high school, after a day of stamping a batch of early acceptance college applications, I, too, had some strong feelings:

Pat / October 30

> *In one of Adam's favorite preschool books, P. D. Eastman's* Are
> You My Mother? *a little bird hatches from its shell and then falls
> out of his treetop nest while his mother is out worm-shopping. In
> desperate need of food and security, he approaches a set of trucks,
> cars, and mammals. "No, I'm not your mother," they each repeat.
> This sends the little yellow bird into a series of panic attacks. Final-
> ly, a benevolent steam shovel scoops him up and drops him gently
> back into the nest, where his mother, frantic herself with impending
> loss, embraces him.*
>
> *When Adam leaves home, who will bid him good night, check to
> be sure his CD player is off, take his temperature when he's sick,
> straighten out a tangled school schedule? Where is P. D. Eastman
> now when I need a new script?*

I wasn't the only one whose anxieties were sentimentalized in bird/
nest stories. Just when I thought I was at the extreme end of the coping curve, I met Debbie, a social worker mom, who, with considerable
embarrassment, shared her story:

> *The spring before my son's departure for college, I became fierce-
> ly protective of some birds and their little blue eggs at the top of our
> patio umbrella table. I had the binoculars out, the whole bit. When
> the last baby bird matured and jumped from the nest, it became
> lodged in a rock garden crevice. As I watched, terribly involved and
> scared, the parent birds took an entire day to coax their little one to
> a safer launching ground. And when they all finally flew off, I burst
> into tears. Can you believe it?*

I could. Stories from parents about explicit, conscious feelings of sadness and loss are frequent as their children leave for college, particularly as the impending signs of endings begin to dot the family landscape:
applications, graduation announcements, moving boxes. The reactions
range from a few tears to several months of on-and-off low moods. Many
parents find that acutely sad feelings begin to fade once they know their

children have begun to adjust to being away. Others find that loss continues in some form throughout their children's first year away.

You may be more susceptible to significant feelings of loss if:

- This is your first, last, or only child leaving home.
- College is considerably far from home.
- Your relationship to your child has been like a close friendship.
- Your child has played a significant helping or mediating role within the family.
- Your child is the first in many generations to go to college.
- Your only work has been inside the home as a parent and homemaker.
- There have been other significant losses in the family or other challenging family problems.
- Your own leaving home experience was very sad or anxiety-filled.

For some parents of nearly launched teenagers, anxiety—not sadness—is the pervasive feeling. Anxiety is a heightened sense of alarm set off by uncertainty. Almost every parent has this feeling when a child sets off in a new direction. It is closely connected to our protective instincts. It makes sense, then, that as parents we become anxious when we try to anticipate our children's leaving home.

I remember the high anxiety I felt when our first child walked home alone from kindergarten. Fifteen years later I had similar feelings when he boarded a plane for Spain. Perhaps it is a family anxiety pattern. My mother, now aged seventy-four, says she always worries when her adult children travel until she knows we've arrived safely. More likely, it's a universal, biologically driven instinct.

Chances are you will not fully understand all the meanings behind your child's leaving home until after the fact (see chapter 8). After our first son left for college, I realized that my emotional reactions to his departure had more to do with my loss of role, a more acute sense of my own aging, and a nagging need to begin reshaping my life. Parents I know whose adolescents were companions as well as children felt they had lost a best friend. Many, many mothers and fathers are agreed that the move to college is the end—or the beginning of the end—of an era in family life.

SADNESS
WHAT PARENTS CAN DO

Recognize your sad or anxious feelings as normal and allow them some space in your daily mood. Try viewing your sadness as a celebration of the positive attachment between you and your child. If you *aren't* having strong feelings, that's normal as well.

Consider what a change in parenting roles will be like. What will be positively and negatively different for you?

If you have a strong friendship with your departing adolescent, accept that the change may be especially hard. Plan how you will stay in touch and begin developing other day-to-day supports for yourself.

If issues of aging (for instance, irksome physical problems) are beginning to overlap feelings of loss as your child gets ready for college, tackle those head-on. Get a physical, assess your fitness levels, plan regular activities to help you feel more agile and strong. If aging means a decline in attractiveness to you, renew your wardrobe, get a new haircut, start spending time on yourself.

Begin imagining ways you might still gather as a family during holidays and at your son's or daughter's college.

DREAMING OF THE FUTURE

As our children reach one developmental milestone, we dream of the next. Think of the string of "firsts" in your child's life: birth or homecoming, first steps, first birthday, first days at each school or away at camp, first day driving, first date, first job—they are countless. For parents launching adolescents, there are many events on the not-so-distant horizon. Dave, a father of two launched children and one getting ready to go, reflected on how focus on the future was helpful to him:

> On days when I was somewhat sad about Elizabeth and Ian, and now Owen, leaving home, I tried to think, "Hey, you've already dealt with many of these issues of change. The transition to college is just another one. Later on it will be their first marriage, their first professional job, first child, first home." This really helped me, got me over some bumps.

Parents of children leaving home for college often report that they spend time daydreaming, or what I would call "life dreaming." Some are trying to anticipate the changes in children, themselves, and their family. Others are dreaming about how their offspring will "turn out," or how they *hope* they will turn out. Donna reveals:

> One evening when Toby was about sixteen, I had one of those defining moments when you get a glimpse of what your child might be like as an adult. He was giving a speech at a choir banquet and he was talking with such ease in front of the audience. What struck me was how comfortable he was telling a few stories, using his wit. That quality reminded me of Bruce, his father, and I had a quick flash of a future, confident, all-grown-up Toby who was going to make it. I felt proud but also relieved.

This mother's future vision of her son will be positive for him; optimism about children can lead them to successes. Occasionally, however, envisioning the future gets us into trouble. We turn a pleasing picture or strong hope ("I think she'll be an engineer just like her dad") into an agenda ("She needs to find a good engineering school"). Conversely, negative daydreaming ("He'll never make it at a college that far from home") can set up sure failure. The point is to recognize that dreams are dreams, not realities or certainties.

As our children graduate from high school and get ready to leave home, we tend to imagine them as "finished" products and parenting as "over." If they look good to us, then we sit back with satisfaction, proud of a job well done. If they look flawed in some serious way, we are despondent and anxious, thinking that we failed somehow as parents.

Neither situation is close to the truth. Our adolescents may be leaving our daily lives and our daily influence, but they, like us, will continue to grow and change in substantive ways across the lifespan. Their futures as adults, even aspects of their personalities, are quite uncertain at age eighteen. As many parents of college graduates recounted to me, our job is not over when we wave good-bye at the college dormitory. Parents—whether we relish it or not—continue to be very important in the lives of all adults, young or older.

Yet, most parents experience a sharp decline in worrying as their teens go off to college. And they catch up on sleep. "Out of sight, out of mind" takes on new meaning as children begin to leave home. Parenting a son or daughter through adolescence is an intense experience. There are rich times we want to hold onto forever, but many moments are filled with anxiety, worry, and dread: the midnights when curfew has been breached, the call from your child about an accident ("I'm basically okay, Mom, but the car . . . well, it's not"), or the morning-after search for the meaning behind a pair of bloodshot eyes.

Most parents report a surge of relief as these daily worries disappear, as these two mothers reveal:

> *I just don't worry anymore and that's enormously relieving to me. I think it's because it is beyond my control to do anything about Jenny's choices. That responsibility has been transferred to her. Now I sleep through the night.*

> *Ignorance is bliss! Currently my youngest is doing her spring semester with the National Outdoor Leadership School. This involves skiing, camping, rock climbing, and kayaking in the wilderness areas of Wyoming, Utah, and Colorado. I worry less about her doing these things than I do about her going to a local rock concert!*

It's not that we care less or have fewer concerns about young people after they leave home. In truth, we watch intently for signs of adjustment or problems. But the daily, almost habitual practice of keeping track of children fades rapidly for most parents. And with that comes relief. As Marion Howard, an anthropologist, educator, and mother, wrote as her youngest son returned to college after a break at home:

I do admit to a muffled sniffle as I heard the unmuffled cough of his truck as it turned out of the driveway and down the hill. I walked back to the empty house—even the old black cat had died last summer—but under the held-back tears and the sense of loss, I felt the ease of . . . relief. At that moment, I hadn't identified what I was feeling as relief. Our cultural stories do not include the joy of autonomy for middle-aged women.

The departure of one person from the household also means more order for some families and less work for the hearth keepers. In my son's senior year I anticipated this change, figuring that while I would certainly miss him, I wouldn't miss his lifestyle.

Pat / March 17

> *Although Adam spends less and less time at home, the signs that he's been here are unmistakable. He moves between rooms dropping CDs, peach pits, magazines, and tennis clothes, like some animal marking territory. A few years from now I want to leave the house tidy and attractive and have it stay that way until I get home. I want to show up in the kitchen wearing whatever scanty robe I choose. I want to read a newspaper that hasn't had the sports page ripped from its body. I want to work however long I need to without worrying about whether or not the boys have gotten home safely. I want to drive in a car that isn't littered with burger boxes, pop cans, and spiral notebooks.*

LOOKING TO THE FUTURE
WHAT PARENTS CAN DO

Give yourself permission to daydream about your child's leaving home for college. Imagine the many possibilities for your child's future without clinging to any particular one.

Dream not of the day parenting is over (it's never really over) but of the kind of parent you want to be for an adult child. Begin to imagine how you might spend time together and continue to share life with one another in the future.

Start to fantasize about the freedoms that will come with a child's leaving home. Tune in to the non-parent part of you by nurturing your own interests and developing other aspects of your identity.

THE PRESENT

Remembering the past, dreaming of the future: Life with an adolescent can be like riding—or clinging to—a pendulum swinging between "Remember when . . ." and "Someday . . . ." What about the present? Are the days with an adolescent just to be endured, or are they to be celebrated and remembered? True, some days we want simply to get them all over with. Arguments over just about anything increase this urgency:

- cars
- curfews
- schoolwork
- money
- chores
- rooms
- drinking
- sex
- smoking
- friends
- dating
- telephones
- eating
- sleeping
- bathrooms
- college
- spring break

The checklist is long and tiresome. Even a look or a silence can spark an argument. A youthful-looking stepfather in a workshop about midlife was incredulous about his son's angry reaction to a simple greeting:

> Yesterday Andy looked really sleepy at breakfast so, over cereal, I said, "Good morning." Well, that began a tirade about why I am so sarcastic, why I shouldn't care when he goes to bed, isn't it his

*choice if he stays up until midnight and is really tired the next day?
I just looked at his mother and shook my head.*

But there are also many joyous moments in our kids' adolescence. Some of them are predictably attached to accomplishments and achievements, however large and small:

- When your son called to say that he had rescued a runaway camper
- When your daughter had the courage to run for class president
- The Saturday you and your son worked on his video project
- When a son with learning disabilities brought home his first *A*
- When your daughter scored her first varsity goal in lacrosse
- When your son played his first jazz gig at a local restaurant

Other moments arise from sheer spontaneity: the day you bumped into your child in town and had lunch together, the weekend spent painting a mural in your daughter's room, the night you played Trivial Pursuit as a family until three o'clock in the morning.

One spring break our son and two friends caravaned behind us as we drove to South Carolina, heading for separate condos. I imagined that the carful of boys I could see in our rear-view mirror would barely tolerate this highway tether we had imposed. Instead they had us rolling with laughter with their hilarious, slightly shocking jokes told via the CB radio. They were celebrating their impending freedom at a beach resort and for a few hours they opened an audio window onto their joy. We will never forget that day; it will be a story told and retold many times.

To celebrate means to pause, a difficult task in our culture. To live and raise children in the era of year 2000 is like living in fast-forward for most of us. Not only do parents have multiple responsibilities, but the kids are also incredibly busy with school, homework, lessons, groups, friends, and jobs. It is not unusual for parents and late adolescents to see each other only once a day, and for only a few minutes.

And the busier we are, the faster time goes. The last years, months, or weeks our children are living at home can feel like a blur. After they leave for college, we inevitably ask, "Where did the time go?" If we more fully embrace the moments we have with our children, we can also look back and say, "I'm glad we had that time together."

THE PRESENT

WHAT PARENTS CAN DO

Appreciate and embrace the warm connections and interesting moments you now have with your teenager, even if they are only an occasional positive sprinkle.

Don't pass up opportunities to spend time with your adolescent. Most often those opportunities arise spontaneously. The trick is to be around enough to catch them.

If your adolescent resists hanging out with you (many do), take an interest in his or her pursuits. Many delight in the role-reversal of teaching their parents how to do something or educating them about a foreign topic.

CHAPTER FIVE

Parenting the Late Adolescent

Pat / October 16

> *Yesterday was a long day and night of monitoring Dan's comings
> and goings. The phone rang hourly—he's at Taco Bell, then at
> Peter's, going briefly downtown, followed by the video store, then
> David's, now he has bounced back to Taco Bell, he'll be home in an
> hour. At last we heard the garage door opening. I finally relaxed,
> feeling more like an overworked air traffic controller than a mother,
> as Dan launched himself from one densely packed teenage gathering
> spot to another, finally coming home to rest and refuel.*

Adam / May 17

> *I love driving. Now don't get me wrong, my car is a huge tan boat
> with velour seats, so it's not the car I love. It's being able to come
> and go as I please. I like nothing more than escaping out the front
> door with my backpack and tennis racket and a couple of apples and
> Gatorades and heading for the courts. The folks are screamingly
> upset at what my car looks like on the inside, but, hey, it's my home
> away from home. The next time I leave the house, I'll trick them
> and cart out some Windex. That'll keep them calm for a while.
> Yeah, that'll do it, just ask Mom for that little blue bottle as I head
> for school. When I slam the door, I know she'll have that little
> smug finally-you're-growing-up look on her face, and I'll be outta
> there.*

FAMILY AS A LAUNCHING PAD

The front door opens and closes more often during our children's late adolescence than at any other time during a family's development. The front door to my home actually had to be replaced during my younger son's junior year, done in by the countless slams as Dan and his friends went "out." The door stood as a reminder that middle and late adolescents have two complex and rich worlds: life inside with family and life on the outside with friends. This coming and going from one world to the other becomes a steady practice in the junior and senior years of high school, readying adolescents for the next phase of their lives. To live with them during this swinging-door time requires knowledge, patience, and presence. I asked one teenager, Nora, in the throes of defining herself as a tenth grader, to give parents some advice:

> I think that, rather than trying to keep kids close for those last few years at home, parents should give them more freedom so they will all be ready when it's time to go to college. This doesn't mean not spending time with them, but letting kids get used to independence.

Launching our children is not just about letting go. It also requires energy and flexibility. A somewhat cruel irony confronts mid-life parents living with almost grown teenagers. Just when our joints begin to stiffen ever so slightly, we are asked to stretch. And just when we feel strong about living independently as mid-life adults, we learn that it takes teamwork to raise teenagers to adulthood.

"My parents are usually a united front," sighed a young client in my office. "Even though my dad is a softer touch, he usually backs up my mother. If only I could get my dad off to the side, I'd get to do more." Whether two parents live together, apart, with new partners, or with other adult family members, agreeing on the major do's and don'ts for adolescents helps a great deal. Consistency may be especially tricky between divorced parents, stepparents, and grandparents living in the home. Joint agreements take work. At times, it may seem easier to just make a parenting decision by yourself, particularly when adolescents are pressing hard for an answer or co-parenting conflicts are brewing. But, my client's wishful thinking aside, it works best for adolescents and parents when caregivers have one voice about the major issues.

LAUNCHING AS LOVING PARTNERS
WHAT PARENTS CAN DO

Figure out where your differences lie in parenting adolescents, and work toward resolving them by compromise.

Have you been a very child-centered couple? If so, begin to move closer as adults. Be curious about what's going on inside your partner, what kind of growth is occurring, and what you've appreciated and missed about him or her in the intensity of parenting.

Be creative and determined about finding privacy as a couple: for example, regular weekend "dates," short overnight trips for two (but think twice about leaving your adolescent at home unsupervised), a locked bedroom door, mid-week lunches. One couple I know takes an early morning walk every day.

Get on top of college finances early in the game, and set the parameters for discussion of tuition costs. Don't get paralyzed by the number of zeros. Find a way to agree on your child's financial responsibility for college expenses and on what you value and are willing to support financially.

Begin restoring a sagging or on-hold marriage by exploring shared interests and hobbies. Dare to imagine marriage without children; dare to experiment sexually with one another. Talk about what attracted you to each other before you entered the marriage or partnership.

Talk about what mid-life means to each of you and what launching children will stir up.

Launching as Loving Partners

Research tells us that raising adolescents can take a toll on marriages. In one study, ninety percent of wives reported marital difficulty during the period of their first-born's adolescence. Only one-fifth of these couples reported that marital satisfaction had increased during this time. Change may draw people closer, but it also brings stress. Remember your marriage when your child was an infant? Most of us want to forget those sleepless nights, the ear infections and colic—*not* the usual music for romance. Parents of adolescents have other "noise" that affects their partnerships:

- Disagreements over parenting, often fueled by pesky memories of our own adolescent years.
- The increased sexuality our offspring bring to the home. Being around a daughter's boyfriends or son's girlfriends may raise issues of aging and a tired sex life. It can also generate some uncomfortable sexual stirrings.
- The sheer lack of privacy and couple intimacy as adolescents come and go into the night.
- Strains about finances, especially with college tuition bills looming.
- A nagging mid-life review of our goals, values, work life, and identity as men or women.

Launching as Divorced or Separated Parents

Raising an adolescent to adulthood as divorced parents has special, built-in challenges. When physical custody is shared, the tasks of late adolescent parenting take a great deal of cooperation and coordination. If ex-spouses have settled into a friendly, business-like relationship as parents, these tasks are more easily accomplished. If the former partners continue to argue, teenagers may distance themselves from both parents and take refuge with peers as a way of handling their own distress.

At least three issues *require* regular conversation between divorced mothers and fathers of almost grown children:

1. **What do we agree are the consistent behavioral rules across households about cars, curfews, dating, and substance use?** No set of parents, whether divorced or married, sees eye to eye on every aspect of limit-setting and freedoms for teenagers. Divorced parents, however, have much less time and space to reach common agreements. Some face-to-face time, with or without significant others, may be important to iron out some differences. After that, it's a question of staying in touch with one another enough to keep track of behavior and handle new teenage requests.

2. **How will we monitor school progress and coordinate the college search?** By the time children reach late adolescence, most divorced parents have developed some rhythm and vehicle for staying informed about grades and course planning. However, the college search sometimes brings a more distant parent out of the woodwork. (Chapter 3 contains some specific ideas for divorced parents about the college search.)

3. **Who will pay for college, and for how long?** No issue is quite as inflammatory for divorced parents—and potentially destructive for young adults—as the issue of financing college, particularly if the financial settlement was a bitter fight. An adolescent who watches his or her parents fight about paying for college does not launch securely or joyfully.

Some marriages come apart when children leave home. Officials at the census bureau expect that, as baby boomer parents send their children off to school, we may see a rise in the divorce rate. Why? Some parents wait until their children are away at school to dissolve the marriage because they are committed to maintaining an intact family for as long as possible. Others find that long-brewing marital crises boil over once the parenting tasks no longer distract them from real problems in the marriage.

If you are planning divorce, it is optimal to either initiate the separation well before your child's senior year or wait until an almost grown adolescent child has had more than a year away from home. Adolescents do best when they launch from some stability, even if that stability means two nests. Moreover, they need extra reassurance that their job is to settle into college, not to support a distressed parent.

Launching as a Single Parent

To launch an adolescent as a single parent without significant support is a Herculean task. Parents need people in their lives who can be sounding boards, provide alternative suggestions, or simply be there during the many frustrating, confusing, and emotional times of adolescent parenting. Just to separate from an adolescent is a huge job for a single parent. "So much has been invested of your mind, body, and soul," said one single mother, "that it's very scary to wonder whether or not your child will launch and launch well. There's no one to share that tremendous responsibility."

Single parents tell me that several strategies are helpful during adolescence:

+ Find a support network, people who can be sounding boards, brainstormers, and shoulders when you need them.
+ Give your adolescent some time away from you during the summer or school vacations; both of you need to practice separation, and single parents need time alone.
+ Use books, parenting classes, and professional advice when needed for reassurance that you're on the right track and for redirection when you're over- or underreacting.

PARENTING REORGANIZED

To launch almost grown adolescents parents very often must move into the passenger seat or at least downshift a gear or two. (Note that you are still occupying the car, and the motor is still running.) This parenting reorganization can offer a welcome respite to parents as individuals and partners. As Leah, a high school senior, suggests:

Realize that you're in a different role where you make decisions with your kids, not for them. My parents have been moving in that direction for a while, but I see lots of kids whose parents are still telling them what they can and cannot do.

By the time our kids are finishing high school, we:

- Play more of a safety net and safe haven role and fade out daily protective functions in proportion to our adolescents' abilities to make good decisions.
- Let teenagers more and more live out the consequences of their decisions.
- Enjoy the new people, interests, and ideas our almost grown children are bringing to our lives.
- Act as supporters, consultants, and active listeners, helping adolescents think through relationships, academic choices, and areas of interest.

Does it ever really happen this way? Surely not: the list is merely a parenting plan to aim toward. None of us has a perfect parenting track record. Like our adolescents, we make mistakes (like grounding someone for cracker crumbs on the living room carpet), we get off track (looking the other way when some strange teenager with a large grocery sack turns up after midnight in your son's bedroom), and we lose sight of reason (extrapolating a life of crime from one bold lie). But inventing some guidelines for ourselves keeps us from drifting erratically from one parenting strategy to the next. As our son's tennis coach puts it: "Once you're out there, you need to be totally in the game, firing away at every shot. But before you take the court, have a plan. Tell yourself what you're going to do."

As parents of late adolescents, we work toward creating a game plan that lets us:

- Find new, age-appropriate ways to continue to express our *attachment* to our adolescents.
- Create a protective set of *rules,* based on principle, rather than monitoring every behavior.
- *Communicate* our values and opinions, in place of direct teaching.

ATTACHMENT

Pat / March 13

> *"You're patting me again." We both know what he means. When Adam is plopped in the kitchen eating a banana and reading the paper, I sometimes stand behind his chair and pat him on the shoulder. We both know that patting means "I love you, I'll miss you next year, and I can't believe you're almost all grown up." Lucky for me he only gently complains about this rote but aching act of affection. Lucky for him I feel committed to some regular physical contact with him, even this brief shorthand for the big hug and kiss of early years.*

I hope that my instincts for showing affection to a son leaving home were the right ones. Time will tell. In the meantime, college advisors and counselors couldn't be more clear: The adolescent who launches most easily has balanced independence with strong, solid connections to home. Just like an infant who gradually explores a playroom from the base of a parent sitting nearby, the adolescent uses attachments to friends and family to form a solid, secure base from which to widen his or her world. On paper-and-pencil measures of attachment, students who are more securely attached to their parents make a better social adjustment to college than those who are insecurely attached. To be securely attached in adolescence means agreeing with the following statements:

- My parents respect my feelings.
- My parents accept me as I am.
- I like to get my parents' point of view on things I'm concerned about.
- When we discuss things, my parents consider my point of view.
- If my parents know something is bothering me, they ask me about it.

A sophomore at the University of Wisconsin concurs: "I think I never really got too homesick and upset after I left home, even though I came all the way from New York. My parents have always been supportive. I knew they would never abandon me if I needed them."

In her study of college juniors and seniors, psychologist Sherry L. Hatcher relates a story of a student who struggled successfully to build on his attachments to home and thereby achieve some personal mastery over separation:

> *When I first thought of leaving home, I was very excited. Being on my own seemed like a dream come true. I was a little mistaken. I found that leaving home meant feeling alone sometimes. I was homesick for a while. I not only missed my buddies but mostly my family. My parents are very important to me, and not seeing them daily was hard to adapt to. As the days went by, I met new people and began to explore my new surroundings. Pretty soon I felt like I was home, at my new home.*

Despite the large amounts of time spent with peers as college draws closer, the quality of adolescents' relationships with their parents and family have tremendous importance. Impending separations tend to highlight and intensify parent-child connections. If you have a fairly positive parenting relationship with your adolescent, or a good friendship, revel in the times you share together, despite the separation which lies ahead. One mother, Joan, described a sudden positive change in her daughter's senior year:

> *After at least a year of arguing for more and more freedom, Rayna abruptly moved closer to me. Maybe she sensed that we had little of this time left together; maybe I eased up and relaxed more about how she spent her time. We began having lunches together, even with her girlfriends along, talking about things like politics and music. We actually started a friendship, which was shocking to me after all the fighting. Other mothers have reported similar turnabouts. At sixteen they want no part of their parents; by seventeen, they're buddying up. It's odd, but I'm glad.*

Rayna, like some young people, may have instinctually moved closer to her mother in preparation for her move to Vassar College in the next year. She may have needed the reassurance that her mother was emotionally attached to her before they moved physically apart. Becoming "attached," however, does not mean staying physically close to home.

Adolescents who have other independent living experiences (travel, camps, summer school) before they leave for college make better adjustments than those who do not.

Eileen, a mother from Cleveland, wrote me about her conscious efforts to create that for her adopted teenage daughter:

> *Each summer for the past three years, Jessie has practiced leaving home. Choosing an activity and location within our means, she has lengthened her time away from us, from four to six weeks and now, the summer before her senior year, eight weeks away. She has gone from a camp cabin with supervision to a dorm in Washington, D.C., with intermittent supervision to a chaperoned apartment in Greenwich village this summer. I have had to practice taking charge of my reluctance and worry each summer; she has had to learn self-reliance. She has managed the adventure and freedom beautifully. It has been a helpful process for both of us.*

The summer before her senior year, Jessie searched—and was reunited with—her birth mother. Adolescents who were adopted commonly express a desire for information about their biological roots before they leave home, especially if their adoptive parents and siblings are open and encouraging. It seems like ill timing, one emotionally charged process converging with another. But for many teenagers, knowing more about the people and situation behind the adoption gives them a stronger foundation for separation. "I know more about who I am," said Jessie after meeting her birth mother. That surely is an important tool for an adolescent heading into an unknown world.

Has your adolescent had sufficient practice at being away from home? Some, like Jessie and our sons Adam and Dan, have spent time as counselors or campers at recreational or religious camps during high school summers or at sports or art programs away from home. A few have been in outward-bound type programs or worked away from home on service projects. These young people have a fourfold advantage over teens who have spent briefer times away from home:

- They have had to live without a parental safety net of rules and support.

- ◆ Through trial and error they have had to manage freedom and all the challenges that confront them in that context: drugs, alcohol, sex, money, and laundry.
- ◆ They know what it means to be homesick.
- ◆ Most important, they know they can survive on their own. When college comes around with all its uncertainties and fears, they can say assuredly to themselves, "I can do this."

Not all families can afford to finance such outward-bound experiences or choose to spend their money in that way. If that describes your situation, consider arranging for your son or daughter to spend time with out-of-town family friends or relatives. Let him or her travel there independently and manage money and belongings. This practice is not just for your child, but for you as well. Your confidence in your child's ability to survive away from you is as important as the maturity that will develop from these excursions.

As parents our goal is neither to push emotional separation from our nearly grown children nor to overwhelm them with our own adult needs for emotional closeness. The task instead is to do our part in maintaining a closeness that also respects children's need for increased autonomy and experience in the wider world. It is a delicate balance. Parents can appropriately express affection and maintain closeness with late adolescents in a variety of ways, outlined in the accompanying box.

What does this all add up to? Families should promote both connection and independence in order to most successfully launch their adolescents.

At the other end of the continuum, parents and adolescents who have had a particularly stormy passage through high school may well benefit from the coming college separation. If this sounds familiar, you might do best to accept the differences that lie between you, let go of some control, and make a "peace pact" for the last year or months together. A little harmony now may seed a different, more positive relationship later.

There are several myths about raising late adolescents that permeate our parenting practices and are now being challenged:

Myth: Adolescents must detach stormily from their families. Whether your relationship with your adolescent is calm or contentious, chances are good that a mutual attachment underlies the connection.

For decades psychology promoted the belief that the relationship *had* to be a stormy one, that an adolescent *had* to detach emotionally from parents in order to separate and leave home.

This theory is more myth than reality. Some research indicates that only five to ten percent of families with adolescents report severe family stress, with single-parent and stepfamilies reporting more adolescent-family conflict than traditional families. What researchers have found instead is that adolescents *can* grow up—in fact, grow up *best*—while staying emotionally attached to their families.

As psychologist Kathy Weingarten writes in *The Mother's Voice*, "Growing up does not have to mean growing apart." In other words, to launch a child fully is to let go without breaking ties. In fact, the National Longitudinal Study of Adolescent Health reports that the closer teenagers are to their parents, classmates, and teachers, the less likely they are to smoke, use drugs, drink, be violent, commit suicide, or have sex at an early age.

Myth: Adolescents don't want time with their parents. As a family therapist, I have never heard an adolescent object to the suggestion that he or she spend more mutually enjoyable time with a parent (with emphasis on the words *mutually enjoyable*). I have also seen many differences in how families define closeness, depending in part on their particular culture. The common denominators for emotional bonds are both the amount of time and the quality of time families share. Closeness can be felt during shared activities and meals, through physical affection, while working together, even in a good-natured debate with one another.

What about an adolescent's passion for peers and time away from home, the tiresome debates about the rules, the long periods of time plugged into music or on the phone? Aren't these indicators of adolescents' rejection of us? "You could have fooled me," said a client in my office as I suggested that his surly son really wanted attention from him. "He acts like I ought to disappear from his life altogether." Those self-absorbing, peer-driven activities are usually *not* signs of wanting emotional distance from parents but rather of emerging identity, autonomy, and individuality. It's not an either-or situation. Teenagers do not choose peers *instead* of parents. They seem to want and need both.

"Both" is hard to accomplish. Just when leaving home is around the corner, parents of late adolescents may feel frustrated in their efforts to stay connected with them. The usual warm stuff of childhood and earlier adolescence—doing fun activities together, cuddling up together on the couch, working on school projects, riding and talking in the car—seem less welcome, less appropriate, or unappreciated.

You may want to spend as much time as possible with your adolescent as leaving home approaches, but this is not always a good match to a young person's strong desire to cement high school friendships. Take comfort in the knowledge that these hours with friends will yield a high return. They will become important connections to home during the challenging first months of the freshman year.

Lack of time is often a roadblock to closeness between parents and their almost grown teenagers. Busy lives, hectic schedules, demanding work and school tasks, and a generally high-speed culture all work against sharing time as a family and enjoying the spontaneous moments that can arise. One father, Bob, commented on the structure his faith had helped to provide to his family:

> *What we call "family home evening" is a weekly ritual in our family. Part of the time we focus on religious lessons, but it's also an avenue to communication. Time together is so hard to accomplish in the busy schedules of kids and parents, so going to church together and these weekly evening times are important tools.*

Myth: Adolescents need their mothers more than their fathers. Until recently, mothers have typically had closer daily ties to their adolescents, male or female. This may seem like the natural state of affairs, part of the still-debated idea that mother-child attachments are more critical than father-child bonds. However, the consequences of this one-sidedness are not altogether positive. Research points to poorer adjustment in high school and college when adolescents, males or females, are distant from their fathers, both in intact and in divorced families.

For the balance to shift, at times mothers may need to loosen their ties while fathers work to strengthen theirs. Like much in life, the theory is great; the practice is hard. Some mothers will not let go until they see that fathers are earnest about being available to connect to their children. And fathers often will not take those steps until they see that mothers have backed off far enough to give the father-adolescent relationship space.

As my husband has pointed out, he doesn't want me looking over his shoulder to see how well he connects to our sons. I feared that if I left it all to him, not enough would happen. My journal reveals that we had to work on this with our first son:

Pat / May 19

> *I am consciously giving him to his father. This act finally reached my awareness two nights ago when Rob began lecturing Adam about drinking. We were plopped down in his room on the few bare spots available given the shirts, books, papers, and shoes. That night I kept quiet while Rob spoke his mind and spoke it louder than I usually voice my own opinions. My usual instinct is to tone him down, watch to be sure he doesn't lose his temper. That's irrational, since Rob rarely loses it.*

Gender roles can also play havoc with closeness. Affection between grown or nearly grown people is sometimes confused with sexuality. Very occasionally, and tragically, the normal sexual boundary in families is violated. At the other extreme, some parents react to the increased sexual charge in their children's adolescence by suspending affection altogether. Fathers of adolescent daughters who view their daughters more as females than as children or people often curtail their physical affection. While some natural boundaries between fathers and daughters are appropriate, most adolescent daughters welcome appropriate affection from their fathers and need it to develop a healthy sense of themselves.

Almost grown sons are also sometimes shortchanged in affection. Fathers tend to be socialized away from overt expressions of physical love toward their sons. Mothers, both to modulate sexual tension and in response to cultural messages to toughen their adolescent sons for life, may withdraw affection more freely given in childhood.

Pat / August 30

> *I can't find a smooth place on Adam's cheek when I give him a kiss good-bye. It's all beard. Is this a sign I shouldn't be kissing him any-*

more? Is this the way sons separate from their mothers? My friend Sue has two daughters and she looks so comfortable with them physically. Stephanie and Lindsay are forever siding up to her cheek, their long straight hair mingling with their mother's. Why shouldn't boys continue to get their mother's skin, the touch of her hand or cheek next to their faces? Who started this whole hands-off business anyway?

ATTACHMENT
WHAT PARENTS CAN DO

Consider the ways and times you feel most warmly and enjoyably *connected* to your almost grown adolescent. Do your part to make those experiences happen. Invite, but don't insist. Don't be discouraged by an occasional "No, thanks" to your invitations.

Ask your son or daughter: "Do you think we're spending enough time together, in the ways that matter to you?" "Is there something you would change about the way we are close or not close with one another?" "Why do you think we don't feel very connected with one another?"

Take an interest in your son or daughter's activities and opinions. Ask as an interested learner ("What interests you about jazz. Who is doing cutting edge stuff now?"). Don't be a monitor ("Be sure to list jazz on your college resumé") and don't try to be a peer unless you truly share the interest. Invite your adolescent more and more into discussions usually held between adults.

If you can do so comfortably, express physical and verbal affection to daughters *and* sons. An arm around a shoulder or a touch on the hand can speak a thousand words. But respect boundaries and space. If your child is a bit standoffish, ask first ("You look so discouraged. Can I give you a hug?"). Be sincere

("I really admire the way you handled yourself"). And be as direct as you can ("I love you").

If you are divorced from your child's other parent and see an imbalance in the time your adolescent spends with each of you, do your part to facilitate more equal connections. As a remarried parent, spend individual as well as family time with your almost grown son or daughter.

RULES VERSUS CONTROL

I sometimes wish for a simpler, earlier century. I have wished that my job, like my ancestors', was mainly to teach children how to build and keep a frame house, raise livestock, and sow crops. Then I could actually *see* how well I cut the mustard as a parent.

But as we come into the twenty-first century, instead of training adolescents in tangible or trade skills, our charge is largely to teach *psychological* skills, as psychologist Nydia Garcia Preto points out. We dabble in vague concepts like responsibility, interdependence, commitment, self-confidence, decision making, risk taking, relatedness, cooperation, and self-motivation.

Why do all parents need to become unpaid psychologists? Because the family is no longer just a training ground in how to become a self-supporting economic unit. It is now an emotional support system for children who will become players in a diverse world economy. This recent charge, to launch children with a self-sustaining psychological profile instead of just a trade or set of skills, has left most baby boomer parents limping along with a trial-and-error approach to rearing children. As a generation that marched for freedom from oppression, we have especially struggled around issues of authority, limit-setting, and control.

A parent sat in my office recently bemoaning her troubles with her high school daughters: "I simply have no control. They come and go as they please, ignoring my insistence that they stay in touch. They work only occasionally on homework and demand money. I can't stand them at times; they can't stand me. Whatever happened to our free-spirited, happy family?"

Our generation of parents seems to have vacillated perilously between laissez faire parenting philosophies for our eager toddlers or school-age children and a stricter tough-love attitude for our adolescents. When our kids were little, we flocked to bookstores to read Benjamin Spock, Burton White, T. Berry Brazelton, Selma Fraiberg, Anna Freud, Arnold Gesell, and David Elkind. But when our children became adolescents, the bookshelves were empty. Left to our own devices, some of us leaned on our parents' philosophies or simply abdicated our parental role. Now, finally, psychological researchers have begun to rigorously study adolescents. We can name with some confidence the parenting methods that are most likely to be successful in launching teenagers.

In the last decade, research on parenting styles has consistently endorsed what Lawrence Steinberg and others have called *authoritative parenting*. Adolescents raised in this milieu—at least those from white, middle-class backgrounds—have significantly higher self-esteem, do better in school, have fewer problem behaviors, and are much less anxious and depressed as young adults.

One not surprising dimension of authoritative parenting is "warmth." The need for parents to maintain affection for their offspring in early to middle childhood has been well known. Now it appears that adolescents who appear to want distance from their parents also need and benefit from their warmth.

Another dimension, called "psychological autonomy," is also critical to growth in adulthood, especially for late adolescents in the active leaving-home stage. "Psychological autonomy" is what teenagers feel when parents do not attempt to control their individuality, their thoughts and feelings, and their increased need for time and space away from the family. Simply put, the message here is "Don't try to control who they *are*; control only what they *do*." Parents who seek both behavioral and psychological control tend to be too strict, overprotective, guilt-inducing, or intrusive. Many insist that their adolescents conform to a certain image. When these parents are rebuffed (and they usually are), they tend to punish, withdraw their affection, or induce guilt. Their children may develop into rebellious adolescents and may become depressed. These are not usually "bad" parents. Their motivation is less to maintain authority and control and more to maintain a child's dependency or protect offspring from danger.

The third dimension of authoritative parenting is what psychologist/researcher Diana Baumrind calls "authoritativeness" and what Lawrence Steinberg labels "demandingness." Adolescents seem to fare best when their parents exert not *psychological* control, but sufficient *behavioral* controls. Their parents have reasonable *demands* or expectations for responsible behavior in school, community, and home. Authoritative parents do not attempt to control the person of the adolescent. Instead :

- They clearly and consistently draw lines around behavior that they deem physically and emotionally unsafe (such as drinking and drug use, reckless driving, and unprotected sex).
- They expect behavior that reflects deeply held particular family values (like going to church, synagogue, or mosque; taking care of elders).

One father, Charles, offered a story about adolescence that captures the essence of authoritative parenting:

To me, watching my adolescent is like watching the Colorado River rush through the Grand Canyon. The river is bounded by steep walls, controlling its course down a narrow path, just as parents use well-defined rules to manage the household. At times the river is quiet, obedient to the demands of the canyon walls. At other times it gathers its forces into a wild set of rapids that threaten to rip down sections of the walls. If unchecked, the river the would break out, run out of control, and risk losing its identity, its shape. If the walls hold, the river stays within its boundaries, but both the river and the canyon keep changing and adapting to one another.

Sue, a mother of two high school children, describes the need for parents to adapt to a different style of taking charge as their children grow into adolescence: "I'm finding that as David and Stephanie get to be late adolescents, I'm not telling them what to do as often, not demanding things of them. I tend not to say, 'You have to . . .' or 'You must. . . .' My opening lines when I'm concerned are more like, 'Let's go out and have breakfast and talk. I have some worries.'"

When it works well, authoritative parenting has positive outcomes. One mother reported:

> *This whole year I felt like I had an adult in the house. I'm less of a caretaker parent. The rules are looser. He's taking a lot more responsibility. He does his own laundry; sometimes he does the grocery shopping. I don't think about reminding him about things anymore. So I don't feel much anxiety about how he'll handle himself next year in college.*

In contrast to authoritative parenting are parenting styles that are autocratic or *authoritarian* (insisting on strict, unquestioning compliance to many rules because "I say so"), *indulgent* (giving in to too many of teenagers' requests and demands), *enmeshed* (allowing a role reversal in which an adolescent takes care of a parent), and *disengaged* (giving up behavioral control altogether). As clinical psychologist and adolescent specialist Moira Hubbard explains, "Adolescents define who they are by bouncing off a stable, secure environment. They need both the room to bounce and warm, predictable, consistent, yet flexible and available parenting in order to become individuals."

In authoritative parenting, power struggles are the exception, not the rule. Delsa, mother of six children who are almost all launched from home, offers this lesson:

> *With my first daughter there were many arguments. I finally realized that I was in a power struggle with her, to no good end. From her I learned to let go of those power issues and simply try to stay in communication with our kids, find times to convey my values, and share of myself as a person. They all trained me well.*

Negotiating is contagious. Late adolescents who have had a history of collaborating with parents over non-safety issues (rooms, dress, phone time, homework) will more easily negotiate with roommates at college. In significant romantic relationships or close friendships, they will tend to neither give in nor dominate. But most important, these young adults will feel effective in the management of relationships—at school, at work, in romances, in a future family.

There is yet another, more subtle benefit to the negotiating skills learned at home. Adolescents whose parents negotiate with them learn what some psychologists call *interdependence*, a kind of partnership in which *both* persons are important, all opinions are important, and mutual respect is paramount.

On the other side of the equation, parents have needs, too. The adolescent who has practiced negotiation at home is more likely to take his or her parents' needs into consideration. In our home, we insisted that, in exchange for being able to roam freely at night with friends, our teenagers let us know where they were, even at one o'clock in the morning. That rule existed to satisfy our own need to feel less anxious, not to control where our sons were. Our children grudgingly accepted that rule; in exchange, we only occasionally intervened in their plans. As our sons became late adolescents, rules were adjusted according to their age, our trust in them, and the safety of the situation.

But like all teenagers, ours sometimes frankly and flagrantly broke rules. Until our children left home, punishment or "negative consequences" (our term) had to be part of our parenting. We felt strongly that life was about living with the outcomes of decisions. Life metes out negative consequences, often without a fair hearing. One young man in Lawrence Steinberg's psychological research made an important distinction: "A punishment is something a parent does to you; a consequence is something you do to yourself." What this wise young adult implies is that, *if rules are clear, breaking them is a choice.*

Arbitrary or abusive punishment (name-calling, physical hurting), punishment that is too lax or severe (sweeping the garage for drunken driving, or losing the car for forgetting a chore), or inconsistent and half-hearted punishment ("I *should* punish you, but I think you've learned your lesson") are all examples of ineffective consequences. One of the effective ways of handling flagrant rule violations is to allow adolescents to face the consequences in the real world. Another is to require that adolescents propose (stress *propose*) their own negative consequences. Parents who bail out their teenagers repeatedly and always protect them from real-world consequences keep them in childhood far longer than is healthy. Facing the music is facing growth.

Single parents have some extra challenges when it comes to rules and control of adolescents. By high school, the head of steam it takes to raise a child alone has sometimes cooled. No partner helps to reason through parenting strategies or lends support during difficult times. Some single parents are also facing mid-life and longing for a life of less parenting responsibility. The result can be an inconsistent, unclear set of rules and consequences. On the other hand, one study noted that a significant number of single mothers report that raising a child to adulthood without having to negotiate with a male partner can actually be easier.

RULES

WHAT PARENTS CAN DO

Consider your parenting style with respect to rules and control. Is it how you want it to be, or has it evolved by default? It's not too late to make some changes.

To decide whether a rule is reasonable, ask yourself, "What would happen if I didn't control this aspect of my adolescent's life? Is the rule worth the price of conflict and monitoring, or can I let it go?" As your child gets closer to leaving home, emphasize responsibilities that are about his or her own life, not family responsibilities (your laundry versus our laundry).

What is the level of agreement between caregivers on non-negotiable rules (health and safety, major family values)? If the answer is "low" or "non-existent," work toward more agreement through conversation and negotiation.

For non-negotiable areas, be prepared to say why you want the rules; then stick by them.

Support your adolescent's having a voice in setting rules and consequences. In the flexible areas, negotiate; don't command. If you have trouble loosening control, ask yourself why.

COMMUNICATION

Here's a seeming paradox: In an era of rapidly expanding communication devices (computers, faxes, caller ID), parents and children still have significant problems communicating what they need from each other, what they feel, and what they mean. Perhaps it isn't a paradox; advanced technology and problems with face to face communication are about the same thing: speeded up lives, high pressure, and little time and space to be together.

To communicate with adolescents and resolve the inevitable conflicts that arise, it takes *above all* the commitment to place these tasks high on the priority list. Of course, this is easier said than done. One parent, an extremely conscientious and well-intentioned mother of an eighteen-year-old daughter and fourteen-year-old son, recounted this tale of good intentions gone awry:

> *Friday night was a disaster. We had planned to have Shabbat dinner as a family. John and I wanted to just relax with them a little, talk about the weekend, and discuss some tensions that had cropped up during the week. We worked until five o'clock; we counted on Julie to pick up her brother and for them to get the salad made. Wrong. Julie, unbeknownst to us, had been asked to a party, and was skipping dinner. Paul reached me at work to say that his sister never showed up. I was furious, and located her at her girlfriend's.*

She said later that she had called her dad to let him know about the change in plans. Unfortunately, her message only reached his voice-mail, since he was out of the office for the day. So no dinner, no Julie, and no talking. Instead we had a new argument on our hands, and no family time.

Catching up with an adolescent in high school is a challenge. Most parents find that daily or weekly rituals of gathering in one spot, even for just fifteen minutes, can be a stage for communication: breakfast, a weekday or weekend dinner, a meal out, exercising together.

Time is one of those necessary conditions for good communication. Another is being artful about how you invite an adolescent into conversation. Direct questions that ask your son or daughter to reveal private thoughts or behavior are seldom effective.

Don't ask: "Where did you go last night and what did you do with whom?"

Ask: "Did you have a good time last night? Your mom and I went to an awful movie; I suspect you had a better evening than we did."

Nor is it helpful to ask questions that put young people on the defensive ("Why did you leave the car windows down?" "What were you thinking when you took that drink?!").

One image that helped with our teenagers was that of sideways talking and questioning. I learned to stop always approaching them head-on, stop demanding that they answer my questions right then and there. Instead I began asking *indirectly* about certain topics like drinking and smoking, with more success.

Don't ask: "Exactly how much did you drink last night?"

Ask: "How was the drinking scene last night?" or "How are your friends handling the marijuana scene these days?" or "Do your friends think marijuana is addictive, like some people say it is?"

Asking questions for discussion as opposed to lecturing offers parents a chance to share their *opinions*. However, not many parents share their lives. Talking with adolescents about daily ups and downs is also good communication. It takes practice to break down the firm privacy boundary between parents' adult lives and their children. Older teenagers appreciate the chance to hear about their own parents' successes and disappointments; it puts them on equal footing, and they feel like respected, almost grown family members. Let yourself model:

- How to make mistakes and grow from them
- How to say you're sorry
- How to tolerate being unsure of yourself
- How to manage strong feelings

Communicating is not just talking. To communicate well is to *listen thoughtfully*, to try to understand someone's point of view, and be as clear as you can about your own opinion, even if the best you can say is "I don't know how I feel about that." Kathy Weingarten has called this "radical listening": ". . . through listening to each other well, avidly and devotedly, we draw out voice and accompany each other on our separate journeys."

Listening means giving adolescents the floor to express their views and feelings, playing the role of sounding board ("Are you saying that . . . ?") or devil's advocate ("On the other hand, have you thought of . . . ?"), and simply providing a forum for adolescents to hear themselves reason through decisions. As one psychologist noted, "Many teenagers, after they have shared their ideas with a parent, suddenly brighten with recognition and say, 'Gee, that doesn't make sense, does it?'"

We want to talk to our young people *most* when they look troubled, but that's often when adolescents want *least* to talk. One of the biggest mistakes parents can make is giving too much free advice, protecting in a way that does not allow adolescents to begin to solve their own problems. When it's clear that a teenager has run out of solutions or wants to talk, try questions and comments that are nonjudgmental, free of advice, and inviting:

- What are your options?
- Did you see this coming?
- You look a little down. Do you want to talk?
- I'm sad to see you struggling; let me know if you want a sounding board.
- How are you going to handle this situation?

Even the best communication does not prevent significant arguments from developing between young people and their parents. In fact, in the average household, teenagers and their parents quarrel about twice a week. (The usual topics? Chores, homework, cars, and curfews.) Interestingly, the *frequency* of disagreements is less harmful to parent-adolescent relationships than their *intensity*. Yelling, accusations, crying, storming out, and name-calling are disturbing for everyone, including siblings. Arguments of this kind are unproductive and present poor models for young people. Adolescents learn how to fight fairly through interactions with their parents and often carry over what they learn into their own marriages and partnerships.

Some family situations are more vulnerable to conflict. A divorced or single parent arguing with a teenager who is now her size or larger may be reminded not just of the fighting in the previous marriage but of the divorced partner.

> *No doubt about it, when Jim gets in my face and insists that he hasn't been drinking out of control, he reminds me of his alcoholic father. Then I react in precisely the way I used to when his dad and I were living together. I get very angry, insistent, and then withdraw in deep discouragement. I don't know if I'm seeing things that aren't there, or if I'm an expert by now at detecting denial.*

In stepfamilies, confusion over lines of authority—who is in charge of whom—can mean chaos and continual conflict. Unless a stepparent has had a significant loving and caring relationship with a stepchild since early childhood, meting out rules and punishments, particularly to an adolescent, can be toxic. Maintaining parental authority with one's *own* children is an essential ingredient in blended families.

Unfortunately, in most families intense arguing means that someone withdraws in anger, without resolution. Psychologists point to different, more satisfying pathways for conflict resolution, gleaned from standard mediation techniques. If your family is disrupted by regular intense arguments, consider the following strategy:

- Call a meeting among disagreeing parties.
- Set the ground rules: no sarcasm, name-calling, put-downs, or interrupting.
- Work toward mutual understanding through reflexive listening ("Let me understand. Is this your point?").
- Brainstorm solutions. Agree to one or more.
- Write the solution down; follow up one week later.

Good communication and effective conflict resolution in families pay off later on. Sticky situations lie ahead for your adolescent in college and adulthood involving roommates, teammates, bosses, work colleagues, and significant others. If there are severe, destructive conflicts in your family, it is probably best to seek professional help from a family counselor.

COMMUNICATION
WHAT PARENTS CAN DO

Learn to listen fully and respectfully to your adolescent. Work toward understanding first and reacting second. Be curious, not all-knowing.

Find small spaces of time to make the connection. Talking isn't the only way. Doing things together, however briefly, is also helpful.

Give advice when it's wanted, not as a reflex. Say, "Do you want to hear my thoughts?" not "What you need to do is . . ."

Talk about yourself if you expect your adolescent to talk about himself or herself.

Resolve major conflicts and follow up big arguments with discussion.

CHAPTER SIX

The Launch

Pat / August 7

Three of us are home, suddenly. Adam is eating leftover Chinese food, his head buried in a Charles Baxter novel. I'm on a work break from seeing clients, nibbling lunch. Rob is unpacking his briefcase from a trip to Phoenix. An unease drifts over the still August heat. For an instant we stop to look at one another, knowing full well that this is a rare moment, like a cloudless sunset. In one week Adam will be away at camp again, and then just plain . . . away.

Adam / August 23

I bathe
in full-moon-light
under crickets' hum
amid the quiet roar of distant traffic.
Melancholy and euphoria wrestle
as I think of leaving home and those I love
for a far-off place full of strangers and possibilities.
How many more nights will I spend here
amid familiar wooden chairs and pale green curtains?
When I return home, it will be as a visitor.

If your oldest child is heading to college in the fall, flipping the calendar to August will have new meaning. For twelve years August has meant taking a deep breath to deal with September's school tasks, like assembling health forms, class registration deadlines, lesson schedules, school supplies, and lunch bags. This year, August will mean launching your child to college and beginning a new phase of your relationship.

A deluge of meal plan forms, summer orientation packets, and college bills has already flooded your desk, reinforcing the indisputable fact that your child is going to college. The weeks approaching the departure are filled with long lists and a wild mix of emotions for everyone. Excitement and eager anticipation are among them, but you and other family members may also feel moments of sadness, anxiety, and even dread.

You could approach August and September steeling yourself for an onslaught of upheavals. Or you could frame these months as time to relish your child and family, anticipate challenges, and look forward to change. These are night-and-day images, the contrast between a crouching, huddled family looking painfully inward or away from one another, and a strong, energized, well-prepared family peering excitedly around the next corner.

Anticipating change is helpful in almost any transition. As parents you have some power to make the leaving home process as joyful as you want. This chapter is about that process and the choices you have to make it a positive one.

Sue sits across from me at a crowded coffee bar, her eyes not their usual glistening blue. Instead she looks haggard and upset.

I'm so furious at Barry. Last night he and Amanda got into it, just as she left for a farewell dinner with good friends who are leaving early for college. It was a silly quarrel, something about her forgetting to call Michigan State about the date for soccer try-outs. They each hurled words at each other: "You're never going to take responsibility!" "You're treating me like a baby—stop nagging!" I ran upstairs to stay out of it, and found Amanda's new college sweaters on the floor under her wet towel and dirty jeans. Will things ever change? This is how it goes in our house—tremendous tension and a lot of uproar. And poor David—no one is paying the least attention to him, and he's only twelve. This is a time when we should be having warm, fun moments as a family of four. In two weeks, she'll be gone!

What's probably going on in Sue and Barry's family is a normal crisis, a positive one about the successful launching of their first-born, but a crisis nevertheless. The weeks prior to Departure Day are not unlike those family experiences when a family member is coming *into* (through birth, marriage, or adoption) the family home. Like in all of these positive events, celebration and excitement are mixed with high uncertainty and tension.

The backdrop to a major family change usually includes a fair number of physical disruptions in the home as well. Our son needed as much new equipment for his freshman year of college—from microwave to mattress—as he did when he was first born. These items he layered randomly about his room, on top of a senior year residue of tennis rackets, notebooks, posters, and pictures. Whenever I needed something in his room, I became a wide-eyed archaeologist with an arduous dig ahead of me.

SEPARATION RHYMES WITH PREPARATION

Before you begin to make the Big List, take an emotional inventory. How does your family customarily handle good-byes and separations? Are they highlighted or downplayed? Are people emotional or nonchalant?

As a psychologist, I am always impressed by the ways families handle impending separation. Some funnel their emotions into action and tasks and rarely mention the coming change: "We were so busy shopping and organizing and packing, I didn't have time to get sad or worried about her. I was the same way when she left for camp."

Others express their feelings very openly and directly: "I know this really got on Brian's nerves, but the month before he left for school, at almost every family dinner I reminisced about his childhood. He often rolled his eyes in embarrassment, but I know I needed to talk like this to adjust to his leaving."

As a therapist, I'm strongly in favor of anticipating when a potentially difficult challenge awaits us, and then being prepared. Take a moment alone or with your partner to reflect on the impending separation. These questions may help you to focus:

- How do you typically handle major separations from important people?
- How do you anticipate you will positively and negatively cope with your son's or daughter's separation from the family?
- What support do you need from your partner, family, and friends?

The college experience is a significant opportunity for students to learn about independent living and decision-making. Getting ready to depart for college is an important starting point in that process. To a degree partially dependent on your values, culture, and resources, the departure for college will signal a strong shift of responsibility from you to your child. Assess how the shift is progressing for you:

- Can you leave unopened the important-looking mail that arrives almost daily from colleges and let your child deal with it?
- Will you be able to let your child organize the summer orientation weekend and deal with those details?
- Can you leave the organizational scheme for packing and purchasing up to your student?

Most parents fall somewhere on the continuum between "no way" and "yes, absolutely." Try to push yourself harder to leave more and more up to your youngster to negotiate the departure for college. It's a no-lose strategy. If your child begins to assume greater responsibility for getting to college, everyone's confidence builds. If too many balls get dropped, you can more actively teach your student organizational and planning skills. And if all else fails, there is always the lesson of natural consequences.

A friend's son refused to track down his assigned roommate before he left for the University of Arizona. His mother gently reminded him that knowing what appliances each of them was bringing would be helpful. He did not call and she did not nag him. Instead these two young men were dismayed to discover each had brought an answering machine, large fan, and stereo. It became a lesson in planning.

THE COLLEGE-BOUND ADOLESCENT AT LIFT-OFF

All parents, children, and families are coping with change that is normal when one member leaves the family home. The visible changes are minor (like the pileup of boxes and bags) compared with the invisible psychological changes going on during these weeks before college:

Focusing on the future. Most adolescents about to head away from home are living in future time. No wonder they are not easily engaged in decent conversations or relaxed moments. While we strike up grown-up talk about world unrest, new basketball recruits, and the latest mystery-thriller movie, they are busy forming images of their residence halls, roommates, and classrooms. With the little they know about college from visits and stories, your children are attempting to see themselves already *there*. Inside, that makes for large amounts of excitement, as students picture freedom, new friends, fun, and challenges. These internal pictures also produce a considerable amount of worry and fear.

Saying good-byes. At the same time, students about to leave town are making the rounds of friends who will disperse by the end of the summer. The underlying anxiety is about whether the friendships forged in childhood and adolescence will pass the test of time apart and new college peers. Leaving high school chums can feel like a huge change. As one newly graduated senior pointed out, "You know that you won't ever see some of these people again in your life, and even if you weren't friends, you knew who they are and they knew you." Another college-bound student said: "What about all my friends here at home? Will I ever find people I am this close to anywhere else?"

During the transitional summer between high school and college some friendships may get disrupted as adolescents break new relational ground, testing and stretching their capacity to forge different relationships. For parents, this may look like a bad sign, as if the break with some old friends will lead to wild social experimentation in college. In fact, it's only another example of spreading one's wings before a flight. Consider Melissa's story:

> I thought my summer after graduation would be filled with close times with my best friends. After all, we had been together for so many years, and this would be our last summer together this way. It didn't happen that way. I still saw them now and then but actually I got close to some people who had graduated the year before, tennis players like myself who seemed more mature than my old friends. It was like I had outgrown my old group, and now needed to get ready for college.

Ruptured romances. For adolescents facing separation from romantic partners, the summer may be quite difficult for everyone. Impending loss may intensify the relationship or dilute it, and the emotions in either case may spill over onto yearned-for family time. It's natural that parents want to reclaim their sons and daughters for special time together. It's also natural that young people want to grab every last minute with their high school sweethearts.

A single father, Eric, felt this conflict keenly as he struggled to gain time with his son, whose girlfriend was ever-present:

> It really interfered with our opportunities to find the time and space to talk about what was coming for him, to share my experiences about college, and to tell him how much I cared about him. I pictured us looking through childhood albums, taking a camping

trip. Whenever those impulses came up, he was with her. I'm not positive that all of those things would have happened. But rightly or wrongly, I blamed his girlfriend for stealing him at this key time.

There are no easy answers when it comes to finding time with an adolescent who has strong competing interests. Being a good sport helps—for example, including significant others in family outings. So does being patient and lending support to a sad adolescent. Tip from a mother who learned the hard way: This is *not* the best time to unload your advice about whether or not the romance should go forward.

Self-doubts. Even for adolescents who are high on self-confidence and independence and excited about college, new self-doubts may emerge. They often take the form of major and minor "what-ifs":

- ◆ What if I've chosen the wrong college? (You probably haven't.)
- ◆ What if I hate the kids? (You will probably dislike some but be drawn to others.)
- ◆ What if I get homesick? (You may, but it will pass as soon as you get involved in college life.)
- ◆ What if I hate my roommate? (Don't expect to be friends, just respect one another's differences and cooperate with one another. No one spends much time in his or her room anyway.)
- ◆ What if I can't do the work? (If you are accepted by a college, you can do the work.)
- ◆ What if I can't find my way to classes? (All freshmen are in the same boat, and there are staff and upperclassmen everywhere to help you during that first week of classes.)
- ◆ What if I get sick? (You can call us for advice and go to the health service for treatment.)
- ◆ What if someone from the opposite sex sees me getting out of the shower? (Well, a robe would help.)
- ◆ What if I have to ask a question in front of 200 other people

in my calculus class? (You can ask your teaching assistant later in your section meeting or E-mail the professor after class.)

Separation anxiety: You may learn about all, some, or none of these fears from your son or daughter. *If* your student makes these fears known to you directly, you have a wonderful opportunity to reassure and to help. One young man whose father died earlier in his childhood wrote: "In my life, I have come to be very dependent on the support of my mother and sister. Leaving them will be the most trying experience of going away to college."

All parents want to know that they will be missed when their children leave for college. However, it's not always helpful to let adolescents know *how much* you will miss them. A student about to leave for Norwich University in Vermont wrote:

> *Parents shouldn't make kids more nervous and anxious than they already are. At my house my Mom keeps saying, "What am I going to do when you're gone?" My answer: The same thing I'm going to do at school: Live a life! Leaving home for the first time is stressful enough without people telling you that they are going to miss you.*

Some college-bound students seem extremely eager to leave home and can't be bothered with conversations about separations and missing people. For them, the eagerness for adventure, a new start, independence, or freedom from parental control defines their mood before Departure Day. Try not to feel wounded when they don't want to talk. Assume that they love you *and* want to leave. Each adolescent will handle the separation differently.

Pat / May 29

> *Adam has a glaze over his eyes, almost an imperceptible one. Is it fatigue from play rehearsal, or has he pulled a faint screen down between us, one that lets in light but allows no information to escape? I can no longer read those bright blue pupils for signs of anger, fear, and excitement. He has separated, I think, and this is what it looks like.*

FEARS OR ANXIETY
WHAT PARENTS CAN DO

Support your adolescent by asking gentle questions ("How do you think it's going to be, being away from Emily?"), being understanding with the time your student wants with friends, and watching for spontaneous ways the family can spend time together. Above all, acknowledge and respect your child's concerns and offer reminders that fears are a normal part of separating.

Remind your adolescent about other times when he or she has successfully coped with new places and new friends.

Be there. The period shortly before Departure Day is a time when being at home more often may be helpful. If you can put major work or home projects aside, do so. As your child dashes between home and work and friends, an available parent is an important anchor.

ADOLESCENTS LIVING AT HOME OR NEARBY

For students at community colleges, commuting to college, or living close to their families, the launching process is less dramatic but by no means less important. Students in community colleges who will be living at home need to negotiate some clear boundaries with their parents about independence and responsibility. Going to college means their lives are changing dramatically; their parents may not notice much change and carry on as usual. Larry Chamow, a clinical psychologist in the San Diego area who counsels young adults, remembered his own years as a college student living at home:

I didn't know what I wanted at that point in my life but most importantly I didn't want someone telling me what to do. I think that is where things went wrong in my first two years out of high school. My parents tried to control my time, my workload, and with the best intentions, their anxiety, by telling me what to do. If young adults are to live at home beyond high school they need to walk the delicate balance between creating their own life and living with parents who often want to maintain their influence.

If the adolescents are taking up a separate nearby residence, which happens frequently in college towns, moving out may happen very gradually, and parents may see them more frequently. But, they will still be making decisions on their own and be out of sight much of the time. Saying good-bye can still be strongly felt by parents, even though the separation is much gentler. This story is from Karen, whose son will be attending the local university:

Matt is going to college in his home town, only five miles from our door. I cried when he said good-bye to us, even though he was only five minutes away. I knew we would see him, but it was the end of something. Attending the University of Michigan has meant that he shows up nearly every weekend to borrow the car, do his laundry, and play tennis with his brother. It has also meant that we haven't really separated from him yet. He does seem different to me though, more in charge of his life, quite a bit more grown up.

PARENTS AT LIFT-OFF

"Time Flies, But Where Does It Go?" read the headline of a *New York Times* feature on today's fast-paced living. For parents of children leaving home, time is both a friend and an enemy. The last weeks at home before college can be an odd time warp. On one hand, we yearn to stretch the minutes with our almost grown children into hours, even those mundane minutes we used to take for granted. On the other hand, we can't wait for this transition to be over.

Pat / August 23

> *I have a sense that Adam is already a visitor. As hosts, we know*
> *that his eighteen-year-long visit with us in our family has already*
> *crested. Like those awkward moments before beloved guests depart,*
> *we made tiny talk in the living room today.*
> ME: *So . . .*
> ROB: *Well, Adam . . .*
> ME: *Only a few days until you leave.*
> ADAM: (grinning, stretching out on the couch) *Yup!*
> ME: *So . . .*
> ROB: *Well . . . that's great.*
> ADAM: (a solemn nod) *. . . I know.*

Don't panic: They know how to use a microwave. Many of my clients and friends tell me that during their last few weeks as daily parents, they scrutinize their college-bound youngsters for signs of immaturity, irresponsibility, and deficits in common sense. I remember thinking when our older son left for college that my nit-picking must be hard-wired behavior with an evolutionary function. Lionesses must check their brood before turning them into the grasslands, mustn't they? Does this nearly grown cub know how find food, or doesn't he?

I remember big extrapolations from little behavior:

- He left a five-dollar bill on the floor of his bedroom. (Meaning: He doesn't know how to manage money.)
- He slammed the door in his brother's face after an innocent request for the telephone. (Meaning: He will never get along with roommates.)
- He didn't pack his big dictionary and thesaurus. (Meaning: He doesn't plan to do serious college work.)

These were, in fact, meaningless behaviors. But I worried that our child might have needed more or better parenting and probably layered on too many lessons to be learned last-minute. Most students rightly see through this behavior as parental overanxiousness and patiently tolerate a certain amount of it. Other college-students-to-be, particularly if they are extremely anxious themselves, will butt heads with overcontrolling parents.

Separation anxiety: The deluxe version. Parents have many of the same worries, fears, and separation pangs as adolescents do during this launching period, *minus* some of the excitement, *plus* some anticipatory relief that a child is beginning to be more independent. It's a crazy time.

Pat / August 15

> *I counted how many days remain before Adam leaves for college (ten), and then promptly sobbed into the suds while washing my face. It was my first really gut-wrenching cry about his leaving since last spring. It helped that my face was already wet; that kept the crying short and sweet. Then, in a flash, I had a new idea. He's not leaving home, he's beginning to leave home. That had a nice ring to it.*

One mother with an only son who was unsure of his college choice dreamed of starting over again as the mother of an infant:

> *I dreamed we got to the college and an old man greeted us. As I began to feel reassured that someone would be watching over our son, he dwarfed into a baby. Suddenly I knew that my plans to begin a more adult life were finished: I had to raise another baby, and he would take all of my time!*

Depending on temperament, history, and usual ways of coping, parents manage in different ways as Departure Day draws near. Some women distract themselves by adopting a Mother Extraordinaire role. They cook, shop, organize, and attend to their nearly launched offspring as if they were shooting love and care into their very veins. Some fathers distract themselves with work or become obsessed with finding the right computer or bike to take to school (warning: buy the computer on campus at student prices). At the other extreme, some see leaving home as only a beginning stage of adult development, one with very little meaning. These parents find only joy and pride inside, especially if they have worked long and hard to make college a possibility for their youngster. For any parent of a college-bound student, the task is to accept the ambivalent and sometimes intense nature of your emotions and frame these weeks as a normally up-and-down time.

My husband was a case in point. He found himself somewhat puzzled by my strong feelings during August and September. "For me, I am so pleased about his choice, and so happy for him, that I can't locate very much sadness. This move is so very right for him—that's what I focus on."

Some parents react to the impending Departure Date by last-minute overparenting—imposing their opinions and will in a kind of parents' last stand. That reaction usually backfires and produces an angry thank-goodness-I'm-free kind of attitude in students once they get to school, as this student describes:

> *My roommate's parents were strict with her in high school, and things got worse the summer before she left for college. It was like they couldn't trust her or something. So that first month of freedom from them she just went totally wild and, one weekend and a dozen beers later, got herself in a bad situation.*

Understandably, some parents feel they must maintain "house rules" as long as their children reside under their roof. But the trade-off is seldom worth it. Parents who don't relax some rules during the summer before college will find themselves battling adolescents who have one foot out the door. A wiser strategy is to pare limits down to the minimum and begin to trust your child's judgment.

SIBLINGS AT LIFT-OFF

Siblings have a variety of reactions to life in the family before Departure Day, depending in large part upon their closeness in age, sex, and interests to their college-bound sibling. Some are handling impending loss themselves, as in this story from Alex, a usually devil-may-care sixteen-year-old whose sister had just left for college.

> *The last night my sister was home we sat up and talked about stuff, like when we were little, what we remembered, and what we'll miss now that she's going to college. All of a sudden I felt like*

crying, and I held it in. But then I looked over at Lindsay and she was crying, and then we both cried. I'm fine now—we dropped her off today and it was great to see what a beautiful campus it was. My folks are crying now, though.

A few siblings act out to remind parents that they need at least a minimum amount of attention (and share of the goods their brother or sister is receiving). More than a few become increasingly worried that the pressure will increase for them to carry more chores and take on new roles. Some siblings are too little to anticipate the changes. At least two parents I interviewed were also taking their youngest children to kindergarten at the same time the oldest were heading to college, making for doubly empty nests:

We took Hannah to kindergarten one day, and Sarah to Oberlin College the next. It was an unreal time of separation which didn't grab me until one afternoon at home when I walked by Sarah's empty room and listened to the still house around me. This felt so awful, so empty.

For the most part, brothers and sisters, especially if they are adolescents, do well with simple acts of affection and attention, topped off with the reminder that they will have more attention, not less, from parents after their sibling leaves for college.

LAST-MINUTE LESSONS

Some midnight-hour teaching is necessary. When a moment is at hand, and you know that you (finally) have your student's attention, it's not too late to teach your student how to:

- ◆ Use a checking account and balance a statement
- ◆ Keep track of credit card expenses
- ◆ Use a long-distance calling card
- ◆ Sew on a button

- Microwave simple meals
- Make airline, train, or bus reservations
- Use a thermometer and take simple pain pills

Those smaller lessons are often welcomed by students. One young man told his mother during parents weekend at Tufts University:

I thought when I was a senior that I was really independent. You know what I mean: I kept my own schedule, had a job and car, decided when I needed to do homework or not. But you and Dad were always there to back me up. If I didn't know how to do something, I could walk into the kitchen and ask you. Now I have to figure everything out by myself. That's independence.

Some last-minute lessons are less welcomed by students, and parents don't relish them either. These are about money, sex, and substance use.

Money and the Art of Increasing Responsibility

Money is power. Money is often used to communicate love. Money means freedom. Money corrupts. Money is work. In other words, money is not simply money. Research with parents who have college-age children has found that financial and residential independence is the major factor that, in parents' eyes, distinguishes children who have left home from those who have not.

You may have decided long ago that a financial education begins early in a child's development. But more than a few of us, with college only weeks off, rush to teach our offspring about checking accounts, cash withdrawal cards, credit cards, and budgets.

College guidance for students always includes tips for how they can best manage their money and avoid falling into traps laid by credit card companies and banks. Tuition, fees, housing, and meal plan bills are usually fixed prepaid expenses. What remains variable is spending money. As parents, you hope that your child uses that money responsibly. You have the opportunity, in these last weeks, to make that more likely.

TEACHING MONEY MANAGEMENT

WHAT PARENTS CAN DO

If you are providing spending money for your student's freshman year, decide clearly ahead of time how much money to send in the first semester. By second semester you can revise that amount, based on fall spending.

Decide how you will disperse the money. Some parents give their students the whole semester's amount at once; others parcel it out by quarter or month. Some parents want their college-aged children to write the actual tuition checks, hoping they will better appreciate the cost of their educations. If your child is unaccustomed to budgeting money, it's better to give it in multiple small lumps.

Decide what you will do if your child runs out of money and asks for more. This can be a family conversation, a contingency plan worked out ahead of time.

Think twice (or even thrice!) before arranging for your child to have a personal credit card. In the rush of the first weeks when students are furnishing dorm rooms, buying clothes and tickets for special events, and going out with new friends, a credit card can look like free money. On the other hand, you may want students to charge some purchases, like books and class supplies. One solution is to have your child listed as a signer on one of *your* cards, so that you get the statements and help your student to track expenses.

Be sure that your student has ample *cash* for the first week of school. Lines to open checking accounts may be long at banks, and many are reluctant to cash out-of-town checks unless the student has a bank account.

If you feel strongly that college is the place for students to work toward financial independence, hold to your money agreements, barring emergencies and unforeseen academic expenses. That may be difficult to do if your family has ample financial resources, and the children are accustomed to asking for money. Whatever your decision, it should be a reasoned one, with some goal in mind for your child's development as an adult.

Sex and Drugs

If you haven't already—and even if you have—open a serious discussion with your adolescent about sexual intercourse, birth control, and alcohol and drug use. For most adolescents, college means a high degree of personal control without adult supervision (no matter what the college tells you about the resident advisor). This is often a time of experimentation.

Young women and men need education about birth control, condom and dental dam protection from HIV and other sexually transmitted diseases (STDs), and date rape. Drinking and drug use on college campuses remain very high. One parent we know requires her leaving-home children to read a book about how to drink moderately. Frank conversation on these topics can be testy and awkward between almost grown children and their parents, but it is certainly worthwhile, given the grave risks. Useful questions invite conversation and not argumentation—if asked non-accusatorily. They imply that your son or daughter can be responsible and conscious about risk behavior:

- ◆ Knowing what you do about yourself, how will you know if you develop a problem with substance use? What will you look for?
- ◆ What are your opinions about birth control and STD protection? Where do you think you can get it at school and learn to use it?
- ◆ How will you protect yourself against sexual assault, date rape, or accusations of date rape?

(See chapter 1 for a full discussion of adolescent sexuality and substance abuse.)

CELEBRATING A RITE OF PASSAGE

Rituals and ceremonies are effective vehicles for expressing emotions. Other than the bar and bat mitzvah of Jewish culture, there are few Western rituals in adolescence, probably because adolescence itself is a recent twentieth-century invention. In past generations, the marriage ritual signaled the end of childhood and the beginning of adulthood and, along with financial independence, it is still a key ritual to mark the passage into adulthood.

Coming of age among college students often happens gradually, in some far-off orbit quite a distance from their homes. So a ritual, even a small one, would help. Like in weddings, it would be nice to have one's relatives around to help celebrate the success of the next step and bid good luck. Unfortunately, ceremony surrounding college departure is often absent, empty, or overwhelming. Charles McGrath, writing in *The New Yorker* about delivering his youngest child to college, laments:

> *We waited in lines for a while, and we wrote a bunch of checks. Then we went out and wandered around town for a bit, and while we were waiting at a corner for a light to change, the nest suddenly emptied. A quick hug, a wave, a promise to call, and, in an instant, he was gone. It's too late for us now—we will have to work through our grief in other ways, on our own . . . but I kept wishing that the college had arranged some ceremony to mark the occasion. A circling of the Volvos, Cherokees, and Caravans lined up according to age and mileage while the dean affixes a brand-new college decal to the rear window of each. Or maybe an interfaith blessing of the first-year stereos . . .*

Leaving home ceremonies and rituals can be invented, however. Bob, a Mormon father whose college-aged son Sean was leaving for a two-year mission totally separated from his family, told this story:

> *About a week before Sean left I took him to our old house where he had spent much of his adolescence. We stood in the driveway. I said to him, "Sean, you and I played hundreds of one-on-one basketball games here. I used to always beat you, and then by the time you were in high school you almost always beat me. . . . I can see that you're a man now. I want you to have this." I pulled out a solid*

gold chain with a small charm on it that read "Sean" and "Dad" on the front and had a scripture on the back. I told him that I wanted him to wear it and remember our good times together. He cried, I cried. This was a different one-on-one, a time where I told him I loved him.

Having a major good-bye dinner with relatives works well for some families. We had two modest celebrations, one with each side of the family. Over dinner our son heard stories from grandparents about how each left home. We also asked each grandparent to express his or her best piece of advice for Adam. Whether or not these words of wisdom really mattered ("Study hard!" "Expand yourself." "Don't forget about fun." "Call your mother.") was less important to me than the gathering of family to say good-bye, and I will cherish that memory.

Even without a gathering of relatives, a farewell party can include good friends and neighbors. Or you might have a restaurant or picnic dinner with just immediate family members. Small rituals like these celebrate the fact that your child—and your family—is passing on to a new stage in the life cycle.

PACKING

"All my children refused to pack for college," announced Judith, a self-possessed and articulate teacher. She had come to accept the refusals as part of the separation process. And she is probably right. Packing means leaving home, and so it's an activity flooded with meaning for many soon-to-be-freshmen moving away to college. Parents who attempt to move packing along faster than their children want are often met with glares ("You want me to leave, *don't* you?"). Parents who don't help at all may not fare any better ("You don't want me to leave, *do* you?").

I saw college shopping/buying/packing as a repository for all my anxiety. Stopped cold at my son's door ("Stop sorting my room!"), I was aghast that he would not let me ceremoniously pack up a special box of his lifelong treasures that I had moved surreptitiously onto one bookshelf. In the end, he took only a few of them, throwing them into a small brown sandwich bag.

Peggy, a mother whose oldest child was headed to Vassar, had a most dramatic story:

> The night before Emily left for school, her friends were here until midnight. She hadn't packed anything. Nothing. I had pictured us having a big heart-to-heart talk on her bed, or at least packing together. I decided to stay up, but steer clear of her and the private space she clearly needed to separate from us. At about two o'clock in the morning, she began calling for me: "Mom, would you waterproof my shoes?" "Mom, we have to figure out how to thermofax my Van Gogh picture before I leave tomorrow." Slowly she began to pack, and I was her willing servant.

DROP-OFF DAY

Experienced parents who have helped their children move to college agree that *parents who have serious things to say to their children as they leave home should say those things at home.* The transitional day from home to college is too filled with the physical and emotional exertion of moving. And there is little time and space in that intense day for special, close moments.

Some parents, divorced parents among them, will not accompany their children to college. Some students' parents cannot afford to make the trip. Other students are not traveling very far and will move in gradually. Still others will remain at home while attending college. Whatever form going off to college takes, Day One is a defining day. "I knew we would see him," said Karen, whose son would be living very nearby, "but it was the end of something when we took him to his dorm. I cried."

Bidding farewell at home will not doom the new relationship to a bad start. Lia decided with her daughter that her father would take her to college. Their good-bye scene was close and loving:

We cried for two hours before she left with her dad. She sat in my lap. After a bit, I asked her if she was ready to leave. She said no, and so I held her quietly. When I asked a few minutes later, she was. We both knew this was really it. This was really good-bye.

College students, interviewed after the start of their freshman year, report that it almost always helps if their families take them to school. It isn't always possible, and not everyone can always go. But many students make a better initial adjustment if at least one parent can make the trip. And, ideally, siblings can be tucked in among the stereos. There are great benefits to brothers and sisters' being part of the ritual. Later, they will remember the scene and use it to shape their own leaving-home process. And for parents and siblings alike, memories of the dorm room, eating hall, and campus can be enormously comforting during the initial separation.

If parents have separated or divorced, two parental trips may work best. One divorced family arranged that a daughter's father would drive her out, with the mother to follow two weeks later. This was emotionally difficult for the mother. But she rationalized that her daughter and ex-husband, whose relationship had been strained over college costs, needed some mending time before she began her first year at the University of Rochester:

When Grant picked her up and they started loading the car, arguing the whole time about what would and would not fit, I had a terrible ache in my throat, wishing that this moment could be different for all of us. Grant and I just glowered at each other. Just as it looked as though absolutely nothing else would fit inside the car, Holly brought out a huge floor lamp and proceeded to thread it through the car, aiming it directly at the driver's seat. I got the point, so to speak, and so did her father. We stopped glaring, they stopped arguing, and she and I had a last loving hug in the driveway. It felt good to be able to say, "I'll see you in two weeks."

Joining the Herd

Pat / August 26

> *If, as Americans, we ever have to abandon this country with all our belongings, we'll be in serious trouble. I decided this while I joined one thousand college freshmen and their parents with twenty crates and boxes each of microwaves, televisions, stereos, lofts, books, clothes, and sports equipment and moved in a choking throng into elevators and skinny dorm hallways.*

If you drive your student to school, the college or university will send you detailed instructions about when to arrive and where to park for unloading (and how long you have to do that). The printed sheets will *not* tell you that, from most students' perspective, your job is to be as invisible as possible. While you are focused on settling your child physically, your son or daughter is checking out the social layout of his suite, his hallway, the dorm, and the campus. You may be fighting off whiffs of sadness while your adolescent is not paying you the least bit of attention.

Take your cues from your child on this day. Let your first-day freshman be in charge. He wants to carry his boxes up ten flights of stairs himself? Fine. She begs you to go buy her a piece of carpet for her room before her roommate arrives? He absolutely needs to have a burger at 9 A.M. ? She *has* to have that little red-topped cactus plant at a roadside stand? You *forgot* your daughter's phone (umbilical) cord? (Go buy another one!) This is not the time for arguments. These requests are, in part, an attempt to have some control over a day highly charged with uncertainty.

Parents are trying to have control too, but their efforts to cope are not always well received. Ignoring a cautionary voice inside me, I tried to buy Adam some things I thought he needed for his room. It was *not* appreciated. At the checkout lane, he emphatically took them out and put them on the floor. These were the pitifully transparent acts of a mother falling back on what she used to do at home. I didn't know how else to act. Suddenly, I had no role.

Most parents feel awkward and misplaced on move-in day. Dorm rooms in August are usually small sweatboxes filled with boxes and trunks, the plaintive beginnings of your child's new home. Parents stand about trying to be both invisible and essential. A tricky combination, particularly if you're holding back tears. Fathers who don't build anything watch fathers who can build a loft in ten minutes. Career mothers who never made beds at home watch homemaker mothers swiftly assemble a cozy quilted bed with crisp corners. Parents, just to distract themselves, are calculating the cost per square foot of tiny rooms. (Tip: Don't complain too publicly about the awful ambience of dorm rooms. For some students, maybe even your child's roommate, dorm life is an improvement over their living quarters at home).

The culmination of years of visions, planning, talking, searching, and soul-searching are coming down to this one moment, and it happens in the crowded corridor of your child's dorm, at a street corner, out on the asphalt parking lot, or as the elevator doors close. One father recounts:

> *Suddenly, it was time to go. We were in the lobby of a high-rise dorm, a spot crowded with boxes and carts and people all around. We hugged, Bob said he would call, he stepped into the elevator, and the door closed on his smile. I was stunned. I just stood there, about to cry, realizing that this was a defining moment, one of those times in life when, in one instant, your life changes right before your eyes. He was gone.*

College officials are well aware that the moment of departure is powerful and sometimes dreaded by parents. At Duke University the freshman orientation staff arrange for parents to have their own meeting, not just to give out information, but to help them begin to separate from their children, who are self-occupied and getting to know one another. Every college and university is accustomed to tears on move-in day. Dan Walls, Director of Admissions at Emory University, says:

> *Each year there are parents who linger after college orientation on drop-off day and need a hand from us on their shoulders, or a*

gentle word that it's time for them to leave. It's very tough to make that final good-bye. One of our psychology professors, Marshall Duke, gives a talk to parents that day. He describes this day as being a "privileged moment in time" when you say things that you'll remember all your life.

A father, William, says of drop-off day:

> *It dawned on us like a clap of thunder that as he was leaving . . . he was never going to live with us, live at home again, even though there were holidays and vacations stretched ahead. For us, that day was a watershed. Everything before had been in the paradigm of a family that included him. He officially began his own life that day.*

I felt ready to say good-bye, I thought, since my emotional reactivity was strongest during Adam's senior year. At the actual good-bye (we were in the asphalt group) I was excited for him and eager to experience our new, widening family. At my elbow I had another child to launch, which helped to lighten my sadness. Yet, saying good-bye was nevertheless difficult. Like other parents, I had flashbacks to the first day in my son's life:

Pat / August 25

> *When Adam was born, in that instant when we beheld him after delivery in a greenish hushed room, a huge responsibility befell us. As new parents our job was to pick him up and keep him near. We did that for eighteen years. Now our task would be a reverse kind of delivery and another giant shift. On the asphalt of a noisy dormitory parking lot, we needed to wish him well and let him fly. It was hard. We hugged tearfully, Adam, Rob, and I, fully knowing that this was good-bye. We said, "Have fun. We love you." And he dashed across the street. At the dormitory door, he turned and waved. We actually got to see his train pull down the tracks, I thought. After he disappeared inside of his dormitory, I got into the car, numb but smiling.*

Planning the Trip Back Home

Several parents I spoke with who took their children to college strongly urged others to make a definite plan for the trip back home. It's a way to make a good beginning, especially if you incorporate things in the trip that are positive signs of what's to come.

One mother, Linda, described a journey home from Florida to Michigan after dropping her last child at his university. She and her husband planned two diversionary stop-overs: one with old friends (a sign that old friendships can be renewed with children gone to college), another at a resort, just for themselves as a couple (a sign that this marriage can continue to grow). She then spent twelve days alone while her spouse went on a business trip: "Just me and the cats, the first time in my adulthood" (a sign that she has a life without day-to-day parenting).

Another parent, Alice, anticipating a hard separation from her only daughter, planned a circuitous route home, which originally included a second good-bye:

> I thought that it might really be a good thing to have something to do right after the drop-off. So I organized to accept a speech in a nearby city. Then I couldn't fall apart. I also planned to come back to Washington the following week, on my return from a vacation in South Carolina. Seemed like a great plan, until Andrea gently suggested that it would be hard to have to say good-bye a second time. I was disappointed, but of course I agreed. What that brought home to me was the coming change. Now I have to negotiate with her to see her; now she really lives somewhere else. That seems like the hardest thing to grasp.

I heard many stories about families who, after a hectic, emotion-filled drop-off day, did not return directly home. Life had taken a turn and it was good to acknowledge that things would be different. After we dropped Adam off in Madison, Dan coaxed us to wade into the still warm waters of Lake Michigan, clothes and all:

Pat / August 25

> *We took up Dan's bright-eyed idea so happily. He was right; it was the perfect release from an emotional day. There we were, sopping wet and wild, jumping the waves in our jeans as the sun went down over the lake. Dan is so full of sensual fun and spontaneity. This was not just a diversion and a reward for being a patient sibling, but a sign of how our lives will be enriched with him as our only child at home.*

CHAPTER SEVEN

The Freshman-Year Experience

Postcard / August 28

Dear Adam,

The Wisconsin cornfields fly by in the late sun as we head back East. You are 100 miles behind us, tacking up your Rockies poster, assembling your desk, lounging on the new green futon, getting to know Patrick. And the images of you there, in your new dormitory, merge with the ones I hold in my mind from your last week at home: You punching the piano keys, you wrestling with your guitar strings, you sitting on the deck in the moonlight. I hope things are going well. I love you.

—Mom

Voice-mail from Adam / September 1

Hi, guys. You can stop holding your breath now. I'm fine. But the computer is more money than I thought, so I'm leaving out the CD-ROM. Books were out of sight, too. Just wanted to let you know. I forgot my graphing calculator. Could you send it? It's somewhere in my room. Things are going well. Talk to you soon. Gotta run. 'Bye.

With Adam's message came little waves of relief. He was upbeat, he handled his first big purchase well, and he was staying connected. We'll have only brief glimpses like these into his life now. But he still needs us.

THE FIRST WEEKS

"So much is absolutely new for these first-year students. It's amazing that so many of them survive this transition just fine," remarked Penni

Reed, Director of the Office of New Student Programs at the University of Michigan. Below her third-floor window marched a group of newly admitted students on their way to a dormitory for lunch, and she mused:

> *They are totally uprooted from familiarity, thrown in with new people, new living space, a new town, and then given total independence. Eighty-five percent of our students have never shared a bedroom before! We will try to prepare those students you see down there before they get here, but they won't understand the magnitude of the changes until they arrive in the fall.*

Jennifer Cross, Freshman Orientation Director at U.M., agreed:

> *The biggest task for students, besides adjusting to a new living situation, is to find a way of feeling connected with people. They've arrived with a preexisting high school status (like popular, nerd, intellectual, zany, shy) that won't necessarily stick here. So the first few weeks they are asking, "What will it take for me to be accepted here, to fit in, and to be true to myself?"*

Even if your student has already been to campus to register for classes, true college orientation doesn't really happen until parents in trucks, vans, and station wagons pull away from campus. Freshmen spend their first few weeks at school in mild to major culture shock. They begin by adapting physically and socially to a completely new environment. They learn to live in small quarters, or "eighths," as one freshman girl from the University of Arizona called them. Out of their squashed surrounds, they make little homes complete with a tiny "kitchen" (microwave, refrigerator, and phone), "living room" (couch and stereo), "study" (desk and computer under a loft), and "bedroom" (one to four narrow beds). Ingeniously and artfully decorated, these rooms reflect each inhabitant's tastes and interests. Grateful Dead posters live alongside Sierra Club pictures. Roller blades stand propped alongside guitars.

Orienting means not only learning how to get places using maps and buses, but also acquiring the rules and rituals of a new culture. Your freshman may be acclimating to some "foreign" words (in Michigan, they say "pop," not "soda"), a very different climate and geography, and a new nightlife (free symphony tickets are available at intermission, never go upstairs in a frat house, don't drink on the streets).

Students are also orienting themselves *in time.* No one wakes them up and knows when they come home. And suddenly, after subtracting classes and labs, students have lots of unscheduled time to manage. One young man was startled to discover that he needed to buy a watch: "For years, I depended on the clocks at home, at school, and in my car to stay on time. I used my parents and friends as time keepers. No more. Now I have to do this all on my own."

By far the biggest challenge for most freshmen is orienting to a new set of faces, personalities, and living habits. Most students are learning to live with a perfect stranger. This may be the most interesting, enjoyable, and easygoing person your child has ever met, or the sloppiest, surliest, least cooperative student there ever was. Roommate matches are rarely made in heaven and can be difficult to change. All schools have a process for attempting a switch or mediating disputes; parents are advised not to intervene on their child's behalf with the housing office.

Coming to college as a freshman means starting over socially for almost everyone. That means finding one or two good friends and a group of people to dine and hang out with. In high school close friends were those who had known each other for a long time. Now a freshman's best friend may be someone on the floor whom he met only a week ago. As Harvard freshman Chana Schoenberger noted, "'Close friend' meant anyone I saw more than once a day."

Our son Adam didn't skip a beat when asked what the biggest challenge was in his first few weeks: "The hardest part was walking across campus every day for two weeks and *never seeing one person I knew,* and then feeling very alone."

For some students starting over is a breath of fresh air, particularly if they had trouble finding their social niche in high school. A "nerd" reputation, for example, tends not to follow students to college. *By design* a freshman class comprises anywhere from 100 to 8,000 students with a wide range of interests. The student who was hugely popular in high school may find this new social start a bit disconcerting. Said one Rice University freshman:

> *In high school I had this really comfortable spot in a group of girls and guys who hung out together every weekend. We were really, really close in our junior and senior year. I never had to figure out who to call or what to do at night—it just happened. It sounds odd, but now I feel almost naked without a ready-made group. I have to make all the social moves myself.*

Fortunately, everyone is pretty much in the same boat, and any freshman knows someone who is having an even harder time socially. Some students attach themselves initially to people they knew from home, or fall in with an athletic team or other special group, like a music ensemble or engineering program.

Commuting students apparently have to work harder to find a campus-based peer group. Many find themselves unable to resist staying connected to in-town friends from high school. Unlike residents in dormitories, they are not thrown in and expected to cope. In their social favor, commuting students are often sought out as people who know how to navigate the town and campus.

Acclimating to classes and studying is a somewhat easier part of the first weeks' adjustment. Most students simply do what they've always done, in varying degrees of seriousness: go to class, take notes, read, study, write. The real academic orientation is down the road, after the first serious tests or mid-terms. That's when it becomes clearer which college courses are difficult or easy, which are interesting or mundane.

Back home, parents are engaged in their own orientation period, albeit a less exciting and more mundane existence. You may be sad or out of sync (which is normal) or just plain relieved (also normal). You aren't psychotic if, in your adjustment, you visually imagine your child in some of his familiar spots, doing favorite things. This will pass. Find ways to relax and spend some time with your partner and family. Compare notes with other parents and do some gentle reflections on what's *positive* about your child's leaving home. At the least, be reminded that your student has earned both independence and a new place in the academic community. You have successfully begun to launch your child, and chances are good that both of you will adjust well to the many changes ahead.

Passing your son or daughter's empty room in these first few weeks or noting the empty chair at the kitchen table may send bubbles of sadness through you. Sharon Olds's poem "High School Senior" captures this odd feeling:

> I had the daily sight of her,
> like food or air she was there, like a mother.
> I say "college," but I feel as if I cannot tell
> the difference between her leaving for college
> and our parting forever—

If you're like most parents, you won't begin to settle back until you've heard some news from your student that things are going reasonably well. A father recounted his first conversation with his daughter after leaving her at the University of Texas:

> On this, the first weekend of family life without Marla home, I am strangely drained, but peaceful. She called on her third day at school. Even her clipped answers, strung together like a paper chain from Austin to Chicago, are an odd comfort. Roommate? "Fine." Classes? "Seem really good." Finding your way around? "No problem." Homesick? "Not at all." Having fun? "Absolutely."

Note this change. In the past, news of doing well in school has come through periodic reports from teachers and coaches. From now on, no other adult will ever call you with a report. The responsibility for monitoring academic progress has been passed to your student, who may or may not tell *you* about it.

STAYING CONNECTED

Hands down, the best thing for your dispersed family right after the departure to college is to stay connected. That sounds easy enough, given phones and E-mail. But what's tricky is a mismatch in scenarios. You may have a vision of regular phone calls and letters. Your freshman may have a different picture. Some will drop out of sight for several weeks; others will call or send a note right away. Most will oblige parents' requests to call or write weekly or biweekly.

Until some rhythm emerges, it's important to not take any lapse in connection too personally. For most adolescents, leaving home is about what they have *gained* (a high degree of personal control), not what they've *lost* (daily family connections). New college students have to become myopic for the first few weeks in college. Most are very, very busy. They don't tend to think deeply about the separation from their parents. In fact, many are bent on showing their parents how well they can survive without them.

Nevertheless, it's sometimes a puzzling, frustrating, and one-sided dance. Should you initiate contact if you haven't heard from your child for what seems like too long? Isn't that intrusive? Shouldn't your child have to "go it alone" for a while? Freshmen are in strong agreement that it's worse to have *not enough* contact with your parents than *too much*. We think that *not* calling or writing is giving our children their much-desired space, while they wonder if we've stopped thinking about them:

> *After my folks dropped me off, I didn't hear from them for two weeks. I was homesick on and off, but determined to conquer it by not calling home. When they didn't phone me, I thought, "Well, they are giving me some space. Cool." But I also wondered if they didn't care about me, now that I was out of sight.*

On the other hand, to call every day is probably to exercise your own needs, not your child's. The message students may get from daily calling is that either you are suffering or you think they can't cope. What's important is to stay both connected and respectful of your child's new status. Size up your student's needs, consider the kinds of connections that have worked in the past during separations, and use your instincts.

Freshmen report that they like to be connected with everyone in the family, not just the designated hitter, often a mother or stepmother, who is expected to communicate with everyone. Be sure that students hear from both mother and father in the first few weeks. That goes for siblings as well. Divorced parents may benefit from the advice of one father, Mike, an elementary school teacher:

> *The hardest part of being from a divorced family, my college student children tell me, is having to tell each parent the same exact information* twice. *While the children's mother and I both have our own independent relationships with our kids, we worked together to adapt to our college students, who have trouble enough connecting to* one *parent. When it came to basic updates (arriving home safely from a trip, having the flu, passing an important exam), they told me the news and I called their mother, or vice versa.*

Most young people are savvy enough to know that their parents are missing them. Resident advisors (RAs), like the camp counselors before them, urge students to write or call home in the first week. Peterson's *The Ultimate College Survival Guide*, written for students, is more sanguine: "Most parents are notoriously easy to please, as long as they hear something from you regularly."

RAs are very clear about what freshmen want from their parents. Said one Residence Hall Director, "What students love to get from home is *encouragement*! They need to know that their families still think about them and care about them. When you know your child is facing exams, papers, a big game, or has had a disappointment, send a note of support or a care package."

A care package toward the end of September is especially treasured after a month of burritos and burgers. In her book *Bright College Years: Inside the American Campus Today*, Anne Matthews writes: "Postal workers dread September. Campus mailrooms . . . fill and refill with damp bulging packages of emergency rations, mailed express to first-year students: real Tennessee barbecue sauce, homemade salsa and tortillas, a comforting gross of Philadelphia Tastykakes."

STAYING CONNECTED

WHAT PARENTS CAN DO

In the first month, set up a calling system and write or E-mail weekly. An empty mailbox feels, well, empty. Send care packages occasionally, particularly during mid-terms and finals week.

Don't be shy about saying you miss your son or daughter, but try not to emotionally unload.

On the phone, don't cross-examine, lecture, or ask questions you don't really want answers to. Instead, listen well and talk about yourself. Include the mundane. Hearing how you backed into your neighbor's parked truck last night can actually be comforting, a little touch of home.

Don't read too much into phone quietness, unanswered letters, or the sheer lack of information from your student. These are not signs that he or she doesn't love or appreciate you (and your tuition dollars). Your student is busy and distracted getting involved in a new life. Being the anchor that you provide *just by being there* is a thankless and invisible job during this transition. Things will change when your almost grown adolescent is an adult and reaches back toward you.

Decide with your son or daughter whether it makes sense to come for parents weekend. As one guidebook points out, it's not essential that you go, but not going may be wrongly attributed to not caring.

HOMESICKNESS

When college freshmen are asked what they *don't* miss about home in the first few weeks of school, their answers are predictable and painfully honest: "Parents, brothers, sisters, and having to say where you're going." The things they *do* miss, by one account, are: "Food, security, my mom, a bathroom around the corner, towels in the bathroom, and soap." "My mom" is probably shorthand for "home." (Psychoanalysts might have a field day with the preponderance of bathroom items, but most of us can relate to the reluctant daily use of a public bathroom that looks a lot like the ones in airports, except dirtier.)

It's normal for freshmen to be homesick: mildly, moderately, or strongly. Social psychologist Stephen Anderson reports that "feelings of homesickness, grief, loss, depression and loneliness frequently accompany most adolescents' initial reactions to leaving home; these may continue throughout their entire freshman year."

Homesickness makes its appearance during the first few weeks, peaks around mid-terms, and can last until Thanksgiving. Homesickness does somewhat reduce concentration on studies, but not usually enough to affect performance. It fades in most young people by second semester.

The more a student becomes engaged in *rewarding* college activities—academic, social, and extracurricular—the less homesickness he or she feels. In other words, committing to a new environment and enjoying it competes successfully with homesickness. Some factors increase the likelihood of homesickness: no previous extended time away from the family, problems with roommates, a boyfriend or girlfriend back home, and difficulties with classes and grades.

Keep in mind that one panic-stricken phone call does not mean that your child is necessarily in trouble. During the next day—or even the next hour—something may tip the scales in a positive direction. What seemed like "a totally impossible roommate" one bleak day often turns out to be someone your child learns to live with, to everyone's credit.

The usual cure for homesickness is the passage of time or staying a little more connected to home until the feelings pass. Diving more fully into college life is a more long-lasting cure. The student who expresses strong homesickness the first week at school and wants to come home permanently or every weekend needs two kinds of attention: parental warmth *and* support for continuing to stay on campus. Encourage your freshman to connect with the resident advisor, call friends from high school, and attend orientation sessions for extracurricular activities. Your homesick student might well benefit from an Outward Bound motto coined for those who find themselves halfway down a rocky slope or in a canoe two miles away from shore: "When you can't get out of it, get into it."

For especially forlorn students, set up an every *other* day call for about a week. Write regularly; invite other significant family members to do the same. Try to deflect conversations about coming home or transferring. Instead, take an attitude of "Let's wait and see how next week goes." Above all, don't rush to the rescue or solve your student's problems. Don't call your student's resident advisor unless you have strong worries about a health or safety issue. The same goes for driving to the college personally to check out what's wrong.

FIRST-YEAR TASKS

Coping with on-and-off-again homesickness is a minor challenge for most students. Freshmen undertake a number of whoppingly larger tasks during the first year of college.

Freshmen must adapt to a new culture of work. For many students, the college classroom is a far cry from high school. Learning what it takes to be a successful student at the institution is an important first-year task. Inventing a rhythm for studying and prioritizing classes takes time and effort. Their learning environment has probably changed a great deal from last year. Especially for freshmen at a large university, the teacher may be a miniature figure at the bottom of a huge lecture hall writing on a transparency that is then projected on a screen. The final grade in a class may be the average of only two grades, a mid-term and a final. Unless the college is small, your student is likely to be in classes with total strangers, making no easy task out of raising a hand to respond to a question, or asking one. In larger institutions, the professor or even the teaching assistant may be seldom accessible, with limited office hours. Finally, no one insists that your student attend classes. It takes self-discipline to walk to class after only four hours of sleep or when a friend is visiting from home or when a huge test in another class is bearing down.

During freshman year, grades are almost always lower than the student expects, particularly the first semester. Part of learning to work as a freshman means accepting a period of time when your performance as a student is not at its peak. It takes time to adapt to a new culture of grading: what's an *A* versus *B* versus *C* paper, how much do you have to study to pass a test, are late projects graded down or even accepted? College may be many students' first encounter with grading on the curve—at some institutions, a curve is designed such that the majority of students get *C*s and as many receive *F*s as *A*s.

Freshmen construct a home base and then explore. A dormitory room is hardly a home, nor does a dinner group in a noisy dining hall constitute a family. But freshmen who adjust well to college (and most do) learn rather quickly how to set up a base camp of familiar people, places, and routines. Part of establishing that base is establishing a system for studying and coursework. Far from their parents' monitoring eyes, freshmen must find a place and a time to get work done. Tiny desks in dorm rooms are hardly adequate for studying. Instead, students sprawl into libraries, the dorm study or quiet room, the student union, computer rooms, coffee shops, and out of the way nooks across campus. From early morning to late night (or all night!), students can be found studying alone or in groups.

Managing time is an important first-year task. No one will remind students to do their homework or raise an eyebrow if they party on a Wednesday night before a test. Many students are in class only twenty hours per week. Unless they have a paid job to juggle, that means managing lots of free time entirely on their own.

A base includes people to rely on for information and support. For a college freshman that typically means hallmates or roommates. Learning to navigate the system is a major part of the first year. Even in a small school, students must figure out how to buy books, drop and add classes, and register for classes. Where is the best place for live music? Where are the twenty-four-hour stores? Where is the health center?

Resident advisors, if they and the college take those roles seriously, are important links to the institution and a source of support. So are campus priests, rabbis, ministers, and other clergy. Teaching assistants, tutors, and academic advisors are resources as well. The point is made often in freshman orientation that no one is really looking out for individual students. They have to bring themselves to someone's attention before they can get help.

A strong people base, particularly until students form some lasting college friendships, also includes people from back home, from family to friends, some scattered across the country in colleges and universities. With the advent of the Internet and E-mail, staying connected is very easy and inexpensive. Our son's E-mail list was huge by the end of his freshman year. It included many of his friends in other institutions, as well as ("I know, it's silly, Mom") the guy three doors down the hall in his dorm.

Some parents are in almost daily contact with their college students via E-mail. A number of fathers and mothers report a new start to relationships with their sons or daughters, hatched at their offices on the computer.

Freshmen must come to terms with who they are and what they want. One freshman, attending Georgetown University with an athletic scholarship, found himself confronted with a choice between priorities—baseball or academics:

> *After a semester of grueling work, I just couldn't do both. I had classes from eight to two, and then practice from two to six, followed by work-outs until nine, and then I had to study. Being a serious athlete meant not being a serious student, and vice versa. I really got down about Thanksgiving and felt like giving it all up and moving home. Instead, I left the team, which was really hard, since I had been recruited. I don't regret it though. I've concentrated really well on studies, and my spirits lifted.*

Not all students know substantially more about themselves by the end of their freshman year; the process of identity formation is usually more gradual. Almost another whole year will pass before they have to declare a major. But by the end of freshman year, they will have tested some of their beliefs and values through exposure to many diverse people and a host of new situations. They will know something about their capacity to tolerate difference. Most important, they will have more evidence of their own strengths and a peek at some personal vulnerabilities.

Freshmen become interdependent and self-reliant. "Independence," that golden word held out to high school seniors and their parents anticipating freshman year, is a misnomer. The student who walls off support and resources in a quest to be independent will become isolated and lonely. In the first year living at college, a student's task is not to become totally self-reliant, but to learn whom to ask for help. As one student put it, "You learn to be self-motivatedly dependent." "Interdependence" is the goal. Freshmen learn to use each other as resources.

Gradually, these young people wean themselves from their parents as a primary resource. As one young woman from the University of Arizona said during her freshman year:

> While your parents are kind of "there for you," they aren't there. I mean, they aren't living where you're living, in classes, in the dorm, at parties, on campus. So they can't really help you think everything through the way friends can.

On the other hand, a wealth of knowledge also resides within students as gut feelings and reasoning skills. In the first year adolescents will learn to trust a set of developing decision-making skills that are prerequisites for adulthood. They will figure out small and large things like:

- ◆ How to ask a roommate gracefully and firmly to keep the lights off after 2 A.M.
- ◆ Whether or not to get a paid job

- How to find out whether or not a chemistry lab is extremely difficult or an English professor is a great teacher
- Whether to take a winter break at home or in New York City volunteering at a shelter
- How to protect money and possessions from theft
- Which professors will accept late papers, and which will lower the grade

The cousin to self-reliance in the freshman year is responsibility. Two freshmen in a coffee shop, young men from Vanderbilt University, ruminated about the many rude awakenings in their first year at school:

Yeah, when you do badly on a set of calculus problems, you can only blame yourself. In high school, I could appeal to the teacher with things like "We didn't cover this" or "I was absent last week during the review." None of that now. You either get it or not, do the work or not. It's all up to you. After a hard first semester, and a C+ in calculus, I finally got this.

I agree. Last year I played really competitive soccer for my high school and my teachers kind of accepted that my work wasn't going to get in on time. Now, if I have a huge paper due in psychology, my chemistry teaching assistant still expects that I'll get my lab done. Or if I decide to visit a friend at U.T. and miss a test (which I did), I am totally screwed (which I was).

True. For the final my political science professor put the take-home essay part on E-mail. I missed class when he announced this, and I thought we would get it the last day before finals. When I got to the lecture hall, it was empty. It took me many precious days to find someone to give me the question; the professor had already left town for holiday break and her secretary was collecting the essays!

Academic responsibility is an assumed first-year task. Recreational responsibility is sometimes tougher to manage as a freshman. College life offers almost complete freedom to conduct oneself socially with same-sex and opposite-sex peers. Students have it easier if they have already learned to draw clear boundaries around the partying scene, to say "no," and to behave safely in sexual situations and around alcohol and drugs. Those who had difficulty with limits in high school, or very little exposure to partying, may find self-responsibility somewhat harder at first. Freshmen have a responsibility to manage both the *access* and *excess* of parties, drugs, and alcohol on campus.

The other major aspects of self-reliance and independence concern money and health. Both issues fall directly into students' laps as soon as they arrive on campus. Most freshmen find ways of managing their money, especially students who are living on a shoestring and those who have been working, saving, and budgeting through high school. Whether they succeed or not in this important task depends on both their level of past experience in money management and their parents' ability to hold them accountable to a fixed income (for instance, $150 a month in spending money and no more).

Being self-reliant doesn't mean simply writing checks or balancing a checkbook; it means keeping track of money and exercising caution around charge cards. Students who are self-reliant about money live within some spending parameters and pace their spending accordingly. Freshmen who do not may turn to their parents frequently for money and/or get themselves into credit card debt.

"But are you feeling all right? You sound like you have a cold." With children out of sight, parents hope they are taking good care of their health. I even heard myself ask our son (inwardly cringing at my overprotectiveness) if he was wearing a winter hat one cold January night. Learning to be solely responsible for health matters is an important skill during the first year at college. Luckily, it's most often *not* a life-and-death issue if students abuse their bodies. Adjusting to new food, especially if students are used to certain ethnic patterns of eating, and living an almost entirely unmonitored life mean that some young people eat poorly. After all, no one calls them to dinner.

"Well, I ate terribly," said Dave, a rather thin young man, describing his freshman year, "but I sure drank well." The pervasiveness of drugs and alcohol on campus leaves every parent feeling worried and rather powerless. The best we can do is express our strong concerns and watch for signs of heavy or addictive use when our students come home from college.

Partying, dorm or Greek life, and restive roommates can also play havoc with sleep cycles. One mother worried that her freshman daughter from Vanderbilt was sleeping a lot on the weekends: "Does this mean she's into drugs?" A few simple questions put to this young woman home one weekend from college revealed that she used Saturday and Sunday to catch up on sleep; her roommate studied in their room late into the night. Immune systems respond negatively to the physical stress of change in eating or sleeping patterns. And living in rather crowded conditions, students regularly pass around colds or the flu. Learning how to take care of themselves, especially when they're really sick, is one of those begrudging rites of passage all students experience. As one resident advisor lectured her assembled group of new students:

> When you're ill, no parent is around to bring you meals or excuse you from school. No mother or father will check your temperature or buy you drugs to help you feel more comfortable. More importantly, no one will necessarily insist that you go to the health center. It's up to you to ask for help from your roommates or call me or your parents for a consult.

Freshmen make new relationships. From a parent's perspective, it would seem an easy task for freshmen to form new friendships. Isn't college some version of social heaven for an eighteen-year-old? Don't they have anywhere from 200 to 40,000 young people to choose from? Doesn't college life lend itself easily to socializing? Some parents are aghast if a son or daughter writes or calls to say that he or she hasn't really made any good friends or found someone to date. "Are you meeting people and going out?" they ask, with fervent hopes that their almost grown children are bonding to their colleges. In truth, many of us want to allay our own anxieties about our students being alone and disconnected in their new environments. Once they attach to other people, we can sit back with some relief.

Making friends is not as easy as it looks. A mass of new people, no matter how large or small the group, is a group without any shared history. Sizing people up for similarities and differences takes time. Add to that the complexity of being a young person in the throes of identity formation. Toss in a hefty dose of adolescent self-consciousness. And remember that students, as part of the adjustment process, are comparing themselves to others along many dimensions: physical, cultural, intellectual, sexual, and social.

Temperament matters. But even gregarious young people, their social status from high school left behind with their trophies and yearbooks, find the task of meeting new people an awesome one. It is not unusual for college freshmen to take as long as a whole first semester to form some friendships. That's partly what the college experience is about. Your adolescent's social self-confidence will swell with new experiences and a range of like and unlike people. This is a time for social growth and experimentation. Students can make friendships with people who are very different from them in beliefs, or different in racial, sexual, and regional backgrounds. One Midwestern student, Andy, commented:

> *I'm from a very liberal community. We're always marching in our town for causes, we're committed to diversity, we're pretty cynical about patriotism for its own sake. Debate is everywhere. When I walked into my dorm room on day one at the University of Texas, I found that my new roommate had hung the Confederate flag and a noose on the wall. I thought, "Well, this is going to be interesting." It was.*

Even to baby boomer parents who grew up in the '70s, co-educational dorms with no adult supervision seem like overly ripe environments for romantic attachments. "What, a whole year at college, and no girlfriend or boyfriend?" parents ask in befuddlement. Some of us are remembering our own college years in the Free Love era. A few parents are envious of today's students' social (and sexual) freedom. While it's true that some students begin to date almost immediately and soon find a regular partner, other freshmen date sporadically, if at all, in their first year.

A common phenomenon is for today's undergraduates to socialize in unpartnered packs. That sounds more wild than it is. College students are more likely to work toward belonging to an intimate group of male and female peers. One speculation is that "packs" give them a sense of self-assurance and identity, but keep them from deeper, more committed relationships. Many of today's students have lived through a parental divorce. If they haven't, they know the statistics. No longer driven to find mates in college, no longer safe experimenting with casual sex (though many still do), students are finding satisfaction in a small, close group of same-sex and opposite-sex friends. Traditional dating has not become obsolete, but being part of a couple is not the only way to have a warmly connected social life. Most young people like these options.

A significant number of students, depending on the particular college or university, will use the Greek system as the core of their social lives. Fraternities and sororities have doubled memberships since 1971, when living in a "house" was widely unfashionable on campuses peopled by the Woodstock generation. Living within a small, like-minded community as a college student, like a frat or sorority, has some advantages. Especially at large universities, students who are selected into the Greek system feel like they belong *somewhere*. They have a ready-made, highly structured social life and an available group of friends.

By sophomore year, Greek housing may be much more attractive than another year in the dorm and usually not more expensive than sharing a house or apartment. Sororities and fraternities organize many campus-wide, fun-filled activities; they usually perform some service to the larger community as well. Students also have opportunities for leadership and connections within their houses that last beyond the college years.

There are several disadvantages to the Greek system for first-year students. First, many houses rush students in the first few months of freshman year, so that the busy, time-consuming, and expensive swirl of open houses, parties, and impression-making comes just as students are adjusting to living away from home. Second, while the Greek system is making earnest, sometimes effective efforts to curtail and control substance abuse and raucous sexual behavior within its ranks, fraternities and sororities have yet to live down their reputation for excess. Other disadvantages to joining a fraternity or sorority have more to do with the match between students and the panhellenic system. Some students find the population of Greeks too homogeneous or do not like the rankings and rejections inherent in selection (the houses and the students separately and secretly rank their choices, and then hope for a match). A freshman who is crestfallen after a poor match often needs support.

Parents are encouraged to let first-year students make their own choices about whether or not to rush (many do, just for the fun, food, and socializing). If you are disdainful of the Greek system, find a way to be accepting if your son or daughter has a serious interest in making a bid. Or, if you hope your child will carry on a family tradition by joining a certain house, try to keep your hopes and expectations to yourself.

Every college student seeks to find a nest that includes comfortable relationships with peers, whether it's a dorm, cooperative housing, or a fraternity or sorority. Many students are also trying to be accepted into musical groups, theater productions, newspaper staffs, athletic teams, and scores of other organizations. Students at large institutions should be encouraged to find a variety of defining niches for themselves during the first year. Belonging is central to a sense of well-being and helps students make a smooth transition from home.

RETURNING HOME

Most parents eagerly anticipate a visit home by their new college student sometime in the first semester. After several weeks or months of phone calls, they long for some real contact. They are curious to see what changes are underway in a son or daughter's identity and maturity. They want to hear the expanded stories about roommates, classes, and campus life they've heard snippets of on the phone. Most important, parents hope to see the things that will assure them that their children are doing well and that this particular college or university was a good choice. They want to see happiness, enthusiasm, and growth.

They are usually not disappointed. New college students are eager for familiar food and beds and are also looking forward to seeing family. They have tales to tell and want to catch up on the various and sundry events of home. One mother described her daughter's first homecoming:

> She came through the front door, dragging her duffel behind her, looking very much like a college girl now. Her hair was different, I didn't recognize the shirt she had tied around her waist, and she was toting an enormous backpack of books and notebooks. We had a delirious hug and then she went immediately to her room and flopped on the bed. We hung back, her dad and I, not sure how much to crowd her, wanting so much to just be with her.
>
> Thank goodness she felt the same way. She insisted we sit and tell her about what her brothers, the neighbors, and the cats were up to. Then it was a stream of other questions: what was happening at work, had we heard anything about her high school friends, where did we put the bookcase that used to be in the living room, why had we painted the front door blue?
>
> We had a million questions too, but after about an hour of this intense talking, she shifted into the girl we knew. She ran out of her room in search of the phone, in search of food ("What? No Fudgsicles?"), and settled in for the weekend.

On a typical visit, most parents and siblings can count on a long conversation or two, and even a little family time. Students want to rest, sleep in their own rooms, and relish some privacy after communal dormitory life. They want, as one young man put it, "real food." On holidays, almost all want to see their old friends. One late Sunday night our older son and a set of buddies scattered among five different colleges squeezed into our small kitchen, sat on the kitchen counters and floor, and relived the hilarious stories of their senior year of high school. This exhilarating reminiscence seemed liked an important anchor, not just for friendships but for the memories of those times.

Everyone is watching for changes. While returning-home experiences may be warm and connecting, a transition is still very much in the making. You are searching for signs of growth. Your adolescent is watching for new respect. Students hope to see that being a college student affords them some new privilege in the family, a new kind of almost-adult status.

Some assume that their new college lifestyle will be easily accommodated in the family—late nights, music at all hours, drinking and smoking if that's new, sleeping in.

Coming and going as one pleases is an issue to be negotiated in families, particularly those with younger teenagers under a rule structure. Most freshmen are resistant to curfews and check-ins after many months of regulating their own activities. Parents sometimes have difficulty switching quickly to a new operating system, especially when their college students don't look or behave that differently from how they did in high school.

Another issue, especially during longer vacations, is home responsibilities. Aren't college students still a part of the family when living at home? Shouldn't they be expected to help out? Why shouldn't they have meals with the family like they did before? College students often counter, "I have a different life now, I'm happy to be a good guest, but I shouldn't have the same responsibilities as I did before, and I shouldn't be expected to stay at home all the time."

Returning college students are often pulled between friends and family on visits home. Younger siblings can feel like they are last in the line-up of buddies and parents who want time with a college returnee. One mother, whose daughter, Sasha, was like a second mother to a younger sister, recounted the first visit home:

> *Eva was so much looking forward to Sasha's homecoming at Thanksgiving. She had an image, she told me later, of the two of them playing board games, watching videos, taking walks—a return to the way things used to be. Sasha was most intent on reconnecting with her boyfriend and best friend. Her father and I were prepared for that but Eva wasn't. I spent one whole night just consoling her.*

Negotiation is the key to an evolving, positive relationship between new college students and their families. At the least, your freshman will want to have his or her views listened to and respected, even if there are disagreements. No doubt, he or she will want increased freedom and time away from the house. On the family's side, it's perfectly fine to continue some expectations that, when college students are at home, they're part of the family, with obligations to help out and connect with everyone.

Some parents want to treat their returning freshmen as favored guests and do things for them like cooking, laundry, errands, shopping for supplies. Others will expect their college kids to continue handling self-care by themselves. One mother of five announced emphatically: "I *don't* do college laundry; that's where I draw the line. They may get their favorite food at home, but they don't get their clothes washed and folded, bleached and pressed."

TROUBLESHOOTING

Most often, parents can take a back-seat when it comes to the usual set of temporary, normal crises of the freshman year. Many problems are resolved through time, experience, and standard coping skills. Other problems demand parents' attention, intervention, or increased support. These are situations in which backseat parenting is likely to be counterproductive.

Requests to Transfer

A small but significant number of students transfer after their freshman year. Most often the reasons are fears about academic failure, problems finding a peer group, or wanting to be closer to home. Occasionally it is about not fitting in socially, being ostracized for a difference such as race or sexual orientation, or a physical trauma or serious illness. When students ask to transfer during the first few months of school, take their discomfort seriously but encourage them to "hang in there" for a while longer. Extra support is crucial to avoid a hasty decision. Call more, write more, listen empathically, and make a visit sooner than planned. Try to understand which aspect of the college transition is most difficult. Dissuade your student from transferring or leaving before the first semester is over. If your child is adamant about transferring, that is best done after a natural break, preferably after the first year of school. Above all, try to refrain from suggesting that your student change schools or come back home. Should this happen eventually, your son or daughter is better off making the decision, not you.

Parents whose students leave after the first semester or full year face various challenges. They first must lend their advice to the decision and support the transition back home before another launching. More important, parents need to find enthusiasm and a positive frame for a new, more realistic plan. It takes courage for a student to transfer. There are good-byes to friends, questions to face, dreams to exchange. Parents have some of these, too.

Excessive Number of Distress Calls or Visits Home

How much is too much? Some college orientation professionals say that daily calling to report problems or going home every weekend for no important reason constitutes a problem. Trouble may be brewing when, *after the first few weeks*, students are reporting daily distress and making many more family contacts than are typical. In this situation, it is helpful to know whether the problem lies more in adjustment to college or in problems leaving the family. A young woman may return home each weekend ostensibly because she finds the social life at school "boring" or "difficult," but she may actually be worrying about an ill mother or be concerned that her parents will continue to fight or drink in her absence. A young man may insist upon coming home every weekend in order to see his girlfriend, but he may really be having problems feeling accepted by his college roommates.

Most often these students are not attaching well socially to their new environment. Too many things may simply be foreign or feel unwelcoming. This may be a young man or woman who takes a long time to warm up to new places and people or who is exceedingly shy or eccentric. Some adolescents become very anxious when they are on uncertain or unfamiliar ground. If their number one coping strategy in high school was to lean heavily on a parent, they may find coping solo very difficult.

The other kind of attachment problem concerns family problems large enough to override an adjustment to college. Families are systems. When one person makes a major change, other people are affected. An adolescent who leaves home for college temporarily destabilizes a family. Ongoing problems may intensify, particularly if the new college student has been a caretaker of others in the family. A younger sibling who has been used to a second mother or father may act out the loss by becoming difficult to manage. A depressed parent may become more overwhelmed when a daughter or son who has performed important emotional functions is now living away.

Other situations may draw students back to home: a boyfriend or girlfriend in distress, an impending divorce, an ill or handicapped family member, a parent's job loss, or a home where people are periodically out of control. Whenever it is possible, parents are urged to draw upon other resources to avoid pulling a new college student home. They may need to set down some firm boundaries ("You can come home only every *other* weekend") or do some extra reassuring ("We are getting extra support, so don't worry about us") as a way of convincing the student to stay at college.

On the other hand, most college students don't like feeling isolated or protected from family crises that arise after they leave for college. A grandparent's surgery, a mother's threatened job loss, a sibling's school problems—these normal family crises should be reported to students. Otherwise, they feel removed from their families and too far out of the loop. One student remarked:

> *They thought I wanted to be independent—probably because I had been telling them that since I was twelve! But what really bothered me the most was that they didn't tell me when my grandfather had a stroke. Their reason for keeping it a secret was that they didn't want to bother me. But I felt so isolated from the family.*

Debt

When our son was a freshman, his Rollerblades suddenly disappeared from his sports wardrobe. Later he told us that he had to sell them to pay a social debt. We weren't jubilant; after all, we had bought him the Rollerblades for his birthday. But we liked knowing that he was handling the consequences of his spending decisions.

These days, many college students cannot avoid incurring some debt, usually in the form of student loans. Credit card debt, however, may bring them to financial crisis before they are out of college. They may have to work several jobs in order to erase their college debts, or else face ruined credit ratings. One survey of college students found that seventy-six percent held three or more credit cards, and that forty percent—twice the rate of the population at large—had six or more. Credit cards often arrive at students' doorsteps unsolicited, and many do not require a parent's co-signature. Some students see the borrowing limits as a balance to be drawn against instead of a loan that must be repaid, often at very high interest. Financial aid officers who handle emergency requests for tuition money know that it's often because students are struggling with monthly minimum credit card payments. One young woman who racked up $5,000 of bills on credit cards said:

> I was forewarned to get just one credit card and not go crazy, but I did go crazy. . . . I didn't worry about working because I thought, "Oh, I'll just put it on my credit card." It's unfortunate that it affects your credit in the long run.

Students who get into serious debt in the first year can be helped with early intervention. Spending problems can usually be remedied by reducing the amount of available credit and cash. A debit card works well for some young people; it allows a student to charge against a checking or savings account balance, and no more. Parents who shrug their shoulders and pay credit card bills that exceed the agreed-upon amount may be enabling students to remain financially unaccountable and irresponsible throughout college. These young people will start working life already behind the financial eight ball.

Dropping Out

Most students who drop out of college do so because of finances. Scholarships dry up or don't materialize; financial aid is too difficult to obtain; promised support from a divorced parent or other family member doesn't appear. Students who cannot pay tuition or housing costs should appeal to the Financial Aid office for guidance and possible grace. Every college has reserves to help deal with financial emergencies ("My paycheck won't be here for another two weeks, and I have run out of money in my food plan"). Most colleges will make short-term (like sixty-day) loans for these kinds of situations or help students find work to cover a more serious short-fall.

If tuition money dries up for students dependent on their parents' support, this is a matter for parents to handle with the college. Payment extensions are not unheard of. Financial aid packages can be adjusted, or reapplied for, given changed circumstances. If a student must withdraw for a whole semester for medical reasons, tuition is sometimes reimbursed.

Thanks to the art and science of the college admission process, most students don't leave school because they aren't competent to do the academic work. They may, however, leave because of getting seriously behind in school. If your student begins to get poor or failing grades in a class (and you hear about it), there are several possible reasons to check out:

- ♦ Emotional or substance abuse problems. (Have your student call the counseling center for an urgent appointment and then follow up.)
- ♦ Getting behind in class because the material, while understandable, is difficult to absorb through lectures and books. (Suggest your child arrange a tutor through the subject's department; prices are usually reasonable.)
- ♦ Getting behind or depleted because of impossible standards. (Students who read everything on every reading list will not be able to manage multiple classes; suggest they read enough to do the work and save the syllabi for graduate school.)

- Getting poor grades because the material is hard to understand; your student just doesn't "get it." (Suggest your child go and talk with the professor or teaching assistant.)
- Procrastination. (Help your student sift through priorities and develop some time management plan for getting work done. A divide-and-conquer strategy works for many students overwhelmed by a long list of assignments.)
- The same old problems that plagued your son or daughter in high school, like math anxiety, writer's block, fear of failure, or perfectionism. (Encourage your student to get help from the study skills center or a counselor.)

Sometimes problems at home take students out of college. If for any reason your student begins to talk seriously of leaving school, make a trip to the college as soon as possible to discuss the situation with someone in the Dean of Students office.

EMOTIONAL PROBLEMS

Parents are strongly encouraged to intervene when they see clear signs of severe depression, eating disorders, or heavy substance abuse. The trick to detecting any of these major health problems is to know the signs, trust your instincts, and intervene early. That clearly means staying in touch with your student, especially during the first year.

One or two short bouts of feeling down, over- or undereating, and heavy drinking are not necessarily reasons to push the panic button. Ninety percent of all college students have some mild depression during their college careers, usually over grades and relationships. Particularly in the first year, your son's or daughter's weight may suddenly shoot up or down under the influence of cafeteria food and exam pressures. And a few drunken or high weekends do not usually necessitate drug treatment. But when the normal ups and downs in all these behaviors become a regular pattern, or are severe, students need intervention.

"But how will I know?" many parents ask. Again, use your instincts.

If *over a period of a few weeks* your student looks vacant and pretty ill when you visit, does not sound at all like him or herself on the phone, or misses class frequently, something may be wrong. Many of the warning signs of these problems, like changes in eating or sleeping habits (too little or too much), severe lack of energy (or feeling constantly wired), feeling inadequate or panicky, and problems with concentration, are so common among first-year students that it is often hard for *students* to spot them early, let alone their parents who don't see them very much. Often these problems are subtle at first and do not always become dramatic. Substance abuse problems are particularly tricky. Most college students regularly use alcohol and marijuana, sometimes bingeing on the weekends. Society has widely (but not wisely) accepted that drinking and using drugs are a normal part of college life.

It is essential that parents raise concerns directly with a student if there are signs of major depression, panic attacks, or severe substance abuse. As a therapist working in a college town, I have seen more families underreact than overreact to problems, in the interest of giving students their needed space. With too much space, problems can easily grow.

Major Depression

Students at particular risk for depression in college are those with previous histories of major depression or suicidal behavior, young people who have suffered a recent major loss (including a romantic breakup), gay and lesbian students who are closeted or just coming out, individuals who have been raped or sexually assaulted, and high-achieving students whose grades begin to fall (even to *B* levels).

The warning signs of depression are as follows:

- Any attempt at self-harm like cutting, a suicidal gesture, or talk of suicide
- A statement like, "I'm really depressed," or "I'm really worried that something is wrong," or a signal from your child's roommate or best friend
- Change in eating habits (persistent lack of appetite and weight loss or compulsive eating)

- Change in sleeping patterns (persistent insomnia or wanting to sleep all the time)
- Loss of energy and interest in activities, even after adequate rest
- Strong and continual feelings of worthlessness, inadequacy, and guilt, sometimes accompanied by frequent crying
- High irritability or agitation; continually feeling wired and restless in the absence of stimulant drugs
- Great difficulty concentrating
- Frequent thoughts of suicide or death

Panic Disorder

Panic attacks, which are more common than most people realize, may appear for the first time in college students with a biological predisposition. Since panic attacks are often mistaken for physical health problems and vice versa, they must be diagnosed by a physician. Use of drugs, particularly marijuana and hallucinogens (LSD, mushrooms), can bring on panic attacks. The major warning signs are as follows:

- Chest pain or tightness
- Dizziness, tingling, hot and cold flashes, and feeling faint
- Fear of going crazy or dying
- Fears of being closed in or falling, or other irrational fears

Severe Substance Abuse

Any young person who drinks or uses drugs in the face of possible legal penalties is, by definition, abusing a substance. Severe, highly problematic usage in college students is usually indicated by a number of clear signs:

- Any statement like, "I think I may have a problem with drinking or drugs"
- Continued use of drugs or alcohol in the face of severe penalties for usage (e.g., warnings from police or the college, threats to withdraw tuition)

- Missing class regularly, falling grades, dropping classes (in the absence of depression or other emotional problems)
- An arrest for driving under the influence or for drunken disorderly conduct
- Frequent blackouts or being taken drunk or injured to the emergency room
- Reports of date rape while under the influence

Eating Disorders

Students with anorexia and bulimia, almost always female, are usually first noticed by roommates, who may suggest they get help or contact the resident advisor or health service. Parents are not usually aware of these problems until a visit at school or home. Severe weight loss is the first and most important sign of anorexia, which is also characterized by withdrawn, highly controlled behavior and denial that there are problems. Typically, an anorexic young woman does not believe that her body is becoming emaciated; instead, she is on a quest for perfection.

Bulimia, bingeing and then purging by vomiting or laxative use, often combined with extreme exercise, is harder to spot. The adolescent may or may not be thin and typically appears rather happy. Some of the signs are hoarding food, being secretive about eating, and spending unusual amounts of time in the bathroom or at the gym. Bulimia among college women is often discovered by roommates or hallmates. Denial is common among people who suffer from this problem.

EMOTIONAL PROBLEMS
WHAT PARENTS CAN DO

On the prevention side, stay in touch with your first-year student. Not only does contact help problems from intensifying, but it gives you a chance to assess your child's emotional health. Ask not just about how school is going but also about how your son or daughter is coping with stress and change. Don't shy away from asking about sleeping, eating, and partying. Try to visit once during the first semester, or have someone you know look in on your student.

If you feel that a problem may be developing, ask gently about general coping ("How's your mood holding up?"), and then voice your specific concerns ("This is the third time I've found you sleeping in the middle of the afternoon. What's up?" or "You didn't sound like yourself last night, and today you're a little flat. Are you down?") Trust your instincts.

Take any sign that your student is suicidal seriously. Make a visit promptly or arrange for your student to come home. Get help by calling the resident advisor, Dean of Students, and campus counseling center.

If you have a strong sense that your student is experiencing other serious emotional problems, work gently but persistently to get him or her to see a counselor on campus or in the local town. Let your child know that you are very worried by calling regularly, visiting, and, with his or her knowledge, talking to the resident advisor.

If you think you have a student with a serious substance abuse problem, you may need to use your leverage to get the problem addressed, unless your child agrees to an assessment. That may mean withholding a tuition check until a substance abuse evaluation is completed.

CHAPTER EIGHT

New Space for New Growth

Remember the advice we got when our first child came into our lives, and then perhaps a second, or third, or more? "Count on *everything* changing," seasoned parents told us, shaking their oh-so-wise heads. I didn't believe them. Surely some things always stay the same, I tossed back, like how I brush my teeth, the way I cook, my love for books.

I was right—and wrong. I did have to learn how to groom, cook, and read *faster,* and at times I gave up all three while I went to school, worked, and struggled to keep up with relationships. But more or less I held onto some core sense of my self. More or less my marriage clung to its strengths through those whirling years of raising children. Out of the stuff of love and chaos, we made a family, and then it *too* became an entity with its own qualities and quirks.

The advice I now hand back to parents whose almost grown children are leaving their daily lives is similar: "Count on *big* changes." Parents can expect significant changes in themselves and the family as it widens to include an almost grown adolescent living away from home:

- ◆ "Home" will take on new meanings and include not just a physical home or, in the case of divorced parents, two houses. Home will also mean your child's new home, or wherever your family finds places to gather as children grow into adulthood. Home is a concept, not a place. It is, one essayist noted, "the mixture of memory and longing."

- ◆ Some time-honored rituals—like birthdays and holidays—will change, and new ways of connecting as a family will be invented in their place.

- ◆ The structure of the family minus the college freshman will be reshaped as siblings begin to occupy different places in the family structure. There may be *no* children in the nest, requiring parents to redefine "family" dramatically.

- ◆ Gender balances will shift noticeably. As either a male or female child departs, the family may become more feminine- or masculine-oriented.

- ◆ New images of "family" will emerge in anticipation of some firsts: first weekend visits to your son or daughter's college, first homecoming, and, further down the road, career choices and college graduation. The faint outline of events like engagements, weddings, or even grandchildren may take form.

As children leave home, changes will reverberate throughout this vital, living system of sustenance and growth we call family. The way the family functions will be different; the way you think and feel about your family will change. No matter. Families, we know, can stretch to accommodate change, grow new branches, and stay whole.

Peggy, a mother of three with a daughter at Wesleyan College, saw the change happen before her eyes: "As we waved good-bye to Emily, all of us—her brother Peter and sister Laura, Dick and myself—clung tightly together. It was as if her leaving had loosened the bonds suddenly and we had to quickly re-glue."

The families of new college students can be as vital and thriving as families of new kindergartners. What helped my transition was an image of a widening circle, not a broken line. Our family surely had not ruptured as one child left to begin his adulthood. It had grown larger in heart and spirit to hold everyone's growth.

A NEW PARENTHOOD

For their souls dwell in the house of tomorrow, which you cannot
visit, even in your dreams.
You may strive to be like them,
but seek not to make them like you.
For life goes not backward nor tarries with yesterday
                    —from *The Prophet,* by Kahlil Gibran

As adolescents carry out the tasks readying them for adulthood, mothers and fathers begin a new parenthood. This new phase will draw upon the strengths of earlier years and seed the beginning of a new adult child-parent relationship. Some parents eagerly await this new alliance. They are more than ready—by virtue of their own mid-life changes and/or exhaustion—to begin separate but connected lives with their children. Others are not yet ready. They are suffering too acutely from the sadness and anxiety generated by leaving-home children.

Most of us fall between the extremes. We waft between nostalgia for the past and excitement for the changes beginning to brew in our children and ourselves. We have memories of being eighteen to twenty-one years old, and we remember our own parents at that turbulent time. Those stories weave themselves into a story of the future and a different set of roles open to us as parents of college students: anchors, comforters, and counselors.

Be an Anchor

My interviews with college freshmen and college counselors have revealed a host of ways parents can effectively and importantly "anchor" their students:

Maintain a connection. In the first year, most students away from home want a tie to their families. They love letters and care packages, like E-mail and phoning, don't mind occasional calls initiated from home, and look forward to a visit or two. Most prefer this more distant contact to lots of face-to-face time. A natural rhythm will emerge some-time during the first semester; most freshmen want to set the pace themselves for contact. Parents who call frequently, show up unan-nounced, or expect a lot of contact are often simply endured or even rebuffed.

Listen. Being unhappy and confused is part of living through the freshman year. Many students who turn to their parents during stress-ful times simply want someone at home to listen, to know they are struggling. Venting their feelings to a family member who knows and cares for them can help. With a call to home, the problem can fade.

A friend's daughter called her frequently and miserably about a roommate, grade, or boyfriend, and called much less when she was happy. "She feels better after the call, but now I have a new worry to shoulder," my friend said. She's right. Parents of freshmen rarely learn about the *resolutions* to problems. The next day, a follow-up call about a problem may reveal a cheery student: "Oh, I don't feel bad about that now. I talked to the professor yesterday and he understands. Gotta run."

Steady them. A good anchor keeps a ship from straying too far off a charted course. The excitement and stress of the freshman year transi-tion, coupled with living away from home, may provoke some students to make impulsive decisions. Parents don't always hear about these decisions. While some major change may have been in the works for weeks or months, parents are in the dark until a phone call. Suddenly you hear that your son or daughter:

- Wants to change fields "because I can't stand physics (or lit-erature papers or computer programming) another minute"
- Has decided to transfer to a bigger or smaller college "because I know this place just isn't *me*"
- Needs to move back home "to pull myself together"
- Will be spending the summer in Madagascar
- Wants to drop out of pre-med and become a woodwind major

When students signal some need to make big changes, they are often floating trial balloons to gauge their parents' reactions. It's best not to respond too negatively or judgmentally. Instead, listen fully, then help anchor them in the possible consequences of their decisions. Often students are reacting to minor setbacks in their work and need help to find their bearings. Big changes, like transferring schools and changing a long-standing academic or artistic interest, are not unheard of in the freshman year. But major departures like that need to be thought about carefully.

Comfort and Encourage

Whether or not we believe that our kids will make it in the world, or that we did our best to raise them through adolescence, one of the best things we can do for almost grown children is to have faith in them. Regular pats on the back are important. So is an occasional shoring up. The freshman year, with all its promise, is fraught with crises in confidence:

I got a C–, can you believe it, a C– on my history mid-term, and then in composition, my best subject, I'm getting Bs on my papers. I don't know whether I'm smart enough for this place, and I don't think I can study any more than I already am. As it is, I'm exhausted.

My roommate and I have absolutely nothing in common, we don't keep the same hours, and we hate each other's music. She even thinks I talk funny. I don't know where my money is going. Remember when we made that budget and thought $100 a month was going to be plenty? I've spent that in just two weeks.

I was late to my first chemistry lab because I couldn't find it! It's clear across campus and I have to ride a bus to get there. As it is, I don't have time for lunch, and today I found out that we're expected to show up for extra lab time if we don't finish our experiments in class. How can I do that? Marching band is taking all my extra time.

REASSURING

WHAT PARENTS CAN DO

First, hear their stories fully, and validate their concerns with sympathetic words. "That does sound really hard, Nathan, you do sound discouraged" or "You certainly do seem exhausted, and it's probably hard to live with someone who studies late into the night" or "Yes, that's a long way to travel for a class, especially if you have to go there more than once a day. I can understand it feels like an impossible task."

Reassure students that you have confidence in them and their ability to work out the problem. Remind them of times they coped in the past, with specific examples. Emphasize the quali-ties they have that lead you to think they will solve the problem: "I know this seems like a big problem right now, but usually when you've gotten past the really hard moment, you can see a solution."

Reassure your son or daughter that you hear other freshmen have these kinds of dilemmas. If you have a story from your own past to offer (even from your recent history), some story of when you have felt vulnerable, alone, and discouraged, *and you can tell it without implying a lesson for your student,* then share it.

Try not to accuse your student of whining or complaining or immaturity. Don't expect him or her to figure out the solution all alone.

Most important, don't rush to solve their problems yourself by calling RAs or the Dean of Students or a professor.

Counsel

At first glance, parents of college freshmen don't seem well-positioned to be effective counselors. They aren't living with their children, they are a generation away from the college experience, and their students may have resisted counsel all through adolescence. But, in fact, some newly independent teenagers turn to their families for advice after leaving home.

Many parents are startled to see this happen: "It's like he was saying, now that I don't have to live with you, I can let myself need you," said a father whose son began to rely on him as a sounding board for making decisions about college majors. Students themselves are sometimes surprised at how much they begin talking to their parents at a new level. This story is from a freshman at the University of Arizona:

> *When I was living at home, I really didn't like talking to my mother about things that were important to me. She always acted like she knew the answers to everything, so I dodged all those big talks about my Future. After I got to school, she really treated me differently, like she respected my ideas. Now we have these serious talks and I don't mind hearing her opinions.*

For any good counselor, offering ideas and support requires a little artfulness, tact, and timing. In the accompanying box are tips that came from new college students. Coming from young adults who are in the process of separation, these have a lot to say about what *not* to do.

COUNSELING
WHAT PARENTS CAN DO

Don't offer unsolicited advice. Let your student approach you, unless you sense that attempts for contact are falling short. Say, for example, "I sense that you are stuck about what to do this summer. Do you want to run some ideas by me? Do you want to talk aloud a bit about your decision?" Avoid sentences which begin like, "What you ought to do is . . ." or "I think you should . . ."

Don't do the thinking and problem-solving for your student. A good counselor helps people get into their own process. Students *themselves* should think through possibilities, collect information, get help from resources, weigh advantages and disadvantages, make decisions, and take action. Those who work methodically through problems will be growing toward adulthood. Parents who continue to make—or try to make—the decisions for their students run two risks. First, their son or daughter will learn to be dependent. Second, a student whose parents insist on certain solutions or pathways may run in the opposite direction, and thereby circumvent making a decent decision.

Know the limits of your counsel. Some kinds of counsel are probably out of a parent's purview. Those include complex academic program issues (send to an academic advisor), academic probation (send to the Dean's office), roommate problems (send to resident advisor or housing office for mediation), and feeling sick (send to the health center). On the other hand, students with substance abuse problems or clear signs of depression or eating disorders need your intervention and should have professional input at school or back home.

Finally, when you counsel, say what you mean. If you say "I'm not sure working as a volunteer is a good idea for you" and *mean* "We will not support you over the summer unless you have a paid job," you are giving a mixed message.

STARTING OVER

For some parents, the departure for college is an opportunity to put the strife-torn years of adolescence behind them and begin a relationship with their child anew.

A child's going to college means an end to daily or nightly monitoring of that adolescent's life: the differences of opinion about dress, music, and friends; the struggles for a later curfew, the car, more money, less responsibility at home. This will change. The tension, resentment, and anger that have built over years slowly drain away as a child leaves home for college. Instead there comes a new appreciation of one another. Parents give up control because they have no other choice, and adolescents assume more responsibility for themselves—there's no other choice here either. Suddenly, a young person makes choices based on what he or she wants, not on what his or her parents *don't* want.

Linda, a petite, curly-haired mother and music director, told a story to the assembled group of mothers, all talking about their children's first year away from home:

> *When my daughter lived at home during her junior and senior years, we were constantly fighting. She had become attached to a lifestyle I just couldn't support. Our relationship deteriorated. When it came time for college, she chose one entirely on her own, against my wishes. As she left for school, I felt deep dread that she would really come apart. Quite the opposite happened. She got herself together, became a good student, and our relationship has improved immensely. Now she seeks me out to talk about school, friendships, dreams, and struggles. I never thought it would happen.*

A father of a new freshman living far from home remarked that he and his daughter now have "pretty calm talks together, even intellectual ones. College helped set our relationship on a new track, one of equal respect."

UNDERSTANDING YOUR MIXED EMOTIONS

Children's leaving home provokes all kinds of reactions in their parents. Their departure from home, an *event*, sparks a long-term *process*. Mothers and fathers can expect to cope with a range of emotions and an array of changes in themselves. These shifts, we know as psychologists, take place on the *inside looking out* (how an individual understands and feels about the self and the world), and on the *outside looking in* (how the family reorganizes, changing roles and altering relationships). Passing a marker, like leaving for college, doesn't mean that the transition is over. Parents of college students normally cope with a slew of reactions, all at the same time.

"It's the end of an era and I'm out of a job." Your job as a twenty-four-hour, seven-day-a-week parent has drawn to a close. This role has been an exhausting but a richly rewarding job. Watching and helping your child develop, teaching him or her about the world, nurturing growth, keeping your son and daughter safe and well, and celebrating accomplishments big and small has been a privilege and a passion (and, yes, at times a pain).

Is it no wonder, then, that adolescent leave-taking is a mixed blessing for us as parents? Suddenly, we're out of an eighteen-year-old job that, for the most part, we've loved. And just as suddenly, we begin evaluating our performance. Was this a job well done? Can we give ourselves the gold watch? As our children begin to leave home, we evaluate not only *their* competence to survive without our day-to-day care, but our own perceived competence as parents. Some of the fall and winter after our first son departed for college I reviewed whether or not I had done a good enough job parenting him:

Pat / September 24

Did I raise him to be strong in mind, body, and spirit? Can he survive on his own and be responsible? Did I pass on at least some of our family's values? Is he a nice person? Have I worked hard enough to teach him to like himself and respect others? Did we help him to find his talents and strengths and cope with his shortcomings?

But we were not losing him, to be sure. Over the college years, we kept in at least weekly touch with our son. Phone-rate discounts and E-mail helped make that contact affordable. And the fear that he would be gone from our a family was largely unfounded. The week I forgot to tell him about a distant relative's death, he scolded me roundly.

One mother, a forty-five-year-old former flower child, transformed herself from the role of daily parent to one of connector for her children and their friends who had left home for college. Like many parents, she missed her children *and* their close buddies. To cope, she began an E-mail correspondence with her children's circle of friends and began circulating a monthly letter of their stories and news.

"I'm relieved." Life after one child leaves home is usually easier. Families of college-bound adolescents can definitely look forward to some positive, domestic changes. These are in the "one less egg to fry" category. With one family member ensconced in a freshman dormitory (try not to calculate the cost per day), at home there is obviously less food to stock, lighter laundry, and fewer medical and dental appointments to juggle. The departure of one person from the household means more order for some families, and less work for the hearth keepers.

"I've been downsized." A friend, Martha, whose daughter Tara refused to let her mother buy and send some forgotten items for her dorm, wailed, "I have no role anymore. I've been downsized!"

This loss of role may be keenly felt. Erik Erikson noted the existence of what he termed "transitory identity," assumed in response to the crisis of uprootedness and the loss of assigned or expected identity. Parents are not just parents, in the nurturing, protective, socializing, guiding sense. From infancy they are also housekeepers, cooks, laundresses, chauffeurs, teachers, and nurses. As the parent of an adolescent you have added other roles: driving instructor, tutor, answering service and secretary, detective, banker, coach, purchasing agent. During the college search process you probably took on career counselor, travel agent, and financial planner. Added up, there is no bigger, all-encompassing job than parenting. As one father of two nearly grown children put it: "I have been a parent in every cell of my body."

No wonder, then, as our children leave home, we feel a jolt, especially as the first or last one departs. Temporarily, we are out of work. Parents who experience acute loss of role can take solace from the stories of parents whose children are midway through college. The sting of being downsized subsides. Mothers and fathers realize that they still have important roles to play with their children, even as they enter adulthood. Parenting changes; it doesn't end.

"My best friend just left." For some parents, the departure of a son or daughter for college means the loss of a long friendship or one just forming. "After several years of tension, Jill and I were finally beginning to be friends," sighed Joan, a youthful-appearing mother and high school teacher. "And now she's leaving. We used to have dinner together, see movies, talk late into the night—I will really miss that."

The friendship relationships between adolescents and parents are sometimes hard-won. They are wrought often from years of struggle about power, autonomy, and individuality. In the late years of high school, a new, more egalitarian alliance may begin to bloom. A new mutuality and understanding can develop, signs of a budding daily friendship. The college separation then feels like a sudden loss.

Occasionally, a parent-child friendship is unbalanced, particularly if a parent has leaned heavily on a son or daughter for strong emotional support. One mother mourned, "She always talked with me, she appreciated me, needed me and unconditionally loved me. Now that she's so busy, I don't hear these things." The college separation can become a real gap in a parent's life and provide much anxiety for the freshman headed for college. A female student away from home for the first time wrote for advice:

> I'm so worried about my mom. She's just separated from my dad and is very depressed. I feel really bad because I'm her best friend, and she really needs me right now. Yesterday she cried on the phone, and that made me cry. I miss her too. This is really hard for me. I don't think I should be away right now, and I'm thinking of transferring to a college closer to home.

The advice for this young woman was to call her older siblings and together persuade their mother to get more support and, if necessary, some professional help. Returning home would be a very short-term solution to the problems at home and the separation anxiety for the student. To leave school might impede the growth necessary for this daughter *and* mother to continue their own development.

Fortunately for most parents, a friendship that has its roots in high school usually does not impede growth but rather enhances it. Close relationships tend to remain stable and continue their rich development during the college years. Strong feelings of loss persist only until a few homecomings confirm that—like all good friendships—closeness is not diminished by geographical distance.

"I'm getting old." If you're old enough to have a child going to college, aren't you clearly aging? Or old? Statistically speaking, many baby boomer generation parents are reaching fifty just as their children are beginning the leaving home process. For mid-life adults who associate turning fifty with decline and depression, the addition of a child's leaving home may seem overwhelming. Couple that with an ill parent, and loss issues can easily intensify. "*Sandwich* generation?" queried my husband, whose father is in his eighties. "As long as it's a club sandwich."

In the university town where our children were born, I used to observe parents visiting their nearly grown college students. Under their parents day garb of khakis and sweaters and U.M. caps, they had gray hair, little soft paunches, and wrinkles. They looked distinctly middle-aged, even old. They belonged to a different generation, I smugly surmised as I threaded a stroller across campus.

I am smug no more. A child leaving home came to threaten my youthful self-image. After a span of eighteen years, I no longer look or feel like I did when our first son was born in 1976. Then I had a white woman's Afro, a stable of blue jeans, and still played Beatles records. I was proud of my physical energy and agility and, like many in my generation, clung to a culture that celebrated vitality, youth, and, as Bob Dylan intoned, intended to stay "Forever Young."

Adam's leaving for the University of Wisconsin meant that I would begin to appear and behave like the parents-day parents in Ann Arbor, that weary, dazed, and anxious lot of grown-ups who more resembled my own parents than me and my contemporaries. I coped in my own way. I would handle the gradual sagging of my body by becoming an aging athlete. I ran a half-marathon on the day of Adam's senior prom. While a medal in my age group easily escaped me, the irony of that timing did not.

Staying fit doesn't always change our perceptions that having a child old enough to leave home is connected to aging. Karen, an agile, trim woman who plays competitive tennis, felt a strong sense of aging as her first child went off to college: "All of a sudden I feel rather old, which is odd because I'm probably healthier now than I've ever been in my whole adulthood. It's puzzling that the summer before David went to college I felt like a younger middle-aged woman, and now, with him gone, I feel like I'm in the retirement set."

A NEW SIBSHIP

Pat / September 20

> *We took one leaf out of our oak dining table so the three of us can draw a little closer when we eat. That simple, conscious act to bring us together is a beginning. It's another way I'm trying to open my eyes and heart to Dan. He has been in the background some of the time, despite his strong personality. A lot of his communication is subtle. He tends to slump when he's unhappy. When he wants time with us, he'll often invite us to watch him play video games. I'm noticing these things more with Adam away.*

Siblings have their own strong set of reactions and adjustments to manage while parents and college students are wrapped up in the leaving-home process. They have been on the sidelines during the tension-filled college search process and the high celebrations of senior year. They have watched and learned second-hand how to negotiate with their parents over curfews, cars, and colleges. They may have been drawn into battles, siding alternately with parents and their high school senior sibs. And, like it or not, they have not had their parents' usual attention during the college launch.

As the fall of their own school year begins, some sibs are initially coping with a strong sadness, as one mother described after taking an older daughter to college:

> *Peter wanted to write her the minute we got home and tell her all the ways he's missed her. He always heard her radio alarm come*

on in the morning, they always watched a cartoon together during breakfast, things like that.

Other sibs, even if they feel a sad gap in their lives, are relishing the increased space and resources their elder brother or sister has left behind for them. "Eric has already carved out my bathroom for himself," said one new freshman as she mused on her first weekend at home. Not having to share bathrooms, stereos, cars, computers, and phones certainly is positive for many siblings.

With one child entering adulthood, sibling positions, at least in the family home, change dramatically. A middle or youngest sibling now becomes top dog, a change that is a mixed picture for many children. They may have more privileges as top dog, but they might also now be expected to mow the lawn or wash the car. Moreover, parents' energies are now directed toward them more of the time. This particular change, by some accounts, is positive and negative:

My father finally started to realize that I'm just about as smart as my sister. I can hold my own in a conversation about current events, sports, and world hunger. In fact, I'm even a better arguer than she is.

At dinner, I can hardly breathe or eat with my parents asking me so many questions about school, friends, things like that. I wish my sister was back home again. She could handle them better than I can.

I have kind of missed my dad, who was really involved, really overinvolved, with my oldest brother's high school basketball career. We used to go hiking together, like the same music, hang out more until the last few years. He's coming around me a little more now that Jason is gone. Maybe now that I'm starting high school, we'll do more stuff together.

My brother was a real problem in high school. He skipped a lot of school, drank a lot, argued with our parents all the time. He got it together last year and barely got into college. Now they look at me and have these great expectations. I'm not supposed to screw up like he did. I resent this pressure.

I know they really miss my sister and they're taking it out on me, not letting me get out of their sight, or have my own life. It's like they have this huge need for me all of a sudden, just to have a kid around.

Parents should beware of trying to replace the missing child with another one. Siblings are not always willing to step into another sibling's shoes, particularly if they are big ones. I became conscious of my tendency to assume that my son Dan would talk to me the way his older brother did.

Pat / October 20

I want to be careful not to expect Dan to be Adam. A conversation today was telling. We were on the way to buy tennis shoes.
ME: *Sometimes, Dan, I get the feeling that you're unhappy because you don't say very much.*
DAN: *I don't like conversation, that's all. I don't like to talk very much. That's me. We have way too many serious conversations in this family.*
  The way to be with Dan is to do things with him. This will be good for me, a growing edge. Being a writer and psychologist, I see words as more important than action. Dan can teach me a different way of connecting.

With one bird out of the nest, clearly there is more room and time for the rest, and most siblings flourish. Some find the new environment very pleasant, like this fourteen-year-old girl:

I'm getting all this time from my Mom, now that Evan has gone. She makes me my favorite food, she has more money to spend on my clothes, and we watch the shows we like, not just sports. I don't miss him that much, but I do miss his friends, who used to let me hang out with them. But they're gone, too, and I don't mind not having all that noise and chaos every weekend. I have more sleepovers here now.

The "It's my turn now" philosophy pays off well for siblings who enjoy both their parents' newfound attention and their increased wisdom. One mother of three described a chain of changes she observed in the family since their oldest son left for college:

> *Paul feels a great sadness about not being able to confide in his brother like he used to, and Lynn has lost another caregiver—those are the down side. But the two remaining kids have gotten closer as a result. Dick and I focus our parenting differently, too. Dick has focused more on Paul, who has a new, stronger voice. And Lynn is getting more of my attention now, because Paul is caring more for himself.*

The next child, if he or she heads to college, stands to benefit from the sib who went first. Parents have been acclimated to the process, and they know what changes to anticipate at the next launching. They may also have a new appreciation of the time remaining with young children. Marcie, a mother of three and a psychologist, commented, "Leah's leaving has made me more aware of David and Noah in so many ways. I realize now that these years we have left with them are actually quite short, and I have a new desire to embrace our time together."

Even if remaining siblings gain more of their parents after an oldest child goes off to college, the loss of brother or sister can be hard-felt. Our sons were companionable and congenial but in different stages during childhood. Once they both reached adolescence, they became very good friends. Adam defines his younger brother Dan as his best friend, in fact, and he seeks him out on the phone, on vacation, and for visits to college. Traveling to his brother's school is a highlight for Dan each of his high school years. We cringe at the early exposure to college life he has received but support the camaraderie between our sons. Their relationship, which has grown from time together in Madison and at the camp where they are both counselors, is another ripple on the widening circle.

WHAT PARENTS CAN
DO FOR SIBLINGS

Be curious about the differences in parenting and sibling roles now that one child has gone off to college. What has shifted in your family? Are the changes positive or negative? Ask them these same questions.

Work toward appreciating siblings who remain behind for who they are, not how they compare to the oldest or the one who just left. Avoid expectations that siblings be *more* or *different* than they are. Imagine the parts of you that they complement.

Don't fill the empty space created by a college freshman by overparenting the remaining siblings. Instead, attend to each of their needs, and save the extra time for yourself or your partner.

Be sensitive and understanding of the loss a remaining sibling may feel over a departed college student.

Keep some gentle pressure on siblings to stay in contact. Let them talk on the phone or use E-mail generously in the initial month or two. Some colleges have sibling weekend to foster just such a connection (and market to a new group of students).

THE MARITAL PARTNERSHIP: NEW DREAMS

Pat / August 1, 1994

Adam's leaving will mean another change. Rob and I will have more time to be together and fewer parenting projects to talk about. Despite our rich and solid marriage and a booming optimism about the ability of our relationship to survive almost anything, we have

*yet to look beyond parenthood and confront the next stage in our
relationship. We have yet to invent new dreams and possibilities
and decide if we needed to shore up a few planks in our marriage
given the coming changes.*

Parents often face each other anew as their parenting responsibilities
lessen. This is particularly true for couples when a child's leaving home
opens up significant time and emotional space or when some very close
parent-child bond is stretched against the miles of road and telephone
wire between home and college. Changes in a relationship are inevitable,
not just because you have a child leaving home, but because you have
changed steadily in your mid-life years. These changes may include:

- Becoming reacquainted with each other
- Confronting old problems in the relationship that have been
  deferred
- Creating new dreams and projects

"Are you still the person I married?" For parents who have stayed
together or who have taken new partners, the emptying nest means the
possibility of spending more time together. As daily parenting wanes,
many mothers and fathers take a new look at the wives and husbands
emerging from the whirl and intensity of raising children. We want to
see both the continuity of qualities that formed the attraction and some
new growth that has sustained our relationships through hard times.

When what partners see is generally positive, new energies for the
relationship can gradually pour into the gap left by children. Spouses
announce to themselves that the person they married still has some of
the qualities—and more. Memories of times before children may
appear as well to reconnect "us then" with "us now."

When taking a new look at your spouse is negative, the result can be
a marital crisis. Someone may have changed significantly or individual
growth may have led partners away from the relationship rather than
toward it. This does not necessarily spell the end of the marriage;
instead it may signal the beginning of a positive marital revision.

Some couples have become so organized around their children's lives that they really can't answer the question, "Are you the same person I married?" They don't know. They have spent little time together, just as adults, without the press of children, family, and friends. The best way to explore the marriage at this stage is to turn and face one another without distractions.

"That's tricky," said one wife, who brought her spouse to couples counseling for a mid-life tune-up. "We're both pretty involved in our careers, and we spend much of our remaining time during the week with our youngest daughter. And on the weekend I try to help out with my elderly mother. That means I'm pretty tired by Saturday night. I'd rather watch a video or work out. My health is a priority for me."

Mid-life brings the convergence of many parts of ourselves: worker, mother (father), daughter (son), woman (man). This multiplicity can crowd out couple life, and couplehood may become taken for granted. Relationships need the nourishment of time. Without it, they wither and die on the vine. One couple seized an empty nest opportunity, not without some protest from a clinging college-aged child, as this mother E-mailed:

> *Will be brief. Both children in college. My husband and I had a four-day weekend. Decided to fully enjoy our empty nest. Told kids ahead of time not to come home. Youngest forgot. I reminded him that we were going to be alone those four days. He got a little hurt and angry. I think we have every right to enjoy a few days alone after all the years we had our kids around us. I love them coming home, but at this stage I also want some rest. My son thinks we're weird.*

Confronting Old Problems

A child's leaving home is bound to make old marital problems clearer, at least until some new distraction can be found. Old power struggles rooted in work-family inequities, old resentments about lack of support during trying times, and even old disagreements about parenting philosophies can appear as children leave home.

Sometimes the problems *feel* rooted in the past ("We could never communicate") but are actually triggered by the imbalance due to a child's leaving home. A wife who held a part-time job while her children were growing up and a husband who is a high-power workaholic may clash as a son's or daughter's departure for college leaves the wife more resentful of her husband's job. She now has time on her hands for the relationship, and he does not.

Conversely, and more and more true of today's working couples with children leaving home, a husband who has plateaued or tired of a demanding work environment may be eager to return to the family and his spouse, only to find her heading back into the workforce after deferring her career interests. "I'm here, and you're gone," said one man incredulously. "I was always here, but you chose to be gone," retorted his wife.

This is a couple clearly out of developmental sync with one another. They were helped to solve this problem by inviting the husband to enrich his life with male friends and new interests, and asking the wife to see her husband who could now "be there" for her by encouraging her career development and reducing the burden of her domestic responsibilities. They attended to their relationship by making a commitment to get away for a weekend every three months.

At times the old problem has to do with fears of couple intimacy, a fear easily sidestepped during the rigors of parenting. Children may have filled a partner's need for closeness and warmth. Once they begin to leave the nest, they take that special intimacy with them, leaving behind an empty and sad parent. The couple may be faced with the task of confronting intimacy issues. Sometimes a therapist is needed to introduce the possibility of getting closer and help them to deal with their fears.

Even with help, some marriages dissolve as children leave home. Why then? Some couples report that the relationship really dissolved years earlier, and they waited until the kids were nearly grown before proceeding with divorce. Others take a harder look at one another as the nest empties and decide that they've grown apart or conclude that longstanding problems are irreconcilable. This is always sad and very distressing for everyone. As the family structure shifts, the foundation of some marriages crumbles.

When that happens, therapists advise divorcing partners to begin thinking of ways to establish two homes, a binuclear family, as psychologist Constance Ahrons calls it. Parents maintain some semblance of a partnership in order to continue providing nurturance and guidance for their children, but set up new, separate lives. When young adults stay significantly connected to each parent without choosing sides, and if they are helped to physically establish themselves in each home (with a place to sleep and store belongings), they will continue to have a base, now two bases, from which to grow.

"Home" is not gone when parents divorce. As psychiatrist Vincenzo DiNicola writes, a family is "bound up with, shaped by and situated in the places where we actually live and those that have a hold on our hearts and minds through shared memories and symbols. This mental geography both literally and figuratively, 'holds us in place.'" Divorce or other major loss may temporarily slow the development of everyone in the family as everyone readjusts, but it does not destroy "home" or impede the reinvention of family. For some families, brand-new spaces are needed for significant growth.

Creating New Dreams and Projects

Parenting children together and making a family provides many, if not most, partners with a *raison d'être*, a life-giving, fulfilling, and bonding experience with one another that, for many couples, is a hard act to follow. I first struggled with this as our son left home for college.

Pat / July 6

> *This summer with Rob has been odd. Last night as we sat on the couch watching a Woody Allen movie, I tried to find the delicious feeling I used to feel before the children were born. Was I looking for oneness or security or "I just love this man"? I couldn't tell, which was puzzling. There isn't much tension in our marriage; long morning walks have soothed some minor scratches. Rob has been terrifically attentive, present, domestic, and supportive. He looks great, too. But I sat apart from him yesterday and folded my arms across my chest, not his.*

By the end of the summer, as Adam packed for college, I thought I knew the source of the reluctance. I hadn't been ready to fully rejoin Rob in our life as a couple. I was still gently releasing myself from the big, warm arms of a daily motherhood. Being a mother to our boys has been strong drink: intense, syrupy sweet at times, occasionally bitter, but very much a high. They are in my every cell in ways that Rob is not.

Couples beginning to wind down their parenting projects need new ones to replace some of that high. I felt strangely compelled to have us remodel our kitchen while our older son was away in Spain for his junior year of college. We worked together to shape a new living space, one designed around our needs for more adult socializing or intimate dinners. Down the road we could imagine adult children and grand-children converging in the kitchen for holidays as well.

Friends with an only child leaving for college had a similar fantasy of a life together *sans* children:

> *The future looks like this. We're seriously thinking of moving upstate, maybe giving up this city apartment and buying a house with a little more room, a little more land and privacy. Our most wonderful only child will go off to take care of himself and live hap-pily ever after. We will visit each other. Meanwhile Ken and I will create a wonderful home large enough to accommodate family. Our careers will open up, and I see us studiously plugging away on our writing and painting projects.*

Other couples whose lives have been infused with children turn their nurturing skills to camps, teams, and schools. My cousin and her husband, who live in a small Kentucky town, became very involved with youth groups after their three boys left home. Some join cooking or book clubs or take up a new sport together. Those whose nests are also emptying of jobs and careers as well begin traveling across the country or around the globe.

Like all transitions, reinventing a new life together as a couple with adult children doesn't happen in the month, or the fall, or even the year that children begin leaving home. It occurs gradually—and not very consciously. But it happens easily for couples who take a good look at who they each are and decide there is enough love, attachment, and shared interests to commit themselves to the next phase together.

MEN AND WOMEN AT MID-LIFE

When I left for the University of Michigan in 1967 to begin my emerging adulthood, I was supremely unaware of my parents as real people. My mother and father were, well, my parents. I loved them, even liked them sometimes, but my focus was elsewhere: reading *The Alexandria Quartet,* having a boyfriend, marching against the Ann Arbor sheriff who jailed two anti-war protesters, going to Motown keg parties, analyzing Shakespeare's *Twelfth Night,* even inhaling marijuana.

So when my father, aged forty-seven, called one day to ask my opinion about whether he should take a new job in Minnesota, I was stunned. Now that I'm fifty, I know that he and my mother were struggling to cope with a new life phase. They were focusing on themselves and moving into a time of less intense and—for them, as parents in the late 1960s—bewildering parenting. My parents were straddling the two worlds of parenthood and mid-life growth and change. As their almost grown daughter at the time, I was oblivious to this process. I just wanted to know if a move to Minneapolis would mean I would have to pay out-of-state tuition at my school.

The mid-life stage theories of Erikson, Jung, and Daniel Levinson were primarily descriptions of men's lives. Mid-life was supposed to begin when men began to reconnect with others and face their own mortality for the first time. Many women in my grandmothers' generation had no mid-life except one of loss and decline. With children out the door, their major life function, raising children, was over.

Fortunately, much has changed. First, it is widely agreed that, for mid-life men and women alike, life after children leave home is far from winding down. Studies of adult development reveal that important changes in beliefs, identity, and lifestyle continue throughout life. Research on mid-life is beginning to affirm that this period is not usually about crisis as much as it is about calmness, with happiness peaking at age fifty, not declining. My parents, both over seventy-five, recently sold one house in Michigan, packed up their belongings by themselves, and moved to another house and another culture in Florida. Their relationship has deepened, each has pursued a new hobby since turning seventy, and they continue their mid-life passion, golf, in a warmer climate now.

Men at Mid-life

The transitional identity issues that many (but not all) men face in mid-life are generally not about the loss of parenthood or indecisions about how to shape their lives after children leave home. Some crises are tuned to men's sociocultural upbringing:

- ◆ I'm losing the competitive edge at work to younger workers. I'm falling off my career ladder or feeling stuck on a certain rung.
- ◆ My body is letting me down. I can't do physical things as long or as vigorously as I used to.
- ◆ My wife is leaving me because she says that I don't talk to her, that I'm not sensitive to her needs.
- ◆ My children only want to talk to their mother when they call from college. I don't really know them.

Men who have challenged the traditional social codes for masculinity find themselves at a slightly different place as mid-life rolls inevitably around. As we have seen in this book, some fathers are missing their almost grown children deeply and are making the transition to an adult-adult relationship with a son or daughter. Some are working on other connections. They are moving closer to their wives, their own parents, and other male friends. And they are creating meaning in their lives, finding some new moral purpose in the community or congregation.

Robert Pasick, my husband, who has authored several books about men's development, lists five challenges for men at mid-life:

1. Learn to trust your emotions and rediscover your creative side.
2. Renegotiate and revitalize your relationship with women and children.
3. Reevaluate your sexuality, including your homophobia.
4. Redefine your relationship with your family of origin.
5. Learn to (re)connect with other men.

Rob, part of a new generation of mid-life men who are rebalancing lives once so dominated by the world of work, took up yoga and poetry writing in the wee hours of the morning once absorbed by fatherhood. He wants to resume playing ice hockey and start his own consulting business.

The move by each of our sons toward adulthood was heartfelt, but for Rob, like many fathers, there was a time-lag in those reactions. The college departure barely nicked his emotional jaw. Instead he took a whole two years to come to grips with his sadness over Adam's leaving home. Having learned how much fatherhood meant to him, he is now more in touch with Dan, our younger child.

Men are increasingly coming to terms with women who are a strong force in the workplace and who are adamant that their male partners spend time with children and share mundane domestic tasks. Rebalancing the gender roles so deeply situated in our psyches is not an easy or simple task. It has much promise, however, for the men and women striving to find meaning at mid-life.

WHAT MEN CAN DO

Come to know the emotional and relational parts of yourself as your children are leaving home.

Call or write your college-aged children separately from their mother. No young adult really likes the hear mother say, "And Dad says hello."

Be curious about the creative, playful, and spiritual sides of your life and begin to exercise them.

Reevaluate your significant relationships with others: Is there true connection or just contact? Do you have an intimate, loving relationship with a significant person? What would it take to have that in your life?

Reevaluate work. Is this what you want to do for the rest of your work life? What are the satisfactions and empty places in your work? Is it time to consider a change?

Take your body more seriously, including your sexuality. Is your physical health out of balance? Are there new ways you can feel strong and vital?

Women at Mid-life

Women of our generation have followed so many pathways from adolescence to adulthood that very few general statements hold true for all of us after the children leave home. Mothers in traditional marriages who have been full-time at-home mothers (only half of the population) may approach mid-life with trepidation, like the woman who cried, "I have no role." Or they may be eager for release, as one friend asserted ("Now it's *my* turn"). Recently, my mother said that for the first time she has days when she doesn't think of her four adult children. She said, rather matter-of-factly, "I guess I've finally grown up."

A friend, Martha, wrote to me the spring following her first son's departure to college:

> *Middle-age really is a time for introspections, isn't it? I'm finding that I use "middle-age" far less apologetically than I used to. We are going through a transition from nurturing our kids to nurturing our souls. In some women, it seems to result in an outflow of creativity previously funneled toward child-rearing.*

Mothers who have juggled work and parenthood, with or without partners, may experience relief as they feel the mantle of too much responsibility fall from their shoulders when their children begin to leave home. They may turn their attention to a career kept purposely in lower gear or stimulate the growth of other parts of themselves long hidden or deferred.

Our generation of women has run the gauntlet from traditional homemakers with many children to child-free single women with few commitments to others except their life's work. We have had many more (yet not enough) opportunities to follow our own pathways and, in the words of Mary Catherine Bateson, to compose a life. We have struggled to balance our twin needs for autonomy and attachment, or what psychologist and researcher Ruthellen Josselson terms "competence and connection." We have worked to have a stronger, more resolute voice in the marketplace, in our marriages, and as mothers. No wonder our pathways have been different and our mid-lives so varied.

Josselson studied thirty women in their last year of college during 1972 and followed them for twenty-two years to mid-life. In *Revising Herself: The Story of Women's Identity from College to Midlife,* she describes several differing pathways among the women she interviewed. What is fascinating about their journeys is that no one followed a fixed sequence, a definable stage, or could be easily pigeonholed into "traditional" versus "career" woman.

The women in Josselson's study arrived at mid-life from different trajectories and fell into four groups: the *guardians* (good girls in young adulthood who break loose from expected roles in mid-life), the *pathmakers* (early trailblazers and doers, who balance their own needs with those of others right straight into mid-life), the *searchers* (emotionally expressive, self-doubting women who fight authority early on and by mid-life settle into a more realistic, committed life), and *drifters* (women who were free-wheeling, avoidant women as college students and who "find themselves" by mid-life).

Most contemporary studies of women's development in mid-life conclude that women continue to thrive and grow in mid-life as their children leave home. As psychologist/mother Marcie Plunkett told me, "I feel I am in parallel development with my daughter who left for college this fall—she's growing, and almost magically, so am I."

WHAT WOMEN CAN DO

Accept that, *wherever* you are in the process of mid-life development, you will continue to grow. That may mean amplifying what you like about yourself and your life right now, changing direction in some significant way, or unearthing sides of yourself long dormant.

Continue to resist myths that, with children leaving home, you must be a certain way. Culturally written scripts are for television commercials and magazine ads. They are meant to sell products, not direct your life.

Be curious about your multiple selves (not to be confused with multiple personalities), which take turns coming forward and moving to the background throughout the life cycle.

Review what your particular pathway has been from late adolescence to mid-life, assessing how adventurous and committed you've been, and settled or unsettled. Acknowledge ten things you fantasize about doing from age forty-five to fifty-five.

Review your particular balance of connecting to others and attending to yourself. Does it need fine-tuning? Rebalance your life to bring the two spheres (other and self) into closer harmony.

This book is part of my own mid-life development. As my sons launch to adulthood, I am deep into an evaluation of a life shaped by commitments. My long career as an educator and psychologist continues to be a rudder for my moral sensibilities; I want to continue making a contribution to my community. I will continue to be a mother and partner, daughter and aunt, friend and colleague, sister and niece.

What mid-life and a changing motherhood have brought me most are new energies for old passions submerged by the cumulative strains of work plus parenthood. Writing and reading have become very important in my life, as they were when I was a child and young adolescent. Connecting with women friends and older family members has become very important to me. Surprisingly, I am feeling new energies for domestic life, not to serve others' needs, but to meet a desire I have to make my own physical surroundings more serene.

After decades of moving from home to car to office, I want to be outside more of the time and connected with the earth, a side of me inherited from my ancestors who were farmers. My return to "roots" will also take me to the Philippines, where I hope to reconnect with the Asian heritage on my father's side.

While writing one of the last journal entries before Adam went to college, I sat before still waters.

Pat / July 31

I took a deep breath entering this cottage at Hulbert Lake, a wilderness haven we have visited as a family for over ten years. It has memories that fly at me like harmless bats: the dock where Dan learned to jump into water, the small blue table where we played Monopoly on rainy days, the lake once so hard and frozen in January that we tromped out and made angels in the snow by moonlight.

Here I found a few sad places inside of me. Facing Adam's and then Dan's leaving home has felt stone-heavy. Yesterday, in a ceremony of letting that feeling go, I cast a few rocks off the end of the dock. They rippled away from me toward the beaver dam on the other side of the lake, moving in a series of wider and wider circles.

What I discovered in the long hours facing this shore was that I'm past much of the loss and fear I wrote about a year ago, and I'm beyond the frantic feelings of myself changing. Like the lake, which transforms itself second by second through the sun and wind, like my children, who are probably this moment at some other water's edge, I am changing daily. Adam's departure, and then Dan's, will give me more time to notice that.

Notes

INTRODUCTION

xv Anne Lamott, *Operating Instructions* (New York: Pantheon, 1993).
xv Adrienne Rich, "Prospective Immigrants Please Note," in *Collected Early Poems: 1950–1970* (New York: W. W. Norton, 1993).

CHAPTER 1. ADOLESCENTS FROM HIGH SCHOOL TO COLLEGE

5 *Adolescence begins much earlier:* Jeffrey Arnett and Susan Taber, "Adolescence Terminable and Interminable: When Does Adolescence End?" *Journal of Youth and Adolescence,* 23(5), 1994.

5 Carol Gilligan, *In a Different Voice: Psychological Theory and Women's Development* (Cambridge, MA: Harvard University Press, 1982).

5 Mary Pipher, *Reviving Ophelia: Saving the Selves of Adolescent Girls* (New York: G. P. Putnam, 1994).

5 Olga Silverstein, *The Courage to Raise Good Men* (New York: Viking, 1994).

5 Ann Caron, *Strong Mothers, Strong Sons* (New York: HarperCollins, 1994).

6 *A recent Census Bureau report:* "Change in the American Family: Now Only 1 in 4 is 'Traditional,' " *New York Times,* January 29, 1997.

6 *Further proof of increased diversity:* Edgar F. Beckham, "Diversity Opens Doors to All," *New York Times Book Review,* January 5, 1997, p. 58.

8 *Research also tells us:* J. E. Marcia, "Common Processes Underlying Ego Identity, Cognitive/Normal Development, and Individuation," in D. K. Lapsley and F. C. Powers (eds.), *Self, Ego, and Identity* (New York: Springer Verlag, 1988), pp. 211–25.

10 *as psychiatrist Vincenzo DiNicola calls it: A Stranger in the Family,* (New York: W. W. Norton, 1997).

10 *More so today than ever before:* Edgar F. Beckham, "Diversity Opens Doors to All," *New York Times Book Review,* January 5, 1997, p. 58.

11 *Margaret Mead poem: Blackberry Winter* (New York: Simon & Schuster Touchstone, 1984).

22 *Some researchers point out:* J. Zaslow and R. Takanishi, "Priorities for Research on Adolescent Development," *American Psychologist,* 48, 1993, pp. 185–92.

22 Anne Roiphe, *Fruitful: A Real Mother in a Modern World* (Boston: HoughtonMifflin, 1996), p. 147.

27 *By age twenty:* Alan Guttmacher Institute, as reported in Brent Benda and Frederick DiBlasio, "An Integration of Theory: Adolescent Sexual Contacts," *Journal of Youth and Adolescence,* 23(1), 1994, pp. 403–20.

27 *The bottom line:* Herant Katchadourian, "Sexuality" in S. Shirley Feldman and Glen R. Elliott, *At the Threshold: The Developing Adolescent* (Cambridge, MA: Harvard University Press, 1990), pp. 330–51.

28 *A study reported in 1985:* R. Coles and G. Stokes, *Sex and the American Teenager* (New York: Harper & Row, 1985).

28 *Recent studies of sexual practices:* Tamar Lewin, "Teenagers Alter Sexual Practices, Thinking Risks Will Be Avoided," *New York Times,* April 5, 1997.

28 *Oral sex is fairly common*: Mark Schuster, Robert Bell, and David Kanouse, "The Sexual Practices of Adolescent Virgins: Genital Sexual Activities of High School Students Who Have Never Had Vaginal Intercourse," *American Journal of Public Health,* 86(11), 1996, pp. 1570–76.

29 *related to sexual preference:* Herant Katchadourian "Sexuality" in S. Shirley Feldman and Glen R. Elliot, *At the Threshold: The Developing Adolescent,* (Cambridge, MA: Harvard University Press, 1990), pp. 330–51.

29 *A 1995 report:* Ellen Goodman, "When We Talk about Sex and Teens, Can't We Use Words Besides 'No'?" *Boston Globe,* June 22, 1995.

31 *an emotional roller coaster:* Lawrence Steinberg and Ann Levine, *You and Your Adolescent: A Parent's Guide for Ages 10–20* (New York: HarperCollins, 1990).

31 *The main reasons adolescents use:* Joseph Nowinski, *Substance Abuse in Adolescents and Young Adults* (New York: W. W. Norton, 1990).

32 *". . . we have become":* Nowinski, see above, p. 14.

33 *a University of Michigan study:* "Drug Use Rises Again in 1995 among American Teens," *The University of Michigan News and Information Services,* Ann Arbor, Michigan, December 11, 1995.

34 *The typical progression*: Nowinski, see above, p. 30.

35 *The survey of 17,600 students:* Henry Wechsler et al., *Binge Drinking on Campus: Results of a National Study* (Bethesda, MD: U.S. Department of Education, Higher Education Center for Alcohol and Other Drug Prevention, 1996).

37 *One up-to-date*: Cynthia Kuhn, Scott Swartzwelder, and Wilkie Wilson, *Buzzed: The Straight Facts about the Used and Abused Drugs from Alcohol to Ecstacy* (New York: W. W. Norton, 1998).

CHAPTER 2. SURVIVING THE COLLEGE SEARCH

41 *One recent large-scale study:* National Center for Education Statistics, U.S. Department of Education, Office of Educational Research and Improvement (NCES 96-158), p. 28.

41 *On the other hand, the era of downsizing:* Peter Applebome, "Era of Downsizing Creates Job Boom for Class of '97," *New York Times,* May 19, 1997.

47 *Harvard University turns away*: According to Marlyn Lewis, Office of Admissions, Harvard University.

55 *Minority students now comprise*: Edgar F. Beckham, "Diversity Opens Door to All," *New York Times Book Review,* January 5, 1997, p. 58.

57 *"Rising College Costs":* Peter Applebome, "Rising College Costs Imperil the Nation: Blunt Report Says," *New York Times,* June 18, 1997, p. A1.

57 *"With College Costs":* Editorial, "With College Costs Sky High, It's Time for a Savings Plan," *Los Angeles Times,* May 11, 1997.

57 *This is aptly termed sticker shock:* Neale S. Godfrey, *From Cradle to College: A Parent's Guide to Financing Your Child's Life* (New York: HarperBusiness, 1997).

58 *In 1997 the average tuition and fees:* Louis Menand, "Everyone Else's College Education," *New York Times Magazine,* April 20, 1997, pp. 48–49.

58 *Congress has passed:* Sandra Block, "School Tax Breaks May Need Study," *USA Today,* August 18, 1997.

61 *At one small school:* Pat Wingert et al., "Those Scary College Costs" *Newsweek,* April 29, 1996, pp. 52–56.

61 *Tuition discounting:* Peter Passell, "The New Economics of Higher Education," *New York Times,* April 22, 1997, pp. C1, C6.

62 *Judith Wallerstein's long-term study:* Judith Wallerstein and S. Blakeslee, *Second Chance: Men, Women and Children a Decade After Divorce* (New York: Houghton Mifflin, 1989).

CHAPTER 3. FINDING A COLLEGE SEARCH PROCESS THAT WORKS

66 *As author Thomas Haydn: Handbook for College Admissions* (Princeton, NJ: Peterson's, 1995).

76 *There is some research*: National Center for Education Statistics, U. S. Department of Education, Office of Educational Research and Improvement (NCES 96-158), p 14.

81 Daniel Goleman, *Emotional Intelligence* (New York: Bantam, 1995).

81 *More than nine percent of college freshmen*: Marybeth Kravets, "Hidden Disabilities: Another Diverse Population," *Journal of College Admission,* Summer/Fall 1996, pp. 24–31.

81 *And according to one specialist:* Kravets, see above.

84 *As one author notes:* Charles J. Shields, *College Guide for Parents* (New York: The College Board, 1995), p. 145.

CHAPTER 4. PARENTS' EXPERIENCE OF THE TRANSITION YEARS

89 *" . . . they still must leave"*: Judith Viorst, *Necessary Losses* (New York: Simon & Schuster, 1986).

92 Sharon Olds, "The Lady Bug," *The Wellspring* (New York: Knopf, 1996).

93 Lucien Stryk, "Rites of Passage," *Collected Poems* (Athens, OH: Ohio University Press/Swallow Press, 1994).

96 *family rituals:* Mary Whiteside, "Family Rituals as a Key to Kinship Connections in Remarried Families," *Family Relations,* 38, pp. 34–39.

99 *" . . . It seems no time":* Sharon Olds, "My Son the Man," *The Wellspring* (New York: Knopf, 1996).

100 Sharon Olds, "First Formal," *The Wellspring* (New York: Knopf, 1996).

104 *As an article:* William Davis, "The Empty Nest Blues: It's a Dad Thing Too,"*Boston Globe,* November 13, 1996.

111 Marion Howard, "A Halfway House for Me," *New York Times Magazine*, August 7, 1994.

CHAPTER 5. PARENTING THE LATE ADOLESCENT

119   *Research tells us:* Stephen Anderson, "Changes in Parental Adjustment and Communication During the Leaving-Home Transition," *Journal of Social and Personal Relationships,* 7, 1990, pp. 47–68.

123   *On paper-and-pencil measures:* Maureen Kenny and Kenneth Rice, "Attachment to Parents and Adjustment in Late Adolescent College Students: Current Status, Applications, and Future Considerations," *Counseling Psychologist,* 23(3), 1995, pp. 433–56.

124   *In her study:* Sherry Hatcher, "Personal Rites of Passage: Stories of College Youth," in A. Lieblich and R. Josselson (eds.), *Exploring Identity and Gender: The Narrative Study of Lives,* Vol. 2 (Thousand Oaks, CA: Sage, 1994).

127   *Some research indicates:* Lawrence Steinberg, "Autonomy, Conflict, and Harmony in the Family Relationship," in S. Shirley Feldman and Glen R. Elliott (eds.), *At the Threshold: The Developing Adolescent* (Cambridge, MA: Harvard University Press, 1990), pp. 255–76.

127   Kathy Weingarten, *The Mother's Voice: Strengthening Intimacy in Families* (New York: Harcourt & Brace, 1994).

127   *In fact, the National Longitudinal Study:* Robert Langreth, "Teens' Closeness to Parents and School Helps Influence Conduct, Study Shows," *Wall Street Journal,* September 10, 1997.

128   *Research points to poorer adjustment:* Susan McCurdy and Abraham Scherman, "Effects of Family Structure on the Adolescent Separation-individuation Process," *Adolescence,* 31(122), 1996, pp. 307–19.

131   Nydia Garcia Preto, "Transformation of the Family System in Adolescence," in Betty Carter and Monica McGoldrick, *The Changing Family Life Cycle* (second edition) (Boston: Allyn & Bacon, 1989).

132   *In the last decade, research on parenting styles:* Steinberg, see above.

133   *The third dimension of authoritative parenting:* D. Baumrind, "Child Care Practices Anteceding Three Patterns of Pre-school Behavior," *Genetic Psychology Monographs,* 75, 1967, pp. 43–88.

135   *Adolescents whose parents negotiate:* J. Youniss and J. Smollar, *Mutuality in Parent-Adolescent Relationships* (Washington, DC: William T. Grant Foundation Commission on Work, Family, and Citizenship, 1988).

135   *One young man:* Lawrence Steinberg and Ann Levine, *You and Your Adolescent: A Parent's Guide for Ages 10–20* (New York: HarperCollins, 1990), p. 20.

136   *On the other hand, one study:* Frank Furstenberg, "Coming of Age of a Changing Family System," in S. Shirley Feldman and Glen R. Elliott (eds.), *At the Threshold: The Developing Adolescent* (Cambridge, MA: Harvard University Press, 1990).

139   Kathy Weingarten, *The Mother's Voice,* p. 208.

139   *As one psychologist noted:* Bruce Narramore and Vern Lewis, *Parenting Teens: A Road Map Through the Ages and Stages of Adolescence* (Wheaton, IL: Tyndale House, 1990).

140   *In fact, in the average household:* Steinberg, see above, p. 270.

140   *Psychologists point to different:* Steinberg and Levine, see above, pp. 36–38.

CHAPTER 6. THE LAUNCH

151   *"Time flies":* Suzanne Hamlin, "Time Flies, But Where Does It Go?" *New York Times,* September 6, 1997.

156 *Research with parents:* Jeffrey Arnett and Susan Taber, "Adolescence Terminable and Interminable: When Does Adolescence End?" *Journal of Youth and Adolescence,* 23(5),1994, p. 532.

159 *"We waited in lines":* Charles McGrath, "Empty Nest Blues," *The New Yorker,* September 18, 1995.

CHAPTER 7. THE FRESHMAN-YEAR EXPERIENCE

170 *As Harvard freshman:* Chana Schoenberger, "Am I Really Ready For This?" *New York Times,* November 5, 1996, pp. 17–18.

172 Sharon Olds, "High School Senior," *The Wellspring* (New York: Knopf, 1996).

174 Janet Worthington and Ronald Farrar, *The Ultimate College Survival Guide* (Princeton, NJ: Peterson's, 1995).

174 *"Postal workers dread September":* Anne Matthews, *Bright College Years: Inside the American Campus Today* (New York: Simon & Schuster, 1997), p. 45.

176 *The things they* do *miss are:* George Johnson, "Zen of First Impressions about Being in College," *New York Times,* October 4, 1991.

176 Stephen Anderson, "Changes in Parental Adjustment and Communication During the Leaving-Home Transition," *Journal of Social and Personal Relationships,* 7, 1990, p. 49.

180 *As one student put it:* Schoenberger, see above, p. 18.

185 *A common phenomenon:* Trip Gabriel, "Pack Dating: For a Good Time, Call a Crowd," *New York Times,* January, 5, 1997, p. 22.

192 *One survey of college students:* Robert D. Hershey, Jr., "Graduating with Credit Problems," *New York Times,* November 10, 1996, p. 15.

194 *Ninety percent of all college students:* Robert Oswalt and Sarah Finkelberg, "College Depression: Causes, Duration, and Coping," *Psychological Reports,* 77, 1995, p. 858.

CHAPTER 8. NEW SPACE FOR NEW GROWTH

200 *It is, as one essayist noted:* A. B. Giamatti, *Take Time for Paradise: Americans and Their Games* (New York: Summit Books, 1989).

201 Kahlil Gibran, *The Prophet* (New York: Knopf, 1923).

209 *Erik Erikson noted:* Identity: Youth and Crisis (New York: W. W. Norton, 1968).

220 *A binuclear family:* Constance Ahrons and Roy Rogers, *Divorced Families: Meeting the Challenge of Divorce and Remarriage* (New York: W. W. Norton, 1987).

220 *"bound up with":* Vincenzo DiNicola, *A Stranger in the Family* (New York: W. W. Norton, 1997), p. 84.

222 *Research on midlife:* "The Midlife Calm," *Harvard Magazine,* July/August 1997.

223 Robert Pasick, *Awakening from a Deep Sleep* (San Francisco: HarperSanFrancisco, 1992).

226 Mary Catherine Bateson, *Composing a Life* (New York: Atlantic Monthly Press, 1984).

226 Ruthellen Josselson, *Revising Herself: The Story of Women's Identity from College to Midlife* (New York: Oxford University Press, 1996).

Additional Resources

ESPECIALLY FOR PARENTS

Alexander-Roberts, Colleen. *ADHD & Teens: Proven Techniques for Handling Emotional, Academic, and Behavioral Problems.* Dallas: Taylor Publishing, 1995.

Apter, Terri. *Secret Paths: Women in the New Midlife.* New York: W. W. Norton, 1995.

Borden, M., M. Burlinson, and E. Kearns. *In Addition to Tuition: The Parents' Survival Guide to Freshman Year of College.* New York: Facts On File, 1995.

Boyer, Ernest L., and Paul Boyer. *Smart Parents Guide to College.* Princeton, NJ: Peterson's, 1996.

Coburn, Karen, and Madge Treeger. *Letting Go: A Parents' Guide to Understanding the College Years.* New York: HarperCollins,1997.

Drum, Alice, and Richard Kneedler. *Funding a College Education.* Boston: Harvard Business School Press, 1996.

Gordon, Barry. *Your Father, Your Self.* Secaucus, NJ: Birch Lane Press, 1996.

Hall, Colin, and Ron Lieber. *Taking Time Off.* New York: HarperCollins, 1996.

Osherson, Samuel. *Wrestling with Love: How Men Struggle with Women, Children, Parents, and Each Other.* New York: Fawcett, 1992.

Pogrebin, Letty Cottin. *Getting Over Getting Older: An Intimate Journey.* Boston: Little, Brown, 1996.

Shapiro, Patricia G. *My Turn: Women's Search for Self after the Children Leave.* Princeton, NJ: Peterson's, 1996.

Steinberg, Lawrence. *Crossing Paths: How Your Child's Adolescence Can Be an Opportunity for Your Own Personal Growth.* New York: Firestone, 1994.

ESPECIALLY FOR STUDENTS

Clary, Deborah. *The College Survival Handbook.* Kansas City: Andrews and McMeel, 1997.

Hanson, Jennifer, and Friends. *The Real Freshman Handbook: An Irreverent and Totally Honest Guide to Life on Campus.* New York: Houghton Mifflin, 1996.

Page, Cristina, ed. *The Smart Girls' Guide to College.* New York: NoondayPress, 1997.

Rich, Jason. *The Everything College Survival Book.* Holbrook, MA: Adams Media, 1997.

Turton, Joseph P. *My Freshman Manual.* Westlake, OH: Creative Publishing,1995.

Worthington, Janet, and Ronald Farrar. *The Ultimate College Survival Guide.* Princeton, NJ: Peterson's 1995.

INTERNET RESOURCES

http://www.collegeboard.org./index/html
http://www.kaplan.com/prep/

> Both sites offer information about test preparation (PSAT, SAT, ACT). The College Board Web site also contains information about campus visits, some United States colleges, admission, and financial aid.

http://www.finaid.org/nasfaa
http://www.fastweb.com
http://www.fafsa.ed.gov
http://hispanicfund.org
http://www.collegeispossible.com
http://www.scholarships.com

> These sites offer an enormous amount of important information about obtaining loans and scholarships for college tuition.

http://www.nasfaa.org/public/cashfc.html

> Information about applying for financial aid.

http://www.edonline.com/cq/hbcu

> Contains a list of historically black colleges and universities.

http://www.greekpages.com/

> All about fraternity and sorority life on campus.

INDEX